PRAISE FOR
Christopher Pe

The Witch's Shield

This is a wise, helpful book for beginners
and intermediate students of the Craft.
—PUBLISHERS WEEKLY

A treasure trove of traditional and new,
creative ways to protect yourself, your
loved ones, and your property.
—DANCING WORLD REVIEW

The Witch's Coin

Offers profound healing for the many among us
who possess conflicted relationships with money
and prosperity. I highly recommend this book.
—JUDIKA ILLES, AUTHOR OF
The Encyclopedia of 5000 Spells AND *Pure Magic*

Christopher Penczak provides a refreshing
examination of the connection between money,
magic, and the attitude people put toward both.
—TAYLOR ELLWOOD, EDITOR OF
Manifesting Prosperity: A Wealth Magic Anthology

The cover sigil is formed from five hearts
rotated to the five directions, creating a heart
pentagram. Five is strongly associated with
Venus and love in traditional magick, while
seven (for the seven-pointed star in the center) is
associated qabalistically with Venus. The hearts
create a flower-petal design that resonates with
the nature-magick imagery of the book.

{SIGIL DESIGN BY CHRISTOPHER PENCZAK}

THE
Witch's
Heart

About the Author

Christopher Penczak is an award-winning author, teacher, and healing practitioner. As an advocate for the timeless wisdom of the ages, he is rooted firmly in the traditions of modern Witchcraft and earth-based religions but draws from a wide range of spiritual traditions—including shamanism, alchemy, herbalism, Theosophy, and Hermetic Qabalah—to forge his own magickal traditions. His many books include *Magick of Reiki*, *Spirit Allies*, *The Mystic Foundation*, and *The Inner Temple of Witchcraft*. He is the cofounder of the Temple of Witchcraft tradition, a not-for-profit religious organization to advance the spiritual traditions of Witchcraft, as well as the cofounder of Copper Cauldron Publishing, a company dedicated to producing books, recordings, and tools for magickal inspiration and evolution. He has been a faculty member of the North Eastern Institute of Whole Health and a founding member of the Gifts of Grace, an interfaith foundation dedicated to acts of community service, both based in New Hampshire. He maintains a teaching and healing practice in New England but travels extensively lecturing.

More information can be found at www.christopherpenczak.com and www.templeofwitchcraft.org.

CHRISTOPHER PENCZAK

Witch's
THE

Heart

THE MAGICK OF PERFECT LOVE
& PERFECT TRUST

Llewellyn Publications
WOODBURY, MINNESOTA

FIRST EDITION
First Printing, 2011

Book design by Rebecca Zins

Cover design by Kevin R. Brown

All illustrations by the Llewellyn Art Department except for tarot cards in chapter 4 from the Universal Tarot deck by Roberto De Angelis (reprinted with permission from Lo Scarabeo), pentacles in chapter 7 by Jackie Williams, and the Handfasting card from the Well Worn Path deck (illustrated by Mickie Mueller) in chapter 9

The astrological chart in chapter 9 was created using Matrix Software ©1994 Big Rapids, MI

Llewellyn is a registered trademark of Llewellyn Worldwide Ltd.

Library of Congress Cataloging-in-Publication Data
Penczak, Christopher.
 The witch's heart: the magick of perfect love & perfect trust / Christopher Penczak.
—1st ed.
  p. cm.
Includes bibliographical references and index.
ISBN 978-0-7387-2627-4
1. Love—Miscellanea. 2. Magic. I. Title.
BF1623.L6P46 2011
133.4'3—dc22

2010054164

Llewellyn Publications
A Division of Llewellyn Worldwide Ltd.
2143 Wooddale Drive
Woodbury, MN 55125-2989
www.llewellyn.com
Printed in the United States of America

Love,
well made, can lead to liberation.

—THE MAHABHARATA

Special Thanks

Special thanks to the following people for their advice, stories, and support: Adam Sartwell, Steve Kenson, Rosalie and Ronald Penczak, Alixaendreia, Bonnie Boulanger, Joe and Doug at Otherworld Apothecary, Dorothy Morrison, Sandi Liss, Chris Giroux, Rowan, Kris, Dave, Ellen Dugan, Lisa Dubbels, and Laurie Cabot.

CONTENTS

four} The Quest for Love   57

INTRODUCTION

The Witch's Heart is the third in a series of simple books designed to bring life's magick to both the Pagan and the non-Pagan communities. Originally structured to be a line of easy-to-understand how-to books based in the traditions of Witchcraft, the series has evolved beyond the steps of what to do and explored the "whys"—the philosophies behind the magickal topics they cover—with both practical steps and life lessons to help the reader truly integrate the ideas in each book and live a more fulfilling life.

Both in my own life and in watching the lives of my teachers, friends, and students, I've found that people are fascinated when you make it publicly known that you are a Witch. Sometimes they are frightened, but even those who are scared of the Witch's initial archetype are also interested in what secrets you might have. Invariably, they want to know how your secret knowledge can ultimately better them and their own lives. The three areas they ask the most about are protection—how other people's "negative" energies can be affecting them and their health; money—with all its job- and career-related questions; and of course the most asked about topic, love—the secrets to finding the right partner and how to save a failing relationship. To help answer these questions in a more in-depth manner than the time allotted to a simple tarot reading or afternoon tea, I've created three books. The first is *The Witch's Shield* to answer questions about protection. The second is *The Witch's Coin* for exploring money magick and the philosophies behind prosperity. Now, in this third volume, we will focus on the mysteries of love through the teachings of *The Witch's Heart*.

Witches have long been associated with the power to induce love in others through spells, potions, and charms to bewitch and beguile the heart. Much of the world's folklore and fairy tales center around the power of love spells, and while most people relegate all magick, including love magick, to childhood fantasy, there is still a part of those of us who are old romantics that holds on to the idea and the hope that the power of love spells can be true—and even more, that *we* shall find the right spell and with it find the love of our life.

Love plays an important part in traditional magick. One of the thirteen blessings the goddess Diana gives Witches, through her daughter Aradia in *The Gospel of Aradia*, is "to bring success in love." Yet is that blessing to bring success to other people through spells and charms or to have a healthy religion, a spiritual tradition that brings out the virtue of love and makes healthy, happy relationships a part of its wisdom? By applying the lessons and philosophy of Witchcraft, are we able to find and sustain love for ourselves or are we granted the power to create love for others? While I think it's quite possible to do love magick for other people, I think the Goddess's true blessing is in making and sustaining our own love, starting with ourselves. Self-love was the key for my own spiritual development on this path.

Learning magick brings with it a promise of love magick. If I'm capable of making things happen in my life through magick, and I want a good, loving relationship, I should be capable of creating that as well. Though the road can be hard, the promise of successful love magick is real. Thousands of Witches have found their heart through the Craft. I found my partner through a love spell that I will share with you. The philosophies of magick and Witchcraft have guided us in both creating a healthy and happy romantic life together and sustaining it as it has evolved over time, in new and different ways. On my own quest for love, I made a lot of mistakes, both magickally and mundanely. I've been honored to guide and teach many others who eventually have met their loves and life partners, and they too have made detours along the way.

The magickal philosophies of this book have guided my own counseling practice of singles and couples as an ordained high priest in the Craft. Over the years, I've performed numerous handfastings (Pagan wedding ceremonies), counseled those going through separation and divorce, and focused on the healing work to be done around matters of the heart through tarot divination, magickal healing, and spellcraft, regardless of marital status. Some have been specifically Pagans and Witches. Others have found me because they don't fit into traditional religions and communities. While these ceremonies and spells are part of my trade as a magickal minister, they are all informed by the deeper spiritual principles found in our practice of Witchcraft. Each situation is unique, and while the principles are constant, the rituals and charms are tailored to the individuals in need. Often the remedy is not a charm but deeper healing work through intensive counseling and introspection. I've found that no matter where we are in the journey of life, we can each dive deeper into the mysteries of the heart and find the magick of Perfect Love and Perfect Trust in our lives. That is the true blessing of love magick.

The Witch's Heart is a compilation not just of love magick to attract someone special into your life, but of the ideas and philosophies that prepare you to be ready when you do find someone and how to sustain it to be the love of your life if you so choose. I hope these ideas benefit you as much as they have benefited me.

Blessed be,

Christopher Penczak

ONE

What's Love Got to Do With It?

When doing any form of magick, if you expect success in your working you should have a clear understanding of your magickal goals. If you are going to attempt any love magick, you should probably have a thorough understanding of love. What is love? How would you define it? If you can't describe what you want, it's hard to get it with magick, yet for most of us love is an ineffable concept. We know it when we feel it, but trying to put it into words is like trying to put the ocean in a teacup. However, to do successful love magick, we must do just that impossible task.

For a magician, the word *love*, in English, is an imprecise term. Other cultures with a better understanding of love have different terms for different kinds of love. It's not that modern English-speaking people don't experience all these types of love or understand them, but with our limited vocabulary, we don't take the time to think about them or about what we really mean when we say the word *love*.

Generally, we think of love as an intense emotion, an affection or tenderness for someone or something. Yet the quality—the "flavor," so to speak—of that love depends on the type of relationship. The love between parents and children is different from the love between siblings. Some would go as far as to say that the love between mothers and sons, mothers and daughters, fathers and sons, and fathers and daughters is different. One type of love is not better than the other, just different in terms of how it feels and its role in our society.

The love between family members is different from the love between two passionate sexual partners. We use the term *make love* to denote sexual intercourse, yet sex and love can be two separate things. You can have sex with someone and not really love them or have an emotional connection, and you can love someone and never have sex with them. Romantic love can be unrequited and never consummated through sexual union, but it is still romantic love.

There is love between friends who are not sexually involved nor related by the bonds of family. Because of the relationship we have developed together, we can all have friends who are like family, or simply friends whom we love and adore. Each of our loving friendships will be different and unique from one another, because each person we are friends with is unique.

We use the term *love* for when we really enjoy something or feel we really need something. I love chocolate. I love music. I love walking in the woods. But my love of chocolate, music, and walking is different from my love for my mother or my love for my husband. Yet we use the same word, making it difficult to truly understand the depth of different loves.

Love is also considered to be one of the highest spiritual achievements beyond the personal sphere. Many mystical traditions aspire to unconditional love, or divine love. It is a love that is not based on the personal world, but on the impersonal world. Nothing you do or say can take away this divine love. Mystics can see the universe as being made up of, or held together by, this divine love. Mystics who have embodied this type of love and compassion are considered saints, gurus, and masters. They are holy people, for they have lived a life of divine love and modeled it for others. Modern Witches call this love Perfect Love, the love the Divine has for us, for we are divine. What we might call "imperfect" love, or personal and attached love, is also divine yet fully human, and it is in the experience of any love in the human world that we get a glimpse of the perfect divine love. All love can lead us to the Divine.

The most important key to understanding all forms of love, including divine love, is self-love. You must have self-love and self-esteem before you can really have true love for anyone or anything else.

Cultures with a greater understanding of love as a force, as an energy, usually have a greater understanding of magick. The ancient Greeks were one of a number of cultures that had specific names—eros, phileo, agape, and stergo—to differentiate kinds of love. Understanding the way they see love in an ancient Pagan context and the divine connotations attached with each type of love can help us understand love better and know exactly what we want to create with our own love magick.

> *Eros*—Sexual or romantic love. Eros was a divine force for life, usually paired with Thanatos, the death force, and personified into the son of Aphrodite, giving us the first image that would later develop into our popular notion of Valentine's Cupid, taking its name from Eros's Roman counterpart and portrayed as a beautiful youth with wings and a bow and arrow, "shooting" others to inspire love. In modern Freudian psychology, it is used as a term for the libido, the urge for sexual pleasure and self-preservation.

> *Phileo*—To have affection, not necessarily in a sexual sense. It can refer to the love that comes with a sense of brotherhood.

Agape—A word rarely used in ancient manuscripts, but when it was, it denoted family or spousal love or the love of a particular activity. Sometimes it was used in reference to divinity, as it was used in a Greek title for the goddess Isis, Agape Theon—"beloved of the gods"—and later adopted by Christians to denote Christ's divine, unconditional, voluntary, self-sacrificing love. It is also referenced in forms of modern ceremonial magick.

Stergo—A parental love, used for the love of a parent for children or the love a ruler has for his people. Stergo is how some people see religious or divine love from a parental divinity. Today this is typified by the image of the biblical Father God of Judeo-Christianity. To the mystic and Witch, however, divine love, Perfect Love, is beyond stergo.

Is it any wonder why, for most of us, love is this great quest we spend so much time on, and why so many people feel unfulfilled? We have a romantic, "troubadour-esque" vision of love, and that vision clouds not only what we think about relationships and marriage, but it colors our idea of love with family, friends, and the Divine, creating unrealistic expectations with very little root in nature or history. Looking to the ancient magickal cultures gives us a larger scope of love and expands our view of the many types of love in the context of magick and in life. For the purposes of this book, most assume that love magick is seeking a romantic or sexual love (eros), but it's hard to talk about such love without touching upon these other concepts. While they are all different, there is a reason why we use one word as a translation: to show how they are all connected.

As a modern Witch, I learned that love is the ultimate source in magick. Most Witches believe that what you do returns to you in some way, often known as the Law of Return, or Boomerang Effect, and all magick is fueled by intense emotion, which can be the source of our magickal power. Any emotion will work to propel a magickal intention, but the quality of emotion you use will color your results. Magick done in anger or spite manifests with angry and spiteful qualities, and such qualities can return to you. I have learned that the best magick is fueled by love—not just personal love but unconditional and Perfect Love, divine love. If you make that your focus, regardless of what purpose you are casting a spell for, it will manifest and return to you with the qualities of divine love. You will have a greater chance of not only getting what you want, but of getting what you need and having it manifest in the most perfect and pleasant way possible. If love is also a term used for divinity, a force flowing through us all, then it truly is the ultimate source of our magick and the binding force that connects us all to everything and everyone.

Preparing for Love

In most traditions of magick, one must be prepared for the magick. In some Wiccan and ceremonial traditions, there are rites of preparation and purification before performing a ritual. One might take a ritual bath, be smudged in incense smoke, meditate to clear the mind, or be scourged to purify the spirit. Then specific clothing (if not working skyclad, or nude), jewelry, and specific oils and perfumes are used. One is then considered duly purified and prepared for the act of magick.

In forms of folk magick and cunning craft, there is not the same amount of ritual preparation, yet the practitioner becomes prepared, opened, and aligned with the forces of magick through gathering herbs and other ingredients and walking through nature. Any type of magick requires preparation, even if that preparation is only for a few minutes, to obtain the proper mindset for successful spellcasting.

Love magick is the same as any magick; you must be prepared for it. Love magick is some of the most experimental magick. Many people pick up a spellbook and, with no prior knowledge and training in magick,and not looking at the complete instructions, flip to a spell and do it. When it doesn't work, they assume magick is silly or deceptive and chalk the whole experience up to a wild lark that didn't amount to anything. I'm sure many people will do the same with this book. They were not sufficiently prepared, so the chance of success was slim to begin with. Though I ultimately did experience successful love magick, my first few times were not what I had hoped for, even though I had been formally trained in magick.

Love magick is one of the hardest magicks to be well-versed in. Magick requires a certain amount of detachment, of letting go of your intention, and when you are lonely and desiring a mate, it's hard to let go, even with a magickally trained mind. Since it is so hard for most of us, love magick requires even deeper forms of preparation if you want true and lasting success. Sadly, when people pick up a book on love magick, that's not what they want to hear. They desire a simple series of steps guaranteed to work without any pesky preparation or introspection.

Like Attracts Like

One of the basic magick principles is "like attracts like." In our spellwork, we use magickal correspondences—colors, scents, herbs, and stones—that have a similar spiritual vibration to what we are seeking to create. The qualities of the items denote their signature. Based on a principle known as the Doctrine of Signatures, it's as if Mother Nature has signed everything with little instructions in the item's shape, form, and quality to tell you how it may be used in medicine and magick.

If we are seeking prosperity, we use rich things such as candles or stones colored in royal blue and purple, or herbs that have a rich, full, and spicy flavor like cinnamon or cloves. They have similar spiritual vibrations. These correspondences align with royalty and wealth, as in ancient times the poor did not have access to them. They can be used to create the vibration of wealth. With the vibration of wealth in your ritual, you can attract the energy of wealth and manifest your desire. Likewise, for protection you would use dark, reflective, and dense material—black and brown, lead and iron, or plants with a fiery or spiky signature—to create a boundary. For love, we use material that has the vibration of love. Traditional love correspondences can be found in chapter 6, though we will each have our own personal love correspondences based upon our own preferences, experiences, history, personal symbolism, and even allergies.

The most important tool in any form of magick, but particularly in love magick, is ourselves. Our own body and our own consciousness are the primary instruments to be used. If we cannot vibrate in harmony with love ourselves, we will never be able to attract love. You must be able to feel true love for yourself in order to attract and create love with another. It seems like the classic catch-22: if I'm lonely and depressed and want a relationship, how can I feel happy, fulfilled, and loved while alone? If I felt those things, I wouldn't need a relationship that badly— and that's the key. While magick fills our needs, when you are focused on what modern practitioners call "poverty consciousness"—a level of awareness anchored in wants and needs, a level where you lack—you vibrate with the energy of wants and needs and only attract more wanting and needing.

Ritual and magickal training helps us shift our consciousness, so even while we may feel a lack, we can focus our thoughts on the blessings and, while vibrating in the energy of love and blessings, attract *more* love and blessings to us. Love magick is learning to sharply focus that attraction to get exactly what you want, not just a general love and blessing. It doesn't take away the longing and the need, but if the lack is the predominant factor in your consciousness, you'll never attract what you really want.

Letting Go

A second principle of magick is that we must let go of our intentions so they can manifest. When we hold on to them, unless they manifest instantly, we begin to doubt our magick. As we doubt, we suck back tiny amounts of energy from our spell. The more we doubt and worry, because we are anchored in a place of need, the more we sabotage our spell until it no longer works. Like a magickal leech, we have drained it, and when it no longer has any energy, it dissipates and our spell never reaches fruition.

While letting go of our intentions is a key factor, it's sometimes seemingly impossible, as we are also told to follow up our working with real-world action. How do you detach yet follow up with actions in the real world? You must not be rooted in the poverty consciousness of lacking what you want. Some will say that they found love when they stopped looking for it, focusing on their own goals and dreams, and creating the space and relaxation in their life for love to find them. Though I agree that can work, because desperate hunting only yields more desperation, I do believe in traditional follow-up. Believe it or not, doing a love spell is not enough.

I had one friend who sought magickal training specifically to do a love spell. I give him credit for trying, though so much of his training was done with only his love-spell goal in mind, he missed out on a lot of other deeper, personally fulfilling experiences of spiritual education. He did the love spell and in all likelihood did everything correct and by the book, yet he didn't go out and make an effort to meet anybody. He worked an odd-shift job that left little time to socialize during the week, and on the weekend he stayed at home watching television and movies in his boxers. We joked that unless his dream girl delivered pizza, there was no way he was going to meet her.

If you do a love spell, you have to be open to dates, personal ads, going to clubs, and being social with friends who have single friends. You have to make yourself available. In magick, we call it leaving many doors open for the magick to manifest. If you are set on only one way the magick can manifest, you have closed out many opportunities to success and made your spell less likely to succeed. If you focus on what you specifically want but not on how exactly you will get it, and you are open to seeing it anywhere, you have greatly increased the chances of your success. Put whatever limits are necessary on your magick to make sure you get what you really want, but the more specific, the more limited you get, the harder it becomes to manifest.

Love and Fear

So how do we become more in tune with the vibration of love and release our attachment from our needs and wants? That is where magickal training comes into play. My teachers emphasized that self-love was the key to all magick. Opening the heart and feeling self-esteem opens you to all other blessings and powers. It's not to say that those who feel anger and hate can't do successful magick, but they typically don't have successful lives (as I would define success, by lives I would want) by fueling their magick with anger and hate all the time.

The two major emotional, energetic forces in the universe are not love and hate but love and fear. While love expands, fear contracts. While love brings opportunity and optimism, fear closes us down and gives us a more pessimistic view. I won't tell you one is good and the other is bad, for both are needed. Some fears are sacred. Fear tells us when we are in danger, when we need to run or fight to protect ourselves. Good fear can lead to self-defense and even righteous anger to change ourselves and the world. Fear can also help in initiatory experiences, to make our way through the challenges.

But to live in a state of constant fear contracts us and limits us. When we are anchored in fear, we cannot receive, and we don't feel love. We can be anchored in love and still acknowledge fear and use it appropriately as a tool, without shutting down to other information. So out of the two states of emotion, anchoring in love in the heartspace is much more desirable, both to live a happy life and to make happy, fulfilling magick.

Most spiritual trainings encourage you to face your fears through intellectual examination, magickal exploration, and direct confrontation to determine which fear responses are healthy and which ones are limiting you. Magickal and mystical training also encourages you to experience love. In Witchcraft, we craft our Witch's circles with Perfect Love and Perfect Trust. They are the keys for entering the circle, given in British Traditional-style Wiccan initiations from initiator to student. In such rituals, one is threatened with the point of a sword. If the student cannot enter the circle in Perfect Love and Perfect Trust, then it is better to fall upon the sword than enter.

We all don't have to undergo traditional initiation to understand the power of love. One of the first exercises I learned (and honestly hated when I first did it) was an affirmation mirror exercise. Affirmations are considered basic, and at times trite with modern pop-psychology lingo, but they are extremely effective if practiced regularly. I credit affirmations with changing my life—or at least changing the way I thought about myself and my life. Once I changed my thinking, my life then changed. Doing this preliminary work diligently in my early training made my later, more complex magick much more effective and made me a happier and more effective person in the long run.

EXERCISE} **Mirror Affirmations**

This affirmation exercise can be done with eyes open, staring into a mirror, or with eyes closed, in a deep meditative state. Those with good focus can get into a meditative state while standing before a mirror (or holding a hand mirror) and opening their eyes without breaking the meditative state, finishing the affirmations, closing their eyes, and returning back to a normal state of consciousness.

The purpose of saying affirmations in the mirror is that you are clearly directing them to yourself—you are clearly blessing yourself as well as facing who you are in a given moment. This makes some people feel nervous or silly, but you will soon move through those feelings and get closer to your true self. One of the tools of Witchcraft is the mirror. The glyph ($♀$) of the planet Venus (named after the goddess of love) is said to be a mirror. It is also the modern symbol for woman, the circle topping an equal-armed cross. Mirrors are used for divination and protection magick, and having a hand-held mirror on your altar for magickal work, including affirmations, is of great advantage.

The advantage of saying affirmations in a meditative state is that your full consciousness—the three minds of your conscious self, psychic self, and superconscious self, also known as the middle, lower, and higher selves—hears your program and works together from your new instructions. Meditation aligns all parts of your soul.

The instructions below count you into a meditative state. You can either opt to open your eyes and look at the mirror before you (or a mirror in your hand) or keep your eyes closed and still say the affirmations. Affirmations are best said out loud, but if you are in a deep meditative state, you might find yourself saying them silently, and silent, internal affirmations work too.

1. Start by closing your eyes and relaxing your body. Give your entire body permission to relax, starting at the top of your head and relaxing down through your body, down to the tips of your fingers and the tips of your toes. Imagine waves of relaxation sweeping through your body and releasing any tension or stress out to the universe.

2. Relax your mind. Imagine your mind is like a clear-blue, bright sky. Any unwanted thoughts are like white, wispy clouds, and your will blows through the sky, clearing it, until it's completely peaceful and empty.

3. Feel your heart beating with love. Feel the love flowing through your body, circulating around and inside you. Feel the love you have and the love the universe and the Divine have for you.

4. Within your heart, feel the light of your soul, your inner fire. This inner fire will guide you and protect you in all things, leading the way.

5. Imagine a screen in your mind's eye, and on that screen draw the number 12. Hold it for a moment, and then erase it. Draw the number 11. Hold it and erase it. Continue downward in your count until you reach the number 1. You are now in a meditative state where everything you do is for the highest good of all involved.

6. Release the screen of your mind and hold no image. Simply and silently count backwards from thirteen to one, going deeper into meditation, where anything is possible.

7. If you have a mirror with you or before you, slowly open your eyes and gaze into the mirror. Look deep into your own eyes and say the following affirmations. If you don't have a mirror or simply desire to keep your eyes closed, keep them closed. Say each of these affirmations at least three times in a confident manner, either out loud or strongly but silently in your own mind:

I love myself.
I love others.
I am loved by the universe
(or Divine/gods/Goddess and God/Powers—
whatever term you prefer);
I am able to give and receive love.
I forgive myself.
I forgive others.
I am open to love on all levels.

Feel the affirmations becoming planted in your mind like seeds, and when you repeat this exercise, you are watering and nourishing these spiritual seeds. They will soon take root and grow strong. If your eyes are open, close them and relax for a moment.

8. When done, count yourself up from one to thirteen and then one to twelve, with no visualizations. When you reach the last one, feel your fingers and toes, arms and legs. When you are ready, open your eyes.

9. Bring both hands above the head, with palms facing the crown. Sweep down the front of the body, over the face, neck, heart, belly, and groin, pushing out and then down toward the ground. Say:

   I release all that does not serve my highest good.

   Repeat the sweeping motion two more times, following each with one of these two additional statements:

   I am in balance with myself.
   I am in balance with the universe.

10. Ground yourself as needed. Feel your feet extend into the ground, anchoring your physical body in the physical world.

Not only are positive or constructive affirmations important, but we must also be vigilant in our thoughts to understand our unconscious negative affirmations about love, romance, and relationships. One of the most insidious ways they sneak into our consciousness is through music. When we hear a catchy tune and naturally want to sing along, rarely do we ask ourselves if the lyrics are something we want to reinforce in our personal programming. Most songs about love are about love gone bad, and singing the lyrics over and over again reinforces that imagery and idea in our mind.

Now, before you protest, let me tell you I had a very difficult time with this magickal teaching. I felt it was an attack on my music. I love my music. My college degree is in music; I've been a songwriter; and

I've found dark, depressing, and even angry songs to be very therapeutic. I feel the same way about movies and books. So when a magickal mentor told me this teaching—to purge yourself of such "negative" thoughtforms from your music and other media—I resisted. Yet, looking back many years later, I realize she had a point, but there was something missing from her simple teaching to understand the role of sacred art and healing.

There is absolutely nothing wrong with any art that is considered depressing or angry, and it truly can be therapeutic, giving you a method by which you can express similar feelings. We are all a part of the human condition and go through many of the same basic responses, even though our own situation and perspective is unique. The problem is when we get stuck in them. A really good performing artist in any genre knows how to channel the energy of the art or the energy of the character. They don't get stuck in the song or performance; it moves through them and they let it go.

In magick, we have a practice known as invocation, where we invoke into our bodies an energy, a spiritual entity, and then, when the ritual is done, there are banishings and releasings to bring the magician back to normal. A good performer does that too, though it might be done intuitively. "Bad" performers, who can be very good at their art but not in this release process, find themselves in the tabloid dramas of continually reliving their worst moments. The bad times that fueled their art then become programmed into their consciousness, and they cannot escape them to live a happy and fulfilled life.

If you can sing along with a song and be with it in the moment but not dwell on the times it brings you back to—in other words, to let it pass through you—you are doing well. If you get stuck in a song and, after singing it, you notice it alters your mood or outlook, even though you like the song and think it's fun, you are probably impressing these unwanted programs into your consciousness. You might want to take a break from depressing or angry music, or heartache and break-up songs, particularly when you are feeling like you are blocked to love, romance, and affection. When you do sing them, try to think of such songs as specific performances with a beginning, middle, and end, and when you end, release the spirit of the song.

Love and Healing

Much of our preparation for any magick is through healing. Keeping our thoughts in good order and in harmony with our intention is an integral part of healing. Love magick is a form of healing magick, for we must heal our relationship with, and our connection to, the force of divine unconditional love. Through healing that connection, establishing it firmly in our lives, all things are possible. If fear is a roadblock to love, we must examine our fears in relationship to love. We must be brutally honest with ourselves when it comes to love magick if we truly seek success. Sadly, many people are not reaching for true success and true love but a quick fix without the work. While the spell might last for a bit, you must build a foundation to achieve lasting lifetime results.

Start by asking yourself some questions about love:

- Do you love yourself? Do you have self-esteem and pride in your own being?

- Do you like yourself? While it is possible to love someone without liking that person, it's very hard to love yourself and not like yourself. What about yourself do you not like? What about yourself do you fear or wish you could change? Are these intrinsic qualities and characteristics, or are they changeable behaviors and actions? If they are intrinsic, you must learn to accept yourself to truly love yourself. If they are changeable behaviors, set goals to change them.

- Do you really want love? If so, what kind of love are you looking for? How would you describe it? How do you envision it?

- Do you fear those you are attracted to? If you have self-esteem and self-confidence, you should be able to approach someone you are attracted to without a lot of drama. While this is easier said than done for most of us, it's part of the self-mastery that comes with a serious pursuit of magick. You are confident in yourself and know that if you are rebuffed, there is simply not a connection between you, but that doesn't make you any less of a person or any less attractive.

- Are you really ready for love if you want it? Do you have the space and time in your life, and if not, are you willing to make it? Have you worked on the things about yourself, both personally in the internal world and in the external world, to make sure you are in a place for love? If you are looking for a serious partner, have you "sown your wild oats" and are truly mature and experienced enough to settle down? Do you need that experience, or are you looking for something else? Whatever you are looking for, imagine it happening today. How would your life change? Are you ready for that change? If you truly want it, how would you prepare for that change so you are ready for it when it comes?

- Are you happy and healthy alone? Though you can still want a partner, do you feel secure in yourself and fulfilled in your life? Those who don't feel secure in their life and are seeking to build their life around a partner usually cannot detach from their desire to manifest a successful spell. They are locked in a love poverty consciousness, contracted by the fear of being alone. If you are not happy alone, what steps must you take to gain a greater security with yourself and your own life before finding a partner?

While spells are no substitute for introspection, self-improvement, and, if needed, therapy, they can put in motion the forces to heal and improve issues that can be revealed with the previous questions. Introspection can reveal self-esteem problems and what some would call negative emotions in regard to love—fear, jealousy, loneliness, envy, and a need for control. While such emotions are not helpful in the short term, integrating these feelings into a complete and whole self-image is very important. While many seek a magickal shortcut to banish them completely, healthy Witches know that one cannot be divided from the shadow; we must be aware of it and integrate it.

SPELL} Healing

On the new Moon, prepare two healing potions. One is to cleanse and clear, and the other is to bless and bring harmony. Mix three tablespoons of apple cider vinegar and one tablespoon of sea salt with at least three cups of hot water. Make a second liquid of one tablespoon of honey and one tablespoon of orange juice with three cups of hot water. Also obtain a small rounded stone, such as a white river stone or a tumbled quartz.

Add the vinegar potion to a hot bath. Soak in it and think about what issues you need to transform and reconcile. Let the water drain while still sitting in the tub. Then fill the tub again with hot water and add the second potion to the bath. While in the bath, hold your stone and think about how you would be healthy, whole, and at peace with all your issues, totally prepared for a loving relationship, first with yourself and then with a partner. Carry the stone with you in your left pocket if you are right-handed or your right pocket if you are left-handed.

Repeat this process on every new Moon for five lunar cycles, and you will notice a significant shift in your healing process. Issues of jealousy, loneliness, fear of being touched, and unresolved past relationships will all shift.

TWO

Magickal Partners

Most of us performing love magick are seeking a partner on some level, someone to be in relationship with. We seek to share our life with another. Understanding our views on relationships and both what we expect from a partner and offer to a partner is critical in performing successful love magick. Otherwise we put potential problems on hold for the future. Part of our preparation is understanding ourselves to better understand our desires and what we create.

Relationships

While our culture generally doesn't examine the range and meaning of the word *love*, we also don't look at our relationships with clarity. Before we can do magick for anything, we have to be sure of what we are manifesting. If you are doing love magick with the hopes of a relationship, you need to know what kind of relationship you are looking for. When finding any type of partner, long term or short term, you need to know that both you and your potential partner are viewing the relationship in the same way. If not, you must at least understand your partner's perspective on the relationship if you hope to build something healthy for both of you. Miscommunications and assumptions, both of yourself and of others, are the root for much of our failed relationships. Being honest with yourself and your partner about how you view a relationship is critical in building one and doing magick to manifest one.

Think about how you view a relationship, and see if any of these perspectives fit your view, or is there another way you see a relationship?

Complete Me—Our romantic sense of love, perpetuated by movies and television, tells us that we are incomplete without a romantic partner. Our partner must be our perfect match to us, like the other half of our soul, and once we meet, we are complete. We are looking for someone to bring us happiness, health, and wholeness. Though this is a popular notion, I think it's one of the most harmful views to have and an impediment to a successful relationship. We must complete ourselves, but a partner is a complement to us.

Expectation—A relationship isn't something you have an option about, it's something that you must pursue. Everybody wants a relationship, and if you don't, then there must be something wrong with you. The "normal" thing is to find a partner and settle down for life. Our culture not only expects it, but rewards it. While this view is a norm, it is not necessarily a truth, particularly in our modern society. There are many roles available, and if you don't want a relationship, you don't have to have one. Your first and most important relationship is with yourself, and through your self-relationship, you can find the Divine.

Investment—A relationship is like an investment. When you build a relationship with another, you are both investing in a future together. Your time and effort is like adding to a bank account, and when enough has accrued, you have created stability, a foundation to build the rest of your life on. While this can also be true, it isn't necessarily so. Bank accounts can be dissolved when necessary, and time and effort doesn't guarantee security. While love can be seen as an investment, that puts a lot of conditions and future strings on it, creating a pressure to commit before you are sure you want to commit. To experience unconditional love through relationship, you have to change your expectation of conditional love.

Adventure—Life is an adventure, and every relationship is an adventure. There is no map; there is no goal; there is simply the journey. When two people come together, they are journeying together for as long as they choose, walking side by side. Relationships are exciting and mysterious because you never know what comes next. While this is also true for some, there is a time in a relationship when it can still be an adventure, but the adventurers can have a commitment to plan their journey together, rather than walk blindly without a map.

Hunt—Seeking relationships is like big-game hunting. The thrill and excitement is in the hunt itself and in catching a partner. Many romantic self-help books give you the view of catching a man or woman, as if you have to trap them or become a catch yourself to lure them to catch you. While it might be a fun view for a time, it puts all the emphasis on the dating experience leading up to a relationship but not a lot on actually developing the relationship. If your romantic worldview is centered in the hunt, then you constantly seek out new relationships to be in that "hunt" mode rather than develop any deeper relationships.

Laissez Faire—From a French term meaning "hands off" or "let do" and most often applied to free-market economics, generally meaning to let the economy roam free, hands off. The same idea can be applied to relationships. Some look at relationships in a very relaxed way. Whatever happens, happens with no expectations, commitments, or beliefs. Things will unfold themselves, with no planning or forethought. While that's a nice idea, it doesn't always work in the long run, but those with such a view are not necessarily looking for a long relationship.

Spiritual Work—Any relationship, including a romantic one, is an opportunity to grow and evolve spiritually. We each have something to teach the other, and we stay together as long as we are learning and teaching and growing together. Though this is the ideal for many spiritual workers, it can leave those who are looking for more long-term security feeling insecure, yet life *is* insecure. Just because someone promises to stay with you for their entire life, should they really if it becomes harmful for them or you? The spiritual view of relationships is both a fulfilling and a difficult one.

All of these relationship views have their benefits, but all of them have drawbacks as well. There really is no one perfect way for us to view our relationships, but these are some common paradigms. Your view can change or develop over time, or you can have more than one. Knowing how you look at it, and what benefits and drawbacks your view has, as well as your partner's view, really helps you prepare for a deeper relationship.

In looking at the relationship views you have and the relationships you want, it's important to note there are many different types of relationships out there, and as a general rule, Witches do not discriminate. A modern Witchcraft ethos from the Wiccan Rede is "An' it harm none, do as ye will." Many assume romantic relationships are strictly between a man and a woman, yet most Witches do not discriminate against gays, lesbians, bisexuals, or transgendered people, both in the Craft and in their use of love magick. Some lore dating back to the ancient world gives love spells specifically for attracting a same-sex lover. Specific herbs and spells were used for homosexual love. This doesn't mean that such love is any different from heterosexual love, but it's a different vibration. It's a different expression of love; you are attracting something different, yet both are love. But there is an amazing crossover of correspondences used for both gay and straight people alike, showing that love is love, and the spells contained in this book can work for anyone. For a much more detailed examination of the topic, I suggest my previous book *Gay Witchcraft: Empowering the Tribe*.

Witches are not biased against alternative relationships. Many people in the Pagan community identify as polyamorous, whether they are heterosexual, homosexual, or bisexual. Polyamory is a term meaning "many loves," and today it denotes a wide range of relationships but generally means that two lovers are not completely exclusive to each other. This can work out in many ways but is usually a relationship of two individuals who are free to pursue sexual and/or romantic relationships with others independently, or a relationship consisting of more than two committed partners, such as a triad. While much of the grammatical bias of this book denotes finding a single lover or partner, not multiple ones, the ideas and spells can be applied to any situation or relationship. The dynamics are different and the challenges are different, but relationships are relationships, and there is much that is the same. You may think that such relationships would never be for you but later find yourself in a situation where the opportunity and desire arises, so don't be quick to judge. The wisdom of *The Witch's Heart* will help *all* Witches' hearts: monogamous, open, or polyamorous. As long as you are able to pursue your longings in a way that doesn't hurt yourself or others, then it is fine within the morality and ethics of the Witch. Many Pagans and Witches have championed for the rights of those involved in polyamorous relationships and educated the public about misconceptions, particularly the Pagan elder Oberon Zell-Ravenheart. For deeper wisdom specifically on polyamorous relationships, I refer you to the excellent book *Pagan Polyamory* by Raven Kaldera.

Some in the British Traditional lineages are not as open to polyamory, and some are not open to homosexuality or bisexuality, as many of these traditions focus on the polarity of one man and one woman, or several couples in a coven setting, to work magick. Thankfully, many in such traditions are realizing what works for them both magickally and personally is not what works for all magickal people, and you can separate a traditional teaching for a specific tradition from a guide to life that everyone must follow. If you are practicing those traditions or training in them, it's good to explore the traditional roles in such settings, but it doesn't have to be your lifetime choice. I know many gay Witches who have explored "straight" roles in Gardnerian Wicca and naturally polyamorous people who have focused on a single magickal/sexual partner while training in such traditions.

Understanding "nontraditional" relationship views and the possibility of them in your life, even simply as friends, helps widen your view of love and relationship, and teaches you how to be more open and wise in all situations.

What Do You Really Want?

In my magickal teachings, I tell my students all successful intentional spells have three components in common, regardless of the tradition or method: you must have a method of altering consciousness, clear intention, and a method for directing energy. We use meditation and ritual for the first and third step, but the second step is the hard part: you must have a clear intent. What do you want? What is the purpose of the spell?

When you are doing love magick, what do you want? If you don't know what you want, at least on some level, you will never get it.

A traditional method in love magick to help you prepare and become clear in your intent is to make a list of what you want in a lover or in a relationship.

EXERCISE} List of Qualities in a Partner

In a magickal journal, notebook, or in a computer file where you keep your special and sacred writings, make a list of all the qualities and attributes you would like in a romantic partner and relationship. Your only limits are the ones you place on yourself, but I've found that when you focus on what is truly important rather than on the minor points that don't matter as much, or you phrase your wants in a manner that leaves them more open, you have a greater chance of success.

Simply put, I think it's best to choose qualities more than physical attributes. Only when I let go of my own image of the ideal partner— the stereotypical blond-haired, blue-eyed, tall boy-next-door type—did I open myself to the right person with all the right attributes. Rather than putting specific hair color, eye color, height, and weight for a partner, you could make one of the qualities "is physically attractive to me," and you might discover something beyond your perceived "type." Everybody wants an attractive partner, and there is nothing wrong with that. I think mutual physical attraction is almost mandatory for relationships to work. You can have anything you want but sometimes, by being so specific, you miss out on some amazing people who don't fit into a stereotype.

Once you have made the initial list, go over it a few times, add to it things you might have forgotten, and cross out things that, upon further reflection, don't seem important. Refine your list until it becomes solid and stable.

When you first make the list, reflect on it, then go back to the beginning of the exercise and repeat it. What do you want to keep on the list, and what do you want to change? Rather than rushing into it, give it thought. A new relationship can be a life-altering event, so take some time to make sure you are getting what you want and need. If you prepare and get your intention set beforehand, you will soon be ready to do effective love magick.

Popular author Dorothy Morrison reminds us, in her book *Enchantments of the Heart*, to make sure the list of qualities also includes something to indicate "human," as focusing on the qualities of loyalty or companionship could bring an amazing, loving pet to you, but not necessarily a mate. This may sound silly, as you'd think that many of the other qualifiers would clue the universal powers in on the fact that your goal is a human romantic relationship, but if your own list of qualities is too sentimental and doesn't include things like "has a job" or "someone I'm sexually attracted to," then your spell might work, but you might not get you what you intended. I do know one person who quite successfully conjured a loving Dalmatian with her spell. It was truly guided by divine will, as they make a great pair, and it was also a powerful learning experience. A few years later, she was able to successfully conjure the right man for her and the Dalmatian, and they have all been happily together ever since!

Sometimes making the list of qualities is enough to get the magick started. I have a non-Witch friend who asked me to do a love spell for him. I had him write out his list so it would be clear in his mind what type of person the spell would be attracting. Then I had a family emergency and was out of touch with him for a while—and I never carved, anointed, and consecrated the love candle spell as promised. But he later told me that someone came into his life the next week that matched his intentions, and they began dating. The list really began the magick for him.

When you have your list of qualities that you feel satisfied with, think about yourself. If you are seeking good qualities from someone else, do you offer similar qualities to the one you are in relationship with?

Relationship is always about balance—give and take. If you have a clear intention about what you are seeking, of what you want to receive, do you have a clear intention of what qualities you possess and what you are willing to offer?

EXERCISE} List of Qualities in Yourself

Repeat the previous exercise but this time, focus on making a list about yourself and the qualities you bring to the table. If your potential partner, out there somewhere, was making his or her own list, what would be on that list that would describe you? Refine the list as honestly and objectively as you can.

Upon reflection of your own list, are you a balanced match for what you are looking for, or are you expecting the moon and offering nothing? Do you want that kind of relationship? You could get it, but it won't be very satisfying for your partner, and therefore it won't be very stable for you. Are there things you feel you need to change about yourself to make you a better potential partner? If so, begin making plans to improve yourself in whatever ways are necessary, and seek outside help, outside facilitation if need be. Your personal work might be physical, such as exercising more, eating better, and getting into more attractive physical shape. It could be emotional balance and require a therapist or life coach. Everybody's situation will be different, so find the help that you might need.

The Intention of Love

Intention is such an important part of life. We must balance intention with a balance of being open to unplanned blessings, but intention gives us a direction and impetus forward in the adventure of life. Some people think relationships and romance just happen to them, and it does, yet they keep attracting people who are not balanced and correct because they have never taken the time to think about what kind of person would be right.

My friend Rowan in California is a very loving, very giving person, but after a series of bad relationships with abusive men, she told me that it never occurred to her to ask for what she wanted in a relationship. She is a very magickal person who uses ritual and prayer in all other areas of her life, but she felt like she couldn't be specific with love. For some reason, she felt the universe would send her what was right, without any intention on her part. But she can use magick in love, both for a potential partner and for herself. Her experience in love magick led to a major crisis and healing, working through the issues of self-love and self-acceptance. She performed a ritual for love using a potion I had made specifically for her (see chapter 7's Love Potion No. 13). During the course of the ritual she spilled the potion, and her intuition guided her to anoint her whole body with the entire potion. While she felt great during the ritual, she immediately became very ill in the days and weeks that followed and was bedridden. Throughout the healing process, she was forced by time and solitude to look at all her issues around love and relationship, family and home. She literally couldn't distract herself or run away. Her illness baffled the doctors, and she mysteriously recovered just as she had taken ill but now was in a much clearer, healthier, and happier place, feeling ready for a healthy, balanced relationship. She is still very open to what the universe has to show her, but her boundaries about who she lets into her life, and her intention on the types of men she wants, have become much clearer.

Part of aligning the steps of magick in our ritual space with the follow-up work of life outside of our ritual space is to make sure that our thoughts, words, and actions are truly in alignment with our intentions. Rowan's example was extreme, but we need to get clear in our intentions and follow up those intentions, making sure our actions reflect them in our day-to-day life. Many people say they want something specific, and then their actions do not support their intentions. It's much like lying to the universe, even when we are unconsciously lying to it.

Lying to the universe, to ourselves, and to others devalues the power of our words and diminishes our magick.

The universe understands symbols and actions much easier than words. When we say something in private or in ritual or in our journal, and then our actions are contrary, or out of alignment with what we say we want, the universe doesn't know what to fulfill in terms of intention. Our energy is not clearly attracting what we want, because we are mixing our signals.

Many people will have a clear intention of what kind of relationship they want but then settle for relationships that are obviously not correct for them, not what they are looking for. While we must be open to unexpected blessings in our life, when we settle for a relationship because it's better than being alone, even when it is unhealthy for us, we are not receiving a blessing, we are cursing ourselves. Our self-inflicted, self-chosen jinx is blocking the way for a good relationship to come to us. If we close the avenue of a good relationship, it will never appear.

I have another friend who has been in an unsatisfying relationship for years. This one has turned into a friendship living arrangement with sex but none of the romance he wants. Their relationship is open to other sexual partners, meaning each partner can have sex with someone else without any sense of betrayal. He figures when he finds someone better, he'll just leave. While technically it could happen, this betrays the spirit of his arrangement with his partner. Any truly romantic potential partner who hears about this unhealthy situation will run screaming in the other direction until it all gets settled out. So though he's technically open to finding someone else, he really is closed off to what he wants.

I've had many friends, clients, and students who say they are longing for a life partner, a truly committed person who is their equal, and they put energy into magickal rituals to manifest this. Then they go out and have sex with casual partners right afterward and bemoan the fact they haven't found their partner. While there is nothing inherently wrong with casual sex if it's the right choice for you, it does send mixed signals to the universe. After telling the universe exactly what you want beyond the physical in a partner, you casually pick up and invest a lot of energy in someone who is nothing like for whom you just asked. While it is possible to do love magick for a partner and find that partner through a casual one-night stand right afterward, I've only seen it happen successfully twice; most often I've seen people become miserable when taking this course. There is not an alignment of action and intention.

Love and sexual energy are all different parts of life force, and when you are focused on a goal, you have to focus your energy on the task at hand. That is why many magickal orders and mystic traditions have restrictions on sex. While some are due to politics and a denial of sexual energy, many apply the sexual energy in the pursuit of enlightenment directly with the Divine, rather than the pursuit of enlightenment through the physical world and a relationship with it and others.

Thankfully, Witchcraft is a mystery tradition that doesn't require celibacy on any level. But if you have a specific goal in mind, you should be careful in how you use your life-force energy. If you want to focus your romantic and sexual energy on a partner, and you tell the universe this but take actions to the contrary while you are waiting, scattering your energy in many directions, you are self-sabotaging the working. It's like telling the universe you want to be in shape and healthy immediately, yet eating lots of potato chips while you're waiting for it to magickally happen. There is nothing immoral about eating potato chips, but it does run contrary to your stated goal. The waiting period is what helps shape your internal world to create a change in your external world. Now, if you have no romantic-partner goal in mind, you can have sex with whomever you want, whenever you want. It's just a matter of applying the right energies to the goals you have.

Learning to apply this principle to my own life was very profound and effective. After doing many love spells and having a profound experience during one ritual (see chapter 7's Rose Wish), I still wasn't manifesting a good partner, and I was distracted by someone sexually who I knew was not and would never be my life partner. But I was lonely. We would break things off and then get back together. When I made the clear and final decision to break off all sexual contact with this man, as we were both settling for something less than what we both wanted, and focused on finding the right partner, my future husband showed up three days later. Once I was truly clear in what I wanted, my magick had the energy and space to manifest.

A friend of mine, after a long search for his life mate, was told by an ancestor spirit during a Samhain ritual that he spread his power around too much. He spread his ability to attract around too much, sharing his energy with too many people sexually. By doing so, he couldn't attract "the one" because he was not shining brightly, he was wasting his energy on other tiny flames in his life, thinking he was just killing time and having fun until "the one" showed up. People don't just show up. It's a complicated interplay of forces that brings two people together. Both have to be ready. If you keep telling the universe you are just playing, just "killing time," you continue to attract people who reinforce that status of waiting, killing time. Before you know it, your life has passed before your eyes. Many pop culture self-help approaches to magick sum it up nicely: "You attract whatever you focus on."

EXERCISE} **Sexual Black Fast**

One technique to clearly focus your energy in the direction you want is a variation of the black fast. Traditionally, the black fast is a curse. One curses another individual and then vows to eat nothing but bread, water, and salt until that curse comes true. The idea is that your psyche, pushed to such an extreme with these physical conditions, will work day and night to fulfill your malignant will. Now, I am not suggesting cursing anyone to get the relationship you want, but the principle of forcing your psyche with extreme physical conditions is an interesting and effective magickal technique.

I am suggesting a form of sexual black fast. When you truly decide you are prepared and ready for a long-term relationship and have a clear intention of what kind of relationship you want, abstain from casual sexual encounters. You can still have food normally, so this isn't a food fast. Focus your will and the energy of your body on the goal you have. I'm not saying don't date. Please, *do* date. Get to know the person, and determine if this is a potential partner. If so, then you break the fast. But if not, don't get tied down or engaged in any romantic or sexual relationship with the person. You can be friends, but let go of any romantic notions and continue your quest. We can get bogged down with people who are nice or take months to find out that a person isn't right for us. A good, clear, and level-headed magician will be able to quickly determine if a person comes close to matching their intention and has the same intentions toward you as well. If not, don't settle because you're lonely or you think you can change the person into an ideal partner. A magician knows that lasting change must come from within. A person can change if they want to change. You can change yourself. You can't change someone else into what you want them to be. Even when they appear to conform for a time, it won't be a deep and lasting change.

Making sure you are in total harmony with your intentions is key to any successful magick. Love is messy, and love magick also is messy and difficult. The clearer you can be in yourself, and the more centered you can be in all aspects of your life, the more successful your love magick will be.

THREE

The Ethics of Love, Lust, and Romance Magick

One of the most important aspects of love magick, and one of the reasons that it is so complicated and controversial, is the issue of ethics. I come across quite a few people open to magick and Witchcraft, but aghast that you could use spiritual powers for money, love, or sex. To such people, these are selfish pursuits and are not spiritual at all. Some naively assume that spiritual powers do not work for selfish pursuits, so they don't understand how such magick could work. Due to the fallacies of many television shows about Witchcraft, they believe some sort of cosmic laws prevent it. Those that do believe magick can work for personal gain usually assume that "good" people wouldn't do such a thing because it is somehow evil or harmful to themselves and others.

Yet in my experience as a public Witch, I've found a small percentage of this group who believes love magick is wrong will still come to you in times of desperation and ask you to do something in clear violation

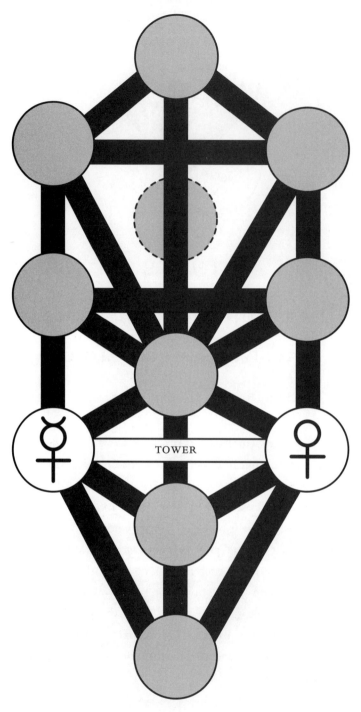

FIGURE} Tree of Life emphasizing Hod (Mercury—
Intellect) and Netzach (Venus—Emotion) with the path of the
Tower card from the tarot's Major Arcana. This image can
be meditated upon to balance our logic with our feelings.

of their proposed ethics and your own, and they feel perfectly justified doing so because their love is "real." Love can make us crazy at times and warp our view of what is right and wrong. I think it is truly impor-tant to reflect and discuss the ethics of love magick, and decide what is right for you far before you get into the situation of casting a love spell. You should clearly define your own morality regarding love magick before you really need it. You can always change your point of view, but at least you will be putting thought and reason into it, rather than bas-ing your decision solely on blind lust, fear, or raging jealousy. Extreme emotions can prompt us to do extreme things. It is important to develop the intellect and reason, the logical mind, to balance the emotions. In the magickal tradition of the Qabalah, the mind is literally balancing the emotions, and the proper proportion of both is needed to be successful in life and magick.

In qabalistic magick, each realm of consciousness, seen both as a spiritual world and an aspect of ourselves, is visualized as a sphere on a glyph known as the Tree of Life. The tree contains ten spheres, properly called sephiroth (sephira, singular), describing both the universe and our own soul. The sphere associated with Venus, as the sphere of love and primal emotion, is called Netzach, and it is directly balanced by a sphere on the other side of the Tree of Life named Hod. Hod is ruled by Mer-cury and embodies the linear mind. The qabalistic tradition teaches us about the balance between our intellect (Hod) and our emotions (Net-zach). For those of us who tend to emphasize one over the other, an understanding of this system can be helpful. It's particularly helpful to rely on the powers of Hod when we feel we are running wild with our Netzach passions and need to find balance.

Each of the spheres on the Tree of Life are connected by a "path," a line originally associated with one of the twenty-two Hebrew letters and then later associated with the Major Arcana of the tarot deck. Each path represents the shift in consciousness that must occur to move from one sphere to another. Climbing to the top of the Tree of Life is the climb to our spiritual source and the experience of enlightenment. The path that traditionally connects Netzach and Hod is symbolized by the tarot card known as the Tower. The Tower's lesson is about how things come crumbling down when we build our life in an imbalanced way. We have to start back at the foundation. When we don't have harmony and balance between emotion and logic, Netzach and Hod, we will soon experience the Tower's lessons and have to rebuild again.

Think about times in your life when your passions regarding relationship are out of balance. When you can't find stability, it truly feels like the world is collapsing; that's the lesson of the Tower. While qabalistic magick is a complex art in itself, the pattern of the Tree of Life can be a good guide to anyone. When your Netzach is out of control, look to the logical mind, Hod, to counterbalance it. Ask yourself the logical, linear, rational questions about the situation. It's hard, but when you do, the process can point out when you've gone a little crazy emotionally and help balance and center you and your actions. Likewise, when you are too intellectual, ask yourself how you feel about a situation. Tap into the powers of Netzach for balance.

Famous Love Archetypes

Part of our own process of building a strong, balanced foundation in regard to love magick is to explore the archetypal wisdom of the Witch through history as it relates to love magick and ethics. Some of the images are steeped in lore and history, the territory of Hod, while others bring up emotional and visceral responses, the realm of Netzach. The Witch's association with love and love spells, both for good and ill, are part of our fascination with Witchcraft and magick. Not all of the mythic and historic figures listed here are role models, but they are teachers. Sometimes they teach by showing us what *not* to do. Both sides are necessary to understand where we as a tradition have come to before we decide where we are going with our magick and ethics.

The Enchantresses

Witches have always had an association with love magick. In fact, it might be one of the reasons for our vilification in Western culture. While we might be most familiar with the image of the Witch as the old hag, the stereotypical Halloween image of the green-faced, crooked-toothed, hooknosed Witch riding her broom and scaring children, the oldest images we have of mythic Witches, coming from ancient Greece, are of beautiful enchantresses and deadly sorceresses.

Two of the most powerful, if not the most ethically flattering in their classic stories, are Circe and Medea. Both are presented as beautiful women, a far cry from the ugly crones of popular European lore. Circe, though portrayed as a Witchlike figure, is actually considered a goddess, the daughter of Helios, a Titan, and Perse, an Oceanid. She has the power of transformation, changing men into beasts. She is most famously known for her love affair with Odysseus and for changing his crew into pigs. Before he set out on his rescue mission, Odysseus was advised by the god Hermes to use the herb moly to block Circe's magickal powers. Circe was so surprised by his immunity to her magick, she fell in love with him and, according to some mythic reports, bore him three sons. She was able to keep Odysseus as her lover in her home for an entire year. Because of her love for him, she eventually assisted him in his quest to return home. She was vilified for seducing Odysseus, a married man, and is portrayed as one of the villains of the story. Did she use magick to seduce him, or was it his own free will? He could certainly blame her magick when rationalizing his immoral activities, but we don't know if it's true.

Medea is also a powerful Witch in the ancient Greek tradition, said to be the niece of Circe as well as the daughter of King Aeetes and granddaughter of the Sun Titan Helios, giving her divine blood, aiding her magick. She was also a priestess to Hecate, and her prayers to this goddess of Witches helped fuel her magick. There are many ancient tales ascribed to Medea, some conflicting in their chronology, outcome, and motives. In the tale of Jason and his quest for the Golden Fleece, she falls in love with Jason and uses both magick and murder to aid him in his adventures as they escape her father. They are married and have children together, but Jason later abandons her to marry another, and Medea seeks revenge by killing his children, his new bride, and his father-in-law with her poison magick.

While both are powerful images of the ancient Witch as lover and beautiful priestess, they are not necessarily the most healthy of role models for the modern Witch. While we can claim a patriarchal vilification of Circe and Medea, even the oldest myths we have of them paint them as villains. The hero's quest is often seen as an initiatory tale, and the female characters can take a difficult but necessary role embodying the dark chthonic forces the hero must face in the quest. Most people don't interpret the stories that way, but rather see them as the villains. In fact, while Witches are almost universally known for their abilities in love magick, there are not many classic stories of the "good" Witch with the "good" love potion, creating a tale of happily ever after.

The Fairy Godmother

Beyond the classic mythology, we have other tales of love magick, Witches, and fairy godmothers, but they too present their share of problems in the archetype of the Witch as enchantress. In the tale of Tristan and Iseult, the couple accidentally consumes a love potion, resulting in their falling in love with each other, creating a difficult affair that, in most versions, ends in tragedy. The potion is not particularly attributed to a Witch, and the magick, while providing the pivotal plot device, does not turn out to be benign in function.

Cinderella is the best tale of the fairy godmother as the benign Witch or otherworldly patron helping the maiden. In early versions, the godmother role is played by her deceased mother, whom Cinderella contacts by praying over her mother's grave, giving the story deeper Witchcraft and necromantic associations, as Witches are known to conjure the dead.

In classic fairy tales, the story of Snow White gives us a stepmother queen villain, described as a Witch figure, who tries to have Snow White murdered so the queen can be the "fairest of them all." She eventually succeeds, at least partially, by poisoning an apple, a symbol associated with Witchcraft and magick, and tricking Snow White into eating it. In the popular Disney version, it is only by being rescued with a kiss by her true love, Prince Charming, that she is returned back to life, similar to Sleeping Beauty's tale. Though we can look at the evil queen as a villain, in terms of an initiatory story, she is the shadow, the dweller on the threshold, and the teacher. She plays a similar role to Snow White that Set plays to his brother Osiris in the Egyptian mythos. In the end, I think many of the tales of "love" involving Witchcraft figures are dark because they provide the impetus to prepare the main character for love, to recognize it and cherish it when it's found. Who said love—and, by extension, life—is going to be easy?

The Venefica

While it's easy for modern-day Neopagans and Witches to blame the Christians exclusively for the Witch hunts and persecutions, we can see that those who identified with the word *witch* in the ancient Greek and Roman world were not lovingly embraced by all of the public. In the Roman Empire, one of the common names for our Witchcraft ancestors was *venefica*. The venefica were thought of as poisoners, for—like the Greek Witches, the *pharmakopia*—they knew the plants that healed and harmed, the blessings and the banes. Pharmakopia is where we get our modern concept of the pharmacist, the one who knows medicines and remedies. The pharmakopia or venefica could use their knowledge of poisons to easily and discreetly kill when they deemed it necessary. The Roman politicians were far more fearful of the unseen toxin slipped into their food or drink than they were of the charging army.

In his book *The Witches' Craft*, popular Witchcraft author Raven Grimassi makes the argument that the venefica were not just considered poisoners of the body, but their earlier association was poisoners of the mind or heart with their love potions and philters. Men in power were afraid of having their minds, hearts, and wills clouded by the attention of a woman and her Witchcraft potions. They didn't want to feel influenced by a "supernatural" agency beyond their control.

Venefica's root word is linked with the term *venereal* as well as *venom*. Venereal refers to desire or "love," such as the term *venereal diseases* for sexually transmitted diseases. All of these words are associated with Venus, the Roman goddess of love, beauty, and sexuality.

Many modern Witches don't have the same spiritual devotion and reverence to Venus as to the darker, more "witchy" goddesses such as Hecate, Diana, Demeter, and Persephone. Equated with the Greek goddess Aphrodite, Venus has associations that put her in touch with the primal Witch Goddess, expanding her realm beyond simply love and romance. Much of the familiar lore has her as a temptress and sometimes trouble maker of the Olympian pantheon, yet she is really an "elder" goddess, somewhat like the Titan Hecate, having peace with the younger generation of Greek gods, but having an older origin.

Aphrodite was born from the ocean when the genitals of Uranus (who kept his children trapped in Gaia's womb) were cut off by his son Cronos. They fell into the ocean, foamed, and Aphrodite rose forth. One of her titles is "foam born," and her oceanic associations link her with the primal ocean goddesses. Three drops of blood from Uranus fell on the land and gave life to the three Furies. So Aphrodite's "sisters" are three powerful, dark, and vengeful goddesses seeking to punish those who are criminals, particularly those who murder family members. They are a primal and violent feminine justice.

As soon as Aphrodite stepped onto the shores, flowers bloomed in her wake. The five-petalled flowers in particular are associated with Aphrodite/Venus and with the pentagram and pentacle. While Demeter is the goddess of grains, Aphrodite is the mother of flowers and the flowering herbs that are the source of many magickal powers (many of the Witch's herbs are flowers and have five petals). She brought forth the powers to heal and to harm, to cure and to curse, to revive and to poison, giving to the root of her name the association with the benign powers of love and life force and the darker powers of poisoning and cursing. Traditional love magick can be seen as a blend of both, depending on your perspective as caster or object of the spell.

The Horned Ones

While many Pagan goddess figures and their priestesses are strongly associated with Witchcraft, we cannot forget the image of the Horned God honored in so many Witchcraft traditions. Perhaps the horned ones are not seen as Witches themselves, as the Witchcraft goddesses are, but they are considered the fathers, or patrons, of Witches. Many types of horned deities exist, differing on location and type of horns—from the familiar goat-horned and -hoofed Greek Pan and his satyrs to the bull horns of Dionysus and the Egyptian Osiris and the stag horns of Celtic Cernunnos.

Pan is probably one of the most sexual of these gods, with many manifestations, ranging from a primal cosmic father (when Pan is translated as "All" and is seen as the Lord of the Witches in a dualistic cosmology) to his fear-inducing image causing "pan-ic" to a more playful, lustful, and seductive figure. It's important to realize that all of these sides have that element of surprise and danger, just like any relationship. Releasing the primal side has its pleasure and drawbacks. In some version of the Greek myths, Hermes is the father of Pan and was originally depicted with horns and hooves like his son. Hermes is a great magician and trickster who eventually morphs into the sage figure of Hermes Trismegistus, akin to a Merlin archetype more than a Pan. Dionysus is the god of ecstasy, wine, and madness. He is beloved by the mad women of the frenzy and inspires these women to acts of violence as a form of worship. Osiris is best known as the brother-husband of Isis, who resurrects him twice, yet through his tale he loses his phallus. His is a tantric tale of divine initiation and rebirth through the goddess Isis as the Lord of the Dead. Cernunnos doesn't have many specific myths, let alone romantic or sexual ones, yet he holds such a fascination in the modern Pagan psyche. He is beloved by Witches and druids, and modern interpretations link him with the Lord of the Dead, the King of Faery, the leader of the Wild Hunt, and an insatiable lover like the goat gods. Though not specifically horned, when looking at Cernunnos as a father figure, he's been linked to the gigantic Dagda, the "Good Father," another very sexual god of the Celts. His enormous club is a euphemism for his phallus and his power of fertility. He mates with the giant Witch goddess the Morrighan to gain the secrets of victory in his people's conflict with the chaotic Fomorians.

All of these male figures found playing such a prominent role in modern Witchcraft have a strong yet dangerous sexual current to them. They are not necessarily speaking to the powers of romance but rather to those of lust and primal urges.

The Daughter of Witchcraft

In later Italian Witchcraft, the daughter of the goddess Diana, Aradia, was said to come to earth to revive the traditions of the old ways and the blessings of the Goddess. Reportedly born in Italy in 1313, she grew to adulthood and taught the ways of the Witch. In *The Gospel of Aradia*, she bestows the thirteen powers of the Witch, including three that are particularly pertinent to our work here: "To grant success in love," "To make those who are ugly beautiful," and "To bless or curse with power friends or enemies." All of these are in alignment with the ancient Witches of Greece, Italy, and elsewhere in the world. Witches have the power of beauty, to be the sirens and enchantresses, as we have seen in the classic Witches Circe and Medea. They can bewitch a man's heart with their beauty. They grant success in love, for both themselves and for others who come to them for aid. They brew the potion and cast the spells for finding and keeping lovers. And, lastly, a gift many fear to talk about, they can bless or curse. They are two sides of the same coin and a reason why Witchcraft has been vilified, but if you don't understand the dark, you can never truly understand the light; lacking the knowledge and power, you become unbalanced. If you don't know how someone can be cursed, you will never be able to heal and break that curse. You need the knowledge and power of both sides, even if you don't use it destructively.

The Wizard Mentor

We don't have many male Witchcraft archetypes in history, but one that is very much connected to our modern images in the Neopagan Witchcraft revival is the figure of Merlin. Merlin is most often thought of as the wizard of King Arthur's court. Most think of him as clad in blue robes with yellow stars and a pointed cap similar to the classic Witch's hat. That image is more akin to the Zoroastrian magi than a Celtic mage, and if there was a historic Merlin, he was far more likely to wear animal skins and look like the wild man of the forest.

Part of Merlin's tale, usually forgotten in the modern retellings focusing on the knights of the Round Table, is his love life. He mentors a young enchantress associated with the Ladies of the Lake. Depending on the version, it is Vivian, Nimue, or even Arthur's half sister Morgan le Fay. In the earliest stories of Merlin (sometimes spelled *Myrddin*), the focus of his attention is his sister, named Gwenddydd or Gandeida, and suggests a possible incestuous relationship. Such themes are quite common in the myths of gods and demigods.

Either he is truly smitten by the young woman who promises herself to the sage or he is simply lonely or lustful. She will not consummate their relationship until she has learned all his magick, creating a dynamic tension between teacher and student where the student seems to have all the power. Some look at Merlin as a fool for falling for this ploy, while others believe he simply knew that his time was done and, through his vision of prophecy, knew this was the way he was taken out of the Arthurian story; the mortals must fend for themselves without his constant guidance. The tension between the two is not unlike the tension found between those occultists of the late nineteenth and early twentieth century who focused on the polarity pairings of a male priest and female priestesses to make a magickal current. While sexuality is the magickal power used, rarely did such magicians ever consummate the relationship in the physical, as it was believed to neutralize the potent magickal current. Author and magician Dion Fortune wrote quite a bit about this type of magickal partnership in her novels, particularly *The Sea Priestess*. While not the preferred method of modern magicians today, living in an age with different sexual norms, it is still quite a potent technique for magick.

Once the young student learns all she can from Merlin, she uses that knowledge to trap him. The cage varies but includes a hawthorn tree, a tomb, a crystal cave, or an invisible tower made of air. In the most mystical versions of the story, he voluntarily retires from the world to a glass house, an astrological observatory, with his sister and others, to continue to prophesize about the future. Merlin's tale depicts the unbalanced relationship between two lovers and poor choices on both sides. While the tale has much stronger mythic themes for semi-divine figures, when brought to the human level in later renditions, it shows a lack of integrity between teacher and student and how denial of the sexual and romantic side for much of your life can lead to obsessive actions later, when you finally allow yourself to express that part of you.

The Chivalrous Knight

While the image of the knight, the warrior, seems disconnected from the archetype of the Witch, there are many myths connecting to the two, particularly in British lore. Many Pagan gods are warriors and hunters. In the Arthurian tales, the noble and romantic figure of Lancelot is raised by the Lady of the Lake, making him Lancelot du Lac, or Lancelot of the Lake, and the most likely to succeed in the Holy Grail quest until he betrays himself with the queen. He was adopted and raised by the Avalonian priestesses. While not a Witch outright, he has a sorcerous heritage. But one of the most interesting tales told among modern Witches involves the Order of the Garter.

In the mythos of Witchcraft, the seemingly mainstream Order of the Garter was actually secretly involved in the Witchcraft cult. Originally, it was founded by King Edward III. While at a gathering with the king, the Countess of Salisbury was dancing, and a garter slipped from her leg. Many jeered and sneered, but the king immediately grabbed it from the ground and tied it on his own leg, with the words *"Honi soit qui mal y pense"* ("Shamed be the person who thinks evil of it"). While today most think of the garter as having something to do with sexuality, Witches claim the garter as a sign of a Witch or even Witch Queen. Modern Witches use the garter and most likely base some of its use upon Stone Age depictions of figures with ropes tied to their legs, presumably to control blood flow and induce trance. More familiar garters became a symbol of rank in Witchcraft traditions.

We believe, at least in the poetic and mythic interpretation of the story, that the slipping of the garter announced her as a Witch, and that King Edward was also secretly a member of a Witchcraft order and gave not only his support but started an entire order. Originally it was twenty-six in number, plus the king. In that numerology, modern Witches see two covens of thirteen "knights" and their Witch King. The order is still in operation today. There are many myths and theories associating the British royal family with various occult groups and conspiracies, as much of Celtic Paganism dealt with the themes of the sacred king uniting with the land.

The magickal origin of the tale probably goes back to the stories of *Sir Gawain and the Green Knight*, another of the Arthurian mystery tales. In *Sir Gawain*, the object is a girdle, not a garter, and the motto translates to "Accursed be a cowardly and covetous heart," but it has similar themes to the founding of the Order of the Garter.

While there is no real evidence to support a Pagan monarchy in Christian times, it is still a favorite myth among Wiccans today. And it paints the image of a male Witch as a chivalrous warrior in service to the crown and the land, and the defender of the lady, particularly the lady of the Craft. Today, some Witches with Celtic leanings use various codes of chivalry to guide them beyond the ethical code of the Wiccan Rede. While this can rile many more feminist-minded modern Witches, it speaks to more British Traditional Wiccans. Such codes can be found popularized in the work of Ed Fitch, particularly in his *Grimoire of Shadows*.

The model of the Witch knight gives men in the Craft some additional inspirational resources to draw upon in a mythos that is heavy with female archetypes. The myth of the Order of the Garter and King Edward, as well as the knights like Gawain, Lancelot, and even King Arthur, can continue to provide a role model to aspire to in terms of the most ethical conduct and a warning of what happens when we fall short in being true to our word and our people. Ultimately, their stories teach the ideal of chivalrous love.

Through these stories, it's easy to see how strongly the Witch archetypes are associated with love and romance, and how often things go wrong when magick is involved. They are tales to urge us to live with the highest integrity and honor in all things, but particularly in magick. Those deeply involved on the magickal path notice they start to live a more archetypal life. Magickal living is a source of strength and enlightenment but can also be a part of our self-sabotage. We can believe we are losing our "humanness" and start to think we are divinely infallible. We are blind to the harmful traits of our developing archetype and often allow its development unconsciously. These portraits are a reminder of the joys, powers, and problems of the Witch as lover. They urge us to remain conscious of all our traits and to choose the path of Perfect Love and the highest good.

Magickal Morality

When modern Witches think about such Old World ideas in terms of morality, they are often repulsed, and understandably so. Yet Witchcraft is the exploration of the dark, of the things other people shun and fear. We must look at that side of ourselves and look at our history and the deeper implications of the entire issue before we judge not only what is right for us but also what has been right in the past and what will be right in the future.

Many of the cultures where magick has been considered "dark" have been cultures with people far less politically, socially, and economically empowered compared to today's standards. Medieval magick has a history of sexual curses, such as spells designed to cause impotence in a man. When we look at these things today, we automatically assume how awful they are. But in the medieval times, a woman was entirely dependent upon her husband, and if he left her for a younger woman or had an affair and had to take care of children from that affair, she was in jeopardy financially and personally. There were no opportunities or options for self-reliance, so such magick kept a man home and faithful. Is it manipulative? Certainly. Yet with a people living in a harsh world with less time to ponder ethics, magick was a practical, problem-solving tradition.

Other cultures that have similar magick, or that advocate and encourage love spells for specific people, such as Voodou, Santería, and Hoodoo, come from economically poor cultures. The practice of these magicks in parts of the United States and Canada has influenced the development of modern Witchcraft in North America, as traditional

Hoodoo and Voodou formulas have made their way into Witchcraft formularies and Books of Shadow.

Voodou developed in a slave culture where the practitioners were completely socially disempowered. Magick was the only way to be empowered, and if you wanted something to happen, you simply wanted it to happen to protect or better your life, which was most likely harsh, cruel, and difficult to change. Love, romance, and sex represented economic avenues to change your condition in life or escape and distract yourself from the difficulties. They did not, and many still do not, have the luxury of contemplating the grander ethical questions, as basic life needs are not being met.

The same magicks have risen time and again, in different form but addressing the same fundamental needs, be it with the peasants in Italy, the rural poor in England, or the slave population in the South. A Witch, priestess, or other magickal practitioner of the community was an expert in these arts and in helping people however the person chose to be helped.

In such times and cultures, it was believed the one who was hiring the Witch to do the spell was ultimately responsible for the consequences of it; the magickal practitioner was just the hired hand who supplied knowledge, information, or technical work but were not morally engaged. And in such cultures, the client simply had to be prepared to pay the consequences of such magick, knowing full well the spell could work to their satisfaction or backfire. And it was most often the client who paid the price, rather than the practitioner, for the client—even if he or she was not present at the ritual—was providing the impetus for the work. Are you prepared to pay the "coin" of your wish, or are the stakes too high for you? Only you can determine where the line is and what stake is too high, for all magick contains risk and nothing is ever 100 percent completely safe, just like life.

The Moral Love Spell

When we look at the history of all forms of love magick, we see a wide range of applications, but the most asked question is, "Can you do a love spell for someone specific?" You most certainly can, but the better question is, "*Should* you do a love spell for someone specific?"—and that opens up a whole different debate.

If you look at folk magick traditions from across the world, you most certainly can do a love spell for a specific person. You can find it in ancient Western magickal papyri, European wortcunning, Hoodoo, and Santería. Much of our magickal culture has traditionally been about getting what you want, and many practitioners of folk magick come from peasant cultures who are looking to survive and thrive in an often hostile world. Magick was a tool to gain a measure of control, safety, and success; it was not necessarily the high spiritual art that most of us think of today. That's not to say that simple folk magick cannot be incredibly spiritual and part of a much larger tradition, but the vast majority of customers for the local cunning woman, root doctor, or *bruja* are not interested in having a deeply moving spiritual experience. They are coming to get physically healed, be blessed, make money, have a healthy crop or herd, and get or keep a romantic or sexual partner.

So there is obviously a history to such magick, and that is where we gain a lot of our lore of aphrodisiacs. The immediate complaint from most people is that doing a spell on someone specific to be your lover is manipulative. You are taking away their free will and thereby doing evil. Yet we use things like aphrodisiacs, which at one time were considered magick. When we are attracted to someone, we flirt. We speak in a way that is not our normal way of speaking, to attract attention, to flatter, and to intrigue. We wear flattering clothing. We wear cologne, perfume, or oils. We give gifts or flowers. If we make it to a social setting, such as a dinner date, we have romantic, sensual foods with tastes and scents that engage an atmosphere of romance. If this all leads to a relationship, the behavior often stops once the relationship becomes more solid.

In retrospect, isn't this a form of manipulation? Is it a form of deception, to make someone do what you want? But the person, your romantic target, agreed to it; no one forced them to pay attention. No one forced them on a date, or to have sex, or whatever the end result was. In many ways, yes, this was manipulation, yet it is accepted as the way things are in our society. This is part of the mating process.

Magickal practitioners who are against specific love magick will be the first to point out that wearing a perfume and performing a magick ritual are two different things. The difference between giving flowers and directing a spell toward someone is like the difference between night and day in terms of the amount of energy, of personal magickal voltage, that is put in each action. And they would be right, to a certain degree, yet a spell is simply an amplification of these behaviors and intentions by someone who knows how to consciously work with energy. There are many people unconsciously working with energy and intention that we would never call spellcasters, yet they can get powerful results.

While I'm not necessarily an advocate for casting love spells on specific people, it's important to look at all sides of the situation and realize that those who do decide to do so are no more despicable or evil than those who are great flirts and seducers. They are simply working with much more potent tools.

Whether you decide to cast a love spell on a specific person or not depends on your own code of personal ethics, justice, and morality. One of the reasons why many modern practitioners will not cast a love spell on someone is that they feel it is unethical. Many adherents of the Wiccan Rede will say that manipulating someone's will violates the Wiccan Rede.

The Wiccan Rede is a much longer section of poetry, but its most important teaching is usually summed up in the lines, "An' it harm none, do as ye will." A rede is good advice, not a law, and basically it says that you can do whatever you want unless you are harming yourself or others. There is a wide range of philosophy and ideas that can be attached to those two simple lines, particularly around the concept of will, but that is how the teaching is conveyed in its most basic form.

So adherents to the Wiccan Rede will say that specific love spells are harmful and that the Wiccan Rede tells you not to do them. Technically it doesn't if you are not harming the person. Yet if you define having someone fall in love with you as harm, then I guess you are. People look at the Wiccan Rede as a variation on the Golden Rule, popularized in Christianity but found in many religions. Basically, if you wouldn't want something done to you, don't do it to someone else. Many modern Witches believe in the Law of Return, or Law of Three, stating that whatever you do comes back to you threefold. If you manipulate someone's will, you are opening yourself up to being manipulated three times as strong. Since no one wants to be manipulated themselves, they refrain from such behavior.

Even though I'm a strong believer in the value of the Wiccan Rede, I was taught that it was fine to do a love spell on a specific person. We end all our spells with these or similar words: "I ask this spell to be for the highest good of all involved, harming none" or "I ask this spell to be in accord with divine will." Basically, we are asking that if the spell was to harm us or another, then the spell should short-circuit and not work, rather than do harm to us or another. I was taught that if you can do a spell for a specific person and keep the spirit of these lines, then it is fine. If a relationship with this person will cause no harm in the big scheme of things, or if it's in accord with divine will, then it will occur. If not, you have to be open to that fact and be okay with the spell's failure.

Easier said than done.

I agree wholeheartedly with the teaching, but I've found personally, and through counseling dozens of Witches in this form of love magick, that by the time you get to a headspace where you've formed a specific attachment to someone that's strong enough that you want to do a spell, then you want what you want and probably don't give a damn about higher will. You assume since you are attracted it must be fate, it must be higher will, but you still need to do a spell to convince your potential partner.

I know a number of Witches who have done this, including a coven-mate who put a lot of energy into the first part of her spell, about what she wanted, and very little into the "harming none for the highest good" part. She got what she asked for, but one could argue if it was for her highest good.

The man she was attracted to did begin a romantic and sexual relationship with her. She didn't know, and he never told her, that he was engaged to be married. Now, the spell did not make him cheat, in my opinion. We later found out that he was with many other women while he was engaged. The relationship only lasted a few weeks. She found out and felt morally compelled to end the relationship, yet she was heartbroken, thinking she had found "the one." For those who see no value in the Law of Three, I could argue that it took her at least three times as long, if not longer, to get over him than it took him to get over her. In some ways, I think even though it was a very hurtful and seemingly unnecessary situation, it still was for her highest good. She learned a valuable lesson on the power of magick, and I got a great teaching story without having to experience it directly myself.

While you can successfully do such magick, I would urge you to think about your long-term goals. What do you want? While I've seen specific magick work, rarely have I seen it evolve into a lifelong partnership. The connection is intense, immediate, and magnetic, and it dissipates quickly unless you put a lot more magick into it. Eventually, you get settled, and without the magick, it dissipates and fizzles out.

I have seen nonspecific love magick that is a spell for a kind of person—the person who matches the qualities on your list rather than for a specific individual you know—bear amazing fruit. I've seen such relationships blossom into spiritual, powerful committed relationships. I feel I'm the recipient of the blessings of such magick in my own life and marriage. If that is what you are looking for, you might consider such nonspecific love magick over specific love magick.

Love magick for a nonspecific person not only circumvents this difficult moral quagmire on ethics but also opens you to potential blessings you did not even know existed. By letting the Divine play matchmaker, you are trusting in divine wisdom to bring you what you need, rather than assuming you know everything you need to know about a specific person, to truly know they are the right match for you. When you let go of your specific-person limitations, you give the magick an opportunity to work on a much deeper level, for much greater success.

When you do a love spell for a specific person, you have two options: either that person responds to it favorably or the person doesn't. If the person doesn't respond to it, there is no other option, no other avenue for that magick: the spell fails. While I do think it's possible to mesmerize and coerce people with some forms of magick, with general love spells, I don't think many people's wills truly can be forced. If someone is utterly unattracted to you or is of a different sexual orientation, there is little magick can do to make you attractive to them in the long term. You can influence thoughts and emotions fleetingly or you can arouse sexual energy in general and make yourself readily available, but it's not long and deep lasting love.

If you do have sufficient magickal strength and lack any concern about higher will or the highest good, and you can bend someone to your will, most people would consider that a form of psychic attack. Even if the target responds with romantic interest in you, it usually doesn't turn out the way you truly desire. The target can become emotionally unbalanced as the psyche attempts to unconsciously fight off this attack, or the target can become obsessive toward you, disregarding your own feelings and boundaries as the spell takes on a stronger life of its own.

When you do a love spell for a type of relationship or a kind of person, you have many options. You have left many doors open, and the universe can align you with someone who fits your criteria and who is also looking for someone whose criteria *you* fit. You might have never guessed this person fit your criteria or, until the magick was cast, have a reason to meet this person, but when you do, the strands of fate move, and your paths cross under exactly the right circumstances.

Soul Mates, Fate, and Ethics

One of the moral issues around love magick is the concept that everybody has one—and only one—person that is right for him or her in this entire lifetime. We call such people soul mates or twin flames and will discuss them more in chapter 9. When you are looking for a partner, I find the concept of soul mates, twin flames, or any other notion that puts the idea that one and only one person is out there for you very destructive. I'm a romantic at heart, and my teachings on this upset many romantics, but it has been my experience personally and the best advice I have in guiding others.

I believe there are many people out there with whom you are mutually attracted, compatible, and able to build a relationship. I think the terms *soul mate* and *twin flame* can denote a deep spiritual connection to someone, but it doesn't necessarily mean a romantic connection. We have had many loves in past incarnations, many connections. In truth, we are all connected by the web of life. I do believe in "life mates," a person with whom you can build a lifetime relationship, but just because you've had a romantic relationship with someone in a past life doesn't mean if you both incarnate in the same place at the same time that you'll be lovers again. You could be siblings, parent/child, friends, or even enemies. Looking for that one perfect fit excludes you from the world of possibilities.

Some who believe in one exclusive soul partner get stuck on a specific person and assume they have greater spiritual knowledge to realize they are soul mates, so they rationalize that the magick to get this person is not manipulative. The target will soon realize "we are meant to be together." To assume you know the fate of another person and not even entertain the possibility you are wrong, and to do magick based on your assumption, is some of the worst magick possible. If it truly is your fate, your higher will, don't try so hard. You will come together. If you feel the need to force it, that's a sure sign that it's not your higher will to be together.

People can become fanatical and not understand why the magick didn't work out, or blame the other person, saying he or she was not "spiritual enough" to pick up on the love vibrations between them. Unfortunately, in that view, if you don't acknowledge your mistake, you'll think you should be alone for the rest of your life because your one true love rejected you. This view creates some pretty tragic situations.

Those who believe in one exclusive soul partner but don't know who it is will often hold potential partners to an unattainable high standard without holding themselves to the same standard. They will dismiss perfectly suitable partners because the partner didn't live up to their expectations of a soul mate. That's why it's important to make a list not only of the qualities you want in a partner, but also of the qualities you are offering. You must make sure you are equal and balanced to each other. You don't need to have the same qualities, but if you are expecting a partner to be perfect for you on all levels, you must be willing to hold yourself to the same standard and be honest with yourself and your qualities. I'd argue that none of us are perfect, so how can our partner be perfect and anticipate all our wants and needs without even knowing us?

Those who can have intention and be open to unseen blessings stand the best chance of having amazingly successful love magick. If you can be clear about what kind of person and relationship you want but be open to how that manifests and with whom you create it, you will not only fulfill your dreams but go far beyond anything you can conceive of now.

EXERCISE} **Examining Your Ethics About Love,
Lust, and Romance Magick**

With all the ideas presented in this chapter fresh in your mind, examine your own thoughts, feelings, and beliefs about love, lust, sex, and romance and the use of magick to get them. What do you believe is "right" or "wrong," keeping in mind that such ideas could be subjective and just for you? What is the line you wouldn't cross, if any? Do you subscribe to the Wiccan Rede, and if so, what does that mean to you? How do you interpret it in terms of love and lust magick?

Before you begin your journey in the ways of love magick for yourself or for others, it's good to have a clear, sober conversation with yourself through journaling. In this way, you put down exactly what you believe in black and white, somewhere you can refer to it again. It doesn't mean that your views won't change over time, but it's very important to have a place to start and refer back to. When you are in the midst of perceived love or lust, it is easy to throw away any code you have and just do what your ego wants to satisfy your needs. When you think about it in a clear space, and write it down (or type it) in black and white, it's slightly harder to ignore your own code even when you want someone really strongly.

FOUR

The Quest for Love

Though life is not a fairy tale, there are some important magickal lessons and mythic truths that can be found in fairy tales, fables, and mythology concerning love. Fairy tales can contain the remnants of old Pagan folk wisdom. As the trials of our popular fairy-tale characters have shown us, no one said love would be easy. Life presents us with challenges to overcome, problems to solve, and quests to fulfill. Though some get lost in the romantic notion of the quest for love and lose track of exactly what they are questing for and why, the quest both for romance and spirituality provides an important model for us to understand.

Though many create personal drama in their own lives, believing they are fulfilling the required drama in the quest for love, they miss a key element. When reading the fairy tales and mythos of lore, try looking at all the characters as parts of yourself. You are Prince Charming. You are the Princess. You are the King. You are the Queen. You are the Fairy Godmothers and the Evil Witch. Regardless of gender or age, they are all within you.

The concept is much like the study of astrology. In astrology, you learn that you contain all of the planets in your astrological chart, each acting as a player in your personal inner drama. Just as you contain all the planets, you contain all the characters of the fairy tale. An astrologer might even align each character with one of the planets.

The resolution of the tale to "happily ever after" isn't the end of the tale but the harmonizing of all the different aspects of our self. We all have a part of us that is questing. We all have a part of us that wants to receive our love. We all have aspects of wisdom, intelligence, power, and magick. Only when we are able to find those powers—to give and receive ourself to ourself—can we then be in a place of true self-love and self-knowledge to have a healthy and appropriate relationship with another person. The fairy tale is much like an inner-world spiritual initiation.

When we fail to realize this and hold the ideal of the Princess or Prince—the ideal of any one character to our self or to a prospective partner—we create a lot of unnecessary drama. I once heard a wise woman say that those who do not enact sacred drama will be forced to live out drama in their daily lives, and I completely agree. By using meditation and visionary pathworking or rituals and ceremonial methods, we must do the inner-world work of sacred drama in order to move these archetypal forces through us, lest they move through us in our daily life and move us to create a lot of unnecessary and unwanted heartache.

When you hold yourself up to the ideal of the fairy tale, book, or movie, which many of us do because it's our role model for what love and relationships are supposed to be in this culture, we try to emulate them. None of us are living in a novel, movie script, or television show, even though it might feel that way. Life does not wrap up neatly in under two hours or three hundred pages. The stories always end happily ever after, and nobody shows the rest. After the meeting, the courting, the problem separating the couple, their triumph and reunion, none of these stories model for us how to deal with the romance once you've had kids, been together for ten years, or you suddenly find yourself seriously attracted to someone else or bored sexually. Classic fairy-tale media is telling a bigger archetypal story of our inner landscape, the story of the soul. It gives us idealized representations of each character, which is, in essence, a part of ourselves. When we erroneously try to apply these idealized roles onto people in our outer daily lives, ourselves included, we fall short of the idealization and think somehow we, or the people around us, have failed.

Learning Love Through the Tarot

While there are some standard parts in the quest for love through fairy tales and stereotypical modern movies and television, I like to look at the highly organized and patterned wisdom of the tarot cards. Each of the four suits represents a quest, and the suit of the cups embodies the quest for love and the highest ideal of love: compassion. As we look at the suit of cups, or chalices, from ace to ten and the court cards, we have a better understanding of the powers of love on all levels, not just romantic.

Ace of Cups—Like all aces, the Ace of Cups is the card of
  new beginnings, of initiation on the quest for love. The
  divine cup of compassion, the Holy Grail of healing and
  regeneration, is divinely granted from the clouded veils of
  the otherworld. This card represents a renewal and rebirth
  on the path to love, wiping away the pains of the past
  without removing their lessons and wisdom, and opening
  the heart to new love and relationship.

Two of Cups—The Two of Cups is the classic love card,
  and when drawn it usually indicates a new or continuing
  romantic relationship. From the solitary but renewed nature
  of the ace, when a second figure is added, as in this card, a

FIGURES} Clockwise from top left: Ace of Cups,
Two of Cups, Three of Cups,
and Four of Cups

relationship can form. Traditionally, in the standard Rider-Waite–style cards, two figures are seen exchanging cups with a divine caduceus figure topped with a winged lion's head overseeing the exchange. Some tarot readers see this as indicating an exchange of vows, or marriage, but most usually read it as the start or continuation of a healthy romantic relationship. The cups exchanged indicate the exchange of energy between the couple as they develop their relationship. The caduceus is the interweaving of their lives together, and the lion is indicative of the sign of Leo, the sign associated with lovers, strength, and beauty. The Two of Cups card is similar, albeit in a lower spiritual octave, to the major arcana card known as the Lovers (see later in this chapter).

Three of Cups—The Three of Cups is known as the abundance card, which might make you think it belongs in the quest for security symbolized by the disc/pentacle cards, but it refers to the abundance of love and friendship. Typically, three women are depicted drinking, cheering, and toasting, showing the relationships of platonic friends, or those who are like sisters to us. This card reminds us of the quest for relationship and love, and to remember and cherish the relationships we already have with friends and family. Without their support, we lose our foundation on the quest for love. Everything, including the drinking depicted on this card, must be done in moderation.

Four of Cups—The Four of Cups is our first semi-difficult cup card. Entitled Mixed Happiness by traditional tarot teachers, it depicts a young man under a tree, with three cups before him and being offered a fourth by a mysterious disembodied hand, much like the descending hand and cup of the ace. The card could be summed up by the question, "Are the cups half empty or half full?" Things aren't bad—the skies

FIGURES} Clockwise from top: Five of Cups,
Six of Cups, and Seven of Cups

are blue and clear—but there is neither satisfaction nor happiness. Things are changing in life and the quest must go deeper, beyond the surface happiness of new relationships or the comfort of friends and family. The realization has begun that the quest for love is also an internal quest.

Five of Cups—The Five of Cups continues the quest as our main figure is now surrounded by five cups, three overturned and spilled and two upright behind him. Fives in the tarot are generally considered destructive, as the power of Mars, their ruling planet, is turned inward to destroy what no longer serves the initiate on the magickal path. It's called the Disappointment card because what you thought you would get is no longer before you—it has "spilled" and been lost. This can occur in love and romance, or just generally in life. It is when we expect things to stay the same, but to evolve we must let go and let things change. When we try to hold on, we simply lose our grip all the quicker. All is not lost, for part of what you wanted is still behind you—if you only look at where you've been to figure out where you are going.

Six of Cups—The Six of Cups is one of the oddest cards in the series in terms of depiction. Titled the Nostalgia card, it signifies a longing for the past, to simpler times. The figures depicted are usually strangely disproportional but usually described as children, with one giving a cup with flowers in it to the other. There is a desire to go back to the innocence and naivety of childhood rather than face adulthood problems of love and serious relationships. Some decks describe this as the pleasure card, depicting fun and frivolity, even sexual pleasure, but still having a fear of going deeper into full intimacy.

Seven of Cups—In this card, the hero of our quest is faced with seven cups, each filled with something strange or

FIGURES} Top, Eight of Cups;
bottom, Nine of Cups

mysterious. Which cup will be chosen? Will the contents be a fulfillment of his dreams or a deadly poison taking him off the path? Will it be anything worthwhile at all? Which should be chosen? Can only one be chosen? This card is known as the Debauchery card, and although it can mean the escapism of drugs, alcohol, or any other addiction—even television or meditation, since any escape that helps us avoid decisions is indicated by this card—it is really the card of muddled thinking, of not being able to choose "correctly" or clearly. When drawn, it indicates that your emotions in the situation, your water element, are muddying your decision-making progress, making it nearly impossible to make a clear, logical, and grounded decision. You are too emotionally close to the situation and fear making a wrong choice, so you often make no choice at all.

Eight of Cups—With the Eight of Cups, a decision is reached and a quest has begun. Everything leading up to this point has just prepared the seeker for the quest. Eight cups are left behind, and he journeys into the night with a walking stick in hand, not looking back. Traditionally, this has been called the Indolence card, using the more archaic definition meaning "one who is free from pain." Perhaps one is not impervious, but with this card's message you begin to understand the true reasons for emotional pain and to seek the inner cure through a relationship with yourself rather than outward selves, numbing your pain through other people. You are the source of your own healing and fulfillment. This card can also be read with a more traditional meaning of indolence, particularly when it's inverted: it would mean "laziness or sloth" and shows someone not dedicated to self-development or personal exploration.

FIGURES} Top, Ten of Cups;
bottom, Page (Knave) of Cups

Nine of Cups—The Nine and Ten of Cups have mixed images, depending on the deck you are using. In the traditional Rider-Waite, this card depicts a powerful man sitting before a table of nine cups, as if he is the patriarch, yet his disposition is welcoming, offering you a place at the table. Many call this the wish card, for it indicates wish fulfillment or satisfaction. It is also known as the card of satiety. In the decks based on the popular work of Aleister Crowley and his Thoth deck, it is called the Happiness card and represents good family relationships.

Ten of Cups—The Ten of Cups in traditional imagery is the happiness card, depicting a family, two parents and two children, with a home, playing under a rainbow of ten cups. While it is a card indicating the happiness of a literal family, like our fairy tales, it is important to realize that each of the four figures, like the king, queen, knight, and page, are aspects of the one person who started the quest. Only when your "inner family" finds happiness will you know the true love and happiness represented in the grail quest. Only then will you find healing and compassion for yourself and for others. Then you will be emotionally fulfilled. In the Crowley deck, this card is named Satiety and indicates the satisfaction of fulfilling the quest for compassion and love.

Page of Cups—The Page of Cups, usually depicted as a female or androgynous figure, is considered a messenger who gives insight to relationships. Sometimes that message is from a person in our lives outside of our relationship, giving us perspective. Other times, it's the inner nagging voice telling us the reality of the situation. In a reading, one of the hallmarks of the Page of Cups appearing is that it is usually good advice, something we need to hear but don't necessarily want to hear. In qabalistic tarot traditions,

FIGURES} Clockwise from top: Knight of Cups,
Queen of Cups, and King of Cups

this page is described as the earth of water, meaning it is
the grounded, practical aspect of emotions, family, and
relationship.

Knight of Cups—The Knight of Cups is the adventurer, the
seeker, and sometimes described as the grail knight of the
Arthurian mythos, or the failed grail knight, for he is not yet
mature enough to find what he seeks in terms of the Holy
Grail or cauldron of the Goddess. Qabalistically, he is the air
of water, the intellectual aspect of love. While we can write
about love, we never quite capture it in words, and if that is
your sole method of experiencing love, the true experience
of love, of the cup, will be just out of your grasp. You will
understand it but not necessarily feel it. The Knight of Cups
is the romantic seeker or the idealist who has a very strong
idea of what love should be but has no idea how to cope
when love turns out to be different from the expectations.

Queen of Cups—The Queen of Cups is the water of water, the
epitome of the water element. On her highest level, she is
the loving goddess, the creatrix. In a reading, she appears
as a human form of both the Great and Terrible Mother,
light and dark. This is the power of true unconditional love,
which on the personal level can be a blessing, a healing,
and a great boon. But unconditional love doesn't mean
unconditional relationships, and sometimes the best thing
someone who loves you unconditionally can do is tell you
or show you something you don't want to experience,
particularly about yourself. Sometimes we expect to be
continually nurtured, but a good mother must push us
out of the nest. The "negative" expression of the card is
the Dark Mother archetype played out in our personal
life. I often call it the Mother-in-Law card, conjuring the
stereotypical bad relationship we have with mothers-in-law,

but it could manifest as a difficult relationship with our own mother or a mother figure.

King of Cups—The King of Cups relates to the fire of water, the passion and intensity of emotion. When that intensity is raised to a spiritual level, it is the successful Grail Knight, the one who seeks the grail, rises above simple intellect, and finds the grail. He finds the Fisher King of Arthurian legend, the wounded guardian of the Grail, and he then becomes the Fisher King. This is the seeker of love who finds and ultimately enters a relationship of service to the Goddess, to the divine feminine, as embodied by the cup.

The Lovers

Beyond the traditional suit, we have two major arcana cards of the tarot that are most often associated with these concepts in a more celestial manner. The first is the most obvious: the sixth trump, the Lovers. In mundane fortunetelling readings, the Lovers is exactly what it appears to be. It is about romantic love, of finding a partner or even marriage or a serious romantic commitment. In a more mystical sense, it is the inner alchemical marriage, the union that occurs between the inner king and inner queen of our soul. Only when these two parts are united in a healthy relationship do we become a balanced and healthy individual.

The concepts of polarity were introduced with the previous trumps of the tarot—the male Magician, the female Priestess, the female Empress, and the male Emperor. Although typically male in artistic rendition, the Hierophant as the inner teacher or guru represents the androgynous component. The traditional pope image is not necessarily sexless but is celibate in the Christian and post-Christian era.

The tradition of the inner marriage is found in many different systems. Most of us first come across the ideas of the inner male self and the inner female self through psychology. In the teachings of pioneering psychologist Carl Jung is the concept of the anima, the inner female part of those who are physically male, and the animus, the inner male part of those who are physically female. Often such selves are personified as inner teachers, wise ones, or angels. Some would equate this other self with the higher self, or the ceremonial magician's concept of the Holy Guardian Angel, though the true higher self, or HGA, is the entity that oversees the sacred marriage. Jung's work has been extrapolated by both psychologists and metaphysicians to the idea that everybody, regardless of gender, has an inner anima and animus, a hidden or idealized inner male and idealized inner female.

This teaching echoes those found in Hermetic alchemy, which influenced both the modern renditions of the tarot cards and the work of Carl Jung. The teachings of alchemy were encoded in graphic plates and engravings. Such engravings were symbolic of the alchemical processes both in the laboratory and their spiritual equivalents in the alchemist's consciousness. They were written in code, with certain symbols, animals, and characters representing the various processes. Many of these teachings contained royal figures such as kings and queens. Each plate furthered the process, depicting kings and queens undergoing some union or merger into a new being with the qualities of both the king and queen, yet something more. The alchemists taught that the two polarities must find union, coagulating into the Philosopher's Stone, the secret inner substance that has the best qualities of all things. Many believe the alchemists were trying to make a Philosopher's Stone in the lab, and perhaps they were, but one teaching says that the alchemist becomes the Philosopher's Stone when the work is done.

In tribal shamanism and forms of more traditional Witchcraft, we have similar concepts with fewer psychological implications and a stronger sense of spiritual partnership. Rather than viewing such entities as part of the mystic's psyche, these traditions see sacred marriage as a partnership with the otherworld and would most likely be highly offended if it were suggested their spirit love or spouse was a part of them in a psychological sense. Shamans often "marry" their tutelary

FIGURES} Top, the Lovers;
bottom, Temperance

spirit, having a spirit wife or husband in the otherworld. In some traditions, it's not a marriage, but there is a psychosexual spiritual exchange with a spirit in a temporary alliance, entered into for the mutual benefit of both beings, human and spirit.

Today, such practices are sometimes referred to as the Fetch Wife/Husband or Fetch Spouse, as well as the Faery Marriage. I believe this lore was corrupted into the Christian mythology of the male incubus and the female succubus, demons feeding on the sexual energy and fluid of sleeping mortals. It only becomes an involuntary or terrifying process when the old ways are forgotten and misunderstood. Those Witches and shamans today who undergo this type of alliance report many of the same effects and benefits the alchemist or psychologist receives, including more balanced awareness and decision making, expanded consciousness, and great capacity for self-knowledge and self-love through the knowledge and love of the spirit ally.

Temperance

The second of the major arcana cards to deal with this theme is the fourteenth trump, traditionally called Temperance. Other tarot innovators have renamed it Art or Alchemy, as the card deals not with the previous partnership crafted between the inner male and inner female, as found in the Lovers card, but with their more sublime union. The alchemical marriage, as depicted in the old engravings of the spiritual scientists, results in a hermaphroditic being of both male and female qualities. The Temperance card depicts the process of that union, which is an art, an alchemical process much like the tempering of steel on an anvil. The traditional image is one of a fairly androgynous angel usually named Michael for the elemental fire triangle in the chest, representing the alchemical fire or forge, mixing various substances, pouring liquids from one chalice to another, with one foot in water and one foot on land. This is a card of transition, of betweenness, and it is that state the mystic ultimately aims for in the quests for love and self-love.

Those who attain this sense of inner balance and union become closer to liminal mythic creatures, not truly belonging to the "ordinary" world of humans with its sharp divisions. This level of spiritual initiation sets the individual apart and gives them traits more in common with the faery folk, angels, and deified ancestors, who stand apart from most of humanity. Those seeking this mystery journey beyond the confines of human society for a time, to the forest, cave, or mountaintop, to create the necessary conditions. Even the artist, alchemist, and blacksmith spend hours in solitude, away from conventional society, among their own creative powers and the primal elements.

The Divine Marriage

One of the first steps in the quest for love, to create the divine drama within us rather than in our daily lives, is to intellectually understand the forces. The next step—in fact, the next several steps—is to work with these inner-world forces directly. As we make changes in our consciousness, beneficial changes in our daily life will occur also.

Doing inner work through visionary images might not be the initiation of the divine alchemical marriage or the union with the fetch mate that occurs on the path of the serious practitioner of the art of magick, but it does help us understand our inner king and queen, and work with them closely to fulfill the inner quest for love so we too can be prepared for the outer quest.

EXERCISE} **The Divine Marriage**

1. Perform steps 1–5 from the mirror affirmations exercise on page 10.

2. Imagine yourself in your own inner sacred space. I call it the Inner Temple, but it is known by many other names—the soul shrine, the interior castle, or even just your "happy place." It can appear as a place you know in the world or

as a fantastic amalgam of otherworldly places. It can be a
sacred temple, a building, or an outdoor scene. In this inner
landscape you are sovereign, safe, and protected.

3. In this sacred space, you will find two gateways. They
   could be doorways to other rooms or, if outside, simply the
   opening between two trees, rocks, or a hole in the ground.
   They will act as magickal portals. When you open the first
   gateway, out steps your inner king, your animus and male
   side. Take a look at your king. What does he look like? How
   does he act? What is your first impression? Do you like your
   king-self? Is your king even a king at all, or is he manifesting
   as something less mature and less powerful? Introduce
   yourself if this is the first time you are meeting. Although
   he knows you, you do not yet know him. Ask him any
   questions you have.

4. Go to the second gateway. Open it, and out steps your
   inner queen, your anima and female side. Take a look at
   your queen. What does she look like? How does she act?
   What is your first impression? Do you like your queen-self?
   Is your queen even a queen at all, or is she manifesting
   as something less mature and less powerful? Introduce
   yourself if this if the first time you are meeting. Although
   she knows you, you do not yet know her. Ask her any
   questions you have.

5. As if you were hosting a party, bring your divine couple
   together, making introductions. Observe their behavior.
   How do they react to one another? Do they know each
   other? Are they long-lost friends, long-lost lovers, or
   antagonistic? Do you have to smooth over their interaction,
   acting as intermediary? Bring the two together as best you
   can, and learn from their relationship.

6. When done, thank both the king and queen, and, unless they have gotten along spectacularly, bring each to their separate doorway and close the gate. If they have gotten along, you can leave them in the inner temple area alone together for their alchemical relationship to grow.

7. Perform steps 8–10 from the mirror affirmations exercise.

The ideal of this exercise is to get the two into a good working relationship, a love or friendship with partnership and balance. They may eventually merge into one alchemical composite, like the old Hermetic engravings. This particular exercise is simply an introduction to the concepts and the forces within you. The work of uniting the two is part of the lifelong Great Work of the alchemist and magician.

Many people think of the alchemical marriage concept as heterosexist. Gay men, lesbians, bisexuals, and transgendered people often ask if it has to be a king and queen. Can it be two queens or two kings? The concept of the alchemical marriage is an inner working, an inner balance of male and female energies, so it is not inherently heterosexist, in the sense that both most modern occultists and most psychologists will agree we all have a unique blend of male and female energies in all of us, regardless of sexual orientation and gender identity. In practical purpose as a teacher, I tell my students to go with whatever the image is that first comes to them. So, when doing this meditation, if you have two kings, two queens, or two beings who defy gender orientation, go with it. If you expected the traditional images and get something else entirely, also go with it. What the meditation reveals is more illuminating and healing than following the images you are "supposed" to see.

Regardless of what you see in your inner vision, work with the beings you encounter. Develop their relationship with your facilitation, knowing that you are really developing an inner-world relationship to change your outer-world life. The more you balance, harmonize, and join together the opposing and complementary natures of your inner self, your king and queen, refining their qualities as you develop and evolve yourself, the more you will have fulfilled the inner quest for love and undergone a level of true initiation with the Lovers card. Be prepared for a healthy, happy, harmonious relationship to manifest in your waking life.

FIVE

The Patrons of Love
and Romance

Many gods and goddesses have been associated with the powers of love, romance, sensuality, and sexuality. Out of all the forces humans have viewed as divine, the first and foremost—beyond the tangible immanent forms of natural divinity such as the earth, moon, sky, or sea—is love. Love, in all its forms, is seen as divine.

Love is the power of connection. On its most cosmic level, it's a primal force. Eros was seen by some ancient philosophers as one of the major creative principles, much like scientists today look at gravity or electromagnetism. Without this power, the world as we know it would not exist. On a personal and human scale, it keeps the human race going, and not just biologically; its higher impulse inspires us to create community and aspire to our more noble urges. On a global scale, it keeps all the races of animals and plants procreating. We might not think of the biological cooperation of minerals, seeds, flowers, and bees as love, but Eros is the connective power drawing these things together. The urge of the Divine to create is based in love. In the atomic and sub-atomic microcosm, the attraction of positive and negative binds particles together to make matter. While that doesn't seem like personal love to us, again, it's the love between subatomic particles.

On some level, we know how important the powers of love are to our happiness and to our continued existence, so we have given a lot of time and attention to the gods and goddesses of love and romance. They have consumed more of our collective psyche and inspired more art, song, music, and poetry than practically any other gods, as love, and perhaps death, are the most common denominators of the human experience. We all seek companionship. We all seek love and contact of some sort. We all desire to intimately connect in some fashion. Through this desire, the goddesses and gods of love move through us.

In terms of ceremonial magick, most deities (often referred to as god-forms in ceremonial magick) are categorized by their archetypal quality and how they would relate to the various points of the Tree of Life or one of the planets. While most Witches see deities as more complicated and personal than "godforms," as independent and divine entities, it's important to understand what certain gods, who are culturally different, have in common magickally, particularly when looked at from the view of a modern magician or Witch. The correspondences of astrology or the Tree of Life are simply one method to organize those similarities.

Most of the gods that are associated with love and romance would also loosely fit into the Venus archetype of godforms. In astrological and planetary magick, Venus plays several different roles. It is the planet of attraction, associated with magnetic forces just as natural lodestones are associated with Venus. The power of beauty, of being the brightest "star" of the morning and evening sky, and the power of beauty to attract are linked. In magick, such power is used to attract whatever you desire, whatever you value or want. Mostly it is used in love, lust, and money magick to get what you want. We say that it attracts what you "love" in a romantic or simply personal sense. We know today that as a planet, Venus's shine is due to the reflective nature of the greenhouse gases creating her beauty. What light and heat that does penetrate the surface is held tight. Once she gets something, she doesn't let go.

Venus's orbit is the closest of the planets to being perfectly circular, associating the beauty of perfection, along with brilliant light, with this planet. Due to the general size and orbit of Venus, it is considered a sister planet to Earth. Venus/Aphrodite is also a goddess of nature as well as love, linking her with Gaia. Many other myths link life on Earth to life on Venus. Lucifer is associated with Venus, and some Italian and Gnostic Witchcraft traditions look at Lucifer as the brother-consort of the Witch goddess Diana and father of Aradia. In Arthurian lore, Lucifer's fallen crown is said to be an emerald from Venus that later becomes the Holy Grail of the knight's quest. The Theosophists have a myth of the earthly lord Sanat Kumara descending from Venus to spark life and consciousness on Earth, echoing some of the Lucifer myths found in Gnostic and Gnostic Faery traditions.

Through our mythology, we intuitively know that we have a strong link to the planet Venus. All of these myths link the light of Venus to starting the cycle of life and procreation on Earth and point to a deeper mystery regarding the goddess Venus, her consorts, and the origin of humanity and our quest for love and union. The powers of Venus are not just for personal love but for the spiritual quest where love is an integral part. Notice how these themes are connected to our love archetypes, including the "fall" of Uranus to create Aphrodite, reminiscent of the fall of Lucifer; Aradia, the daughter of Diana and Lucifer; the faery kings and queens; and the Holy Grail association with Arthurian myths, Merlin, and the various chivalrous knights.

We also know that Venus has a strange rotation, being the slowest of the planets. One "day" on Venus lasts 243 Earth days, as compared to one orbit of the planet around the Sun, which occurs in 224.7 Earth days. Because of this, as an archetypal force Venus is considered slow moving, and some would say lazy. Imagine this goddess lounging, allowing her lovers to come to her. When doing Venusian love magick, it can sometimes appear to be slow moving and slow to manifest, as its power is in the slow and steady work.

Magickally, Venus is the planet of vital magnetism. While we now know that all planets have an electromagnetic field (Earth included), Venus magickally rules over all forms of magnetism and attraction, from the literal power of a natural magnet to animal magnetism, the vital life force that pushes and pulls, used by Witches and magicians to manifest our desires. Vital life force, or personal magnetic energy, is associated with sexual power and charisma, the power to entrance. Venus is the planet of desire and naturally draws to her whatever she wants, like a magnet drawing iron to it. While the Mars godforms are about going out and getting what you want, the Venus godforms are all about attracting what you want to you. That is the true power of Venus as the enchantress, enticing others with sweet songs, smells, and sights. The manipulation of magickal magnetism through poetry and song, perfumery and geomantic talismans is at the heart of how and why Venus magick works.

The following deities either have a strong association with the planet Venus or are considered to be patrons of love, romance, sexuality, and relationship. It is by no means a complete list, as deities are multifaceted and have many attributes over many time periods and cultures, but this gives you a great place to begin in terms of the deities modern Neopagans and Witches have called upon for aid in love magick. If you find an affinity for one, begin cultivating a relationship with that deity, doing your own research on the god's myths, offerings, cultural context, and symbols.

> *Angus Mac Og*—Angus Mac Og, the "Young Son," is of the Irish pantheon of the Tuatha de Danann, the children of the goddess Danu. He is the son of the powerful god Dagda and the goddess Boann. To hide his affair with the married

Boann, the Dagda was said to use his magick to stop the sun from moving for nine months, technically allowing Angus to be conceived, gestated, and born all in one day. Being born out of time is said to make him eternally young. Angus was associated with many love affairs and became known as the god of love, youth, and poetic inspiration. He is also associated with the god Mabon, another "young son" god of the Celtic traditions.

Aphrodite—Aphrodite is the first among deities of love, being the goddess of love, romance, sexuality, and fertility. Her tales in Greek mythology are filled with her exploits and machinations to entwine gods and mortals alike. Sadly, if we go solely by her myths, while she is the force of love personified, she is not always successful in procuring the "happily ever after" scenario most of us desire. While she has steamy affairs with many gods, including her brother Ares, the war god, she is trapped in a loveless marriage with Hephaestus. Those who receive her blessings, such as Paris and Helen, don't always end up happy. Perhaps it is because of the manner in which she was born, rising from an act of violence against a Titan. Her strange myth betrays a foreign origin in culture, most likely coming from the East and linked to Astarte and Ishtar. Despite these factors, many modern Witches have successfully petitioned Aphrodite for aid in love magick, being very specific about their wants, and have had their prayers fulfilled without any harsh and unforeseen consequences.

Astarte—Astarte is a Semitic goddess bearing strong correspondences to the Mesopotamian Ishtar. She is a goddess of love, sexuality, fertility, and war. She was later equated with Aphrodite amongst the Greeks. She is also a goddess associated with the planet Venus.

Bast—Bast is the Egyptian cat goddess. Originally a solar and war goddess, she was later identified with the Moon, perfumes, and ointments. The Greeks equated her with their goddess Artemis, the huntress of the Moon. Later still, due to popular literature and role-playing games, Bast has become regarded as a sensual goddess of pleasure and love akin to the Egyptian Hathor, yet such depictions were not part of her classical attributes. Strangely, many modern Neopagans are far more familiar with her popular attributes as a more Venusian figure than her classical associations with the sun, war, and hunting. She responds quite lovingly in rituals of relationship and romance, demonstrating how deities can change and evolve as their myths and understandings change among humans, even if those changes appear outside the context of religious material and in the domain of pop culture.

Eros—Eros is the Greek god of love. In some myths, he is a primordial god of creation, ushering forth from Chaos with Gaia, Tartarus, and Uranus. His power is the power of love, attraction, and intercourse, giving birth to the universe. In a later version of his myth, he is the son of Aphrodite and either Ares, Hermes, or Hephaestus. In the more familiar image of a winged youth, Eros became the attendant of Aphrodite, working together to inspire love and attraction. That image, particularly of an infant with wings and a bow and arrows, evolved into the Roman Cupid and later into the popular image of Valentine's Day cards. In some myths, Eros is depicted as sober and knowing the power he holds in the lives of god and mortals; other times, he is depicted as childish and ill tempered. Eros's love for Psyche is celebrated in a legendary story, and both are associated with the Eleusinian Mysteries.

Freya—Freya is the goddess of the Norse pantheon most associated with Venus and Aphrodite. In planetary magick, Friday is the day of Venus, yet in English it is derived from Freya's day, though evidence suggests Friday belongs to Frigga, wife of Odin. Freya and Frigga are often erroneously linked and equated, as they belong to two different races of gods. Many magicians believe Freya to simply be a Northern Venus. While she encompasses issues of love and attraction, as well as sexuality, she is much more than that. Her name means "lady," and she is the foremost goddess of the race of nature gods named the Vanir. Even after the Vanir battled the sky gods, the Aesir, and lost, Freya still retained power and prominence, being "adopted" by the Aesir through a battle trade along with her brother. She is a goddess of magick, mysteries, sexual power, and prophecy. She can be benign and she can be fierce. She weeps over the loss of her husband, and her tears that hit the water become amber, while the tears that hit the land become gold.

Freyr—Freyr, or Frey, is the brother to Freya and known as "Lord" amongst the Vanir. He is a god of fertility, virility, and the land. Some see him as the god of the phallus, the embodiment of male virility. Freyr is the god who bestows the blessings on the land and pleasure among mortals. He can be called upon for all blessings, including love, romance, sex, and pleasure.

Guinevere—In the Arthurian mythos, Queen Guinevere is the wife of King Arthur, though in many Witchcraft and goddess traditions Guinevere is seen as an embodiment of the goddess of the land, fertility, and sovereignty. A Venusian and Earth figure to the King's Martial and Sun archetype, we can look to Guinevere as a goddess figure in her own right, even if modern tradition usually depicts

her as human. Older Arthurian lore actually implies she is
a faery queen, with there being three distinct Guineveres
who are seasonally "captured" by an evil king, ushering in
seasons of wither, not unlike the tales of Persephone with
Hades. In many Celtic traditions, the old gods, such as the
Tuatha de Danann, are considered faery folk with the rise of
Christianity, not to displace the image of the monotheistic
Christian god but to retain the interesting semidivine
characters. As the myths are retold, they become more
and more human, making it hard to see who is a god and
who isn't. Most of the Arthurian characters are attaining a
semidivine mythic status in Neopaganism. While her most
popular stories end in tragedy with her betrayal through
an affair with Lancelot, modern Pagans believe there are
deeper, truer stories of this goddess, telling of the mysteries
and sovereignty of the land and how, through love between
king and queen, these mysteries can be experienced and
healing brought to the land and its people.

Hathor—Hathor is the cow-headed goddess of ancient Egypt,
seen as the patron of joy and pleasure, and having roles
as mother, wife, and lover. She is one of the most popular
gods of ancient Egypt, with many festivals in her honor.
She was originally linked with the Milky Way, just as the
cow is linked with life-giving milk, but later Hathor was
identified with other goddesses, such as the gentle side of
the bloodthirsty lion goddess Sekhmet and the horned form
of Isis.

Hera—The later Greek myths do not paint Hera as a very
loving goddess. Most of what we now learn of Hera
involves the difficult aspects of her relationships with Zeus
and her stepchildren. She sought revenge on Zeus for his
infidelity through punishing and tormenting his children

from these affairs, yet she and her Roman counterpart Juno are the Greek and Roman patrons of marriage respectively. The month of June was named after Juno and seen by some as the best month to be married to assure her blessings. The cow, peacock, and cuckoo bird are sacred to Hera. Scholars and Pagans alike speculate that she was a great mother goddess before being absorbed into Greek culture under the guise of Zeus's wife, and that the theme of jealousy was to undercut her own importance. The work of scholar J. J. Bachofen (1815–1887), along with the vast array of ancient temple sites and earliest Greek buildings, suggests a place of greater importance in early and pre-Greek culture, contrasting sharply to her later depictions. From speaking with Pagans practicing a variety of Greek-inspired forms of Witchcraft, I know that my personal experience of Hera in ritual is much different from the later Homeric depictions of her. As long as you show her respect, I've found her quite pleasant and willing to help in love and marriage magick.

Inanna—In the Sumerian pantheon, Inanna is the queen of heaven and earth. Though not specifically a love deity, she is a combination of both earth goddess of fertility and star/sky goddess, and many believe she is the oldest root source of other goddesses such as Astarte, Ishtar, and Aphrodite. Her consort is Dumuzi, a shepherd and vegetation god, and their union is viewed as symbolic both of natural forces coming together and of the tantric sexual practices of her priestesses. In her eyes, Dumuzi later betrays her by his lack of concern over her disappearance into the underworld, and many modern women have used the image of Inanna as the empowered woman as a spiritual aid during breakups and divorces.

Ishtar—Ishtar is the Assyrian and Babylonian counterpart to the older goddess Inanna. She, too, is a goddess of love, fertility, and war, considered the embodiment of the planet Venus. Like Inanna, she has a story of descent into the underworld, shedding pieces of clothing as she descends, until she arrives naked in the underworld. It was the later discovery of the Inanna myths that clarified many points in the Ishtar version for scholars. In her myths, she has a strange relationship with the hero Gilgamesh, both desiring him as a lover and, when he refuses, treating him as an antagonist. Perhaps she is more a tutelary goddess, teaching him through adversity. Her worship is strongly associated with sacred prostitution, dancing, and singing.

Lakshmi—Lakshmi is the Hindu goddess of blessings, wife to Shiva and beloved by Hindus. She shares traits with Aphrodite/Venus, both being born out of a foamy ocean. Ceremonial magicians looking to the Hindu pantheon relate Lakshmi to the Venusian godforms for this reason, as she is generally charitable and good-natured as the goddess of material fortune and beauty, and can be called upon in matters of love and romance. One of her main symbols is the lotus, and she is depicted seated or standing in a lotus, holding lotus flowers, often with four arms.

Morrighan—Though most Neopagans tend to look at the Morrighan as the dark goddess of war and battlefields, she also has associations as a goddess of the land, fertility, and sexuality. Seen as a triple goddess—as Anu, Babd, and Macha or Babd, Macha, and Nemain—some of the attributes of these figures lend themselves to the goddess of the land and sexual union. Her later evolution into the Morgan le Fay figure definitely indicates her as an enchantress. You can draw parallels between the Morrighan and Middle Eastern goddesses such as Astarte and Ishtar as goddesses of both love and war and initiators of heroes. Her relationship with the tragic hero Cu Chulainn is similar to Ishtar's relationship with Gilgamesh.

Venus—Venus is the Roman counterpart of the Greek Aphrodite, so much so that the two are now most often seen as identical. Venus experienced a resurgence in popularity after the Roman Empire though works of art from the Renaissance.

The Temple of Love

One of the experiences that has been most helpful to those coming to me, seeking a deeper relationship with the divinities of love, is to visit the Temple of Love. Many "places" exist on the inner planes that are available to the sincere seeker. When doing my own personal work with a goddess of love, this vision came to me. Since then, I've shared it with others in workshops and private sessions, and many people have had the opportunity to have a profound personal experience with the goddess, whoever is right for them.

The image of the Temple of Love is a psychic amalgam of many places that have existed historically. We know many of the goddesses of love had temples dedicated to them, where rituals of healing, sensuality, and sexuality took place. It is the origin of the "temple prostitutes," who were not prostitutes in the modern sense but temple priestesses fulfilling a sacred function in a society very different from ours today, where sexuality and spirituality had not been separated.

This meditation seems to combine such ideas from the temples of Astarte and Aphrodite in the ancient world with the Venusian correspondences of modern ceremonial magick. Qabalistic magick traditions tell us that each planet is related to a sephira, a point on the qabalistic Tree of Life. Each sephira has its own temple on the inner planes corresponding to its function. Perhaps this Temple of Love is an expression of this Venusian temple associated with the sephira called Netzach. *Netzach* means "victory" and refers to the victory of love, or nature, over all.

Use this pathworking to find your own expression of divine love from the Goddess and to further your own exploration and understanding of what a healthy relationship is. To set the mood, you can burn a green or pink candle and rose or red sandalwood incense if you desire.

EXERCISE} Journey to the Temple of Love

1. Perform steps 1–5 from the mirror affirmations exercise on page 10.

2. Imagine the mirror before you. You don't need a physical mirror to gaze into, but remember the mirror from the mirror affirmations exercise. If using a physical mirror (silver or black) is more helpful for you, then by all means use it. Mirrors are sacred to Venus and can be used as a gateway to her. Even if you don't "see" a mirror in your mind's eye, feel it. Sense it. Know that a psychic mirror is there before you, and it is able to transform into a gateway, leading you to your heart's desire.

3. Ask the powers of the universe, your own higher self and guides, to go to the Temple of Love. Ask the mirror to become a gateway to this temple so you can learn more about the mysteries and power of love.

4. Imagine the mirror's image of yourself shifting like ripples across a pond, distorting the image. Soon it opens up and becomes a gateway. Pass through the gateway and find yourself in a tunnel.

5. The tunnel is warm and wet, but not unpleasant. Water drips from the roof, down the sides. You reach out to touch the water, to feel it, and bring your fingers to your lips to taste it. You taste a faint amount of iron, like the Earth

Mother's blood flows through this tunnel. Or it might have a coppery taste, for copper is the metal of Venus.

6. You continue forward, toward a light at the end of the tunnel; it's a soft and gentle white light, flickering as if generated by candles or torches. You come into the light and move through it, finding yourself in the Temple of Love.

7. Look around. What do you see? To most, this appears as a lavish Old World temple, adorned with jewels and precious metals. It could be entirely constructed by human hands or carved right out of a cavern, working with the natural shapes and curves of the rock. In particular, copper, green, and pink are the dominant colors of the minerals, fabrics, and flowers. Flickering lights from torches, candles, and oil lamps guide the way, and you smell the sweet scents of both flowers and burning resins of incense, slightly intoxicating you. You can see or hear the flow of water, with a fountain or waterfall built into the temple.

8. Unlike most austere temples, the Temple of Love is inviting and comfortable. There are cushions and cots for you to lounge on, and banquets of all manner of delicacies set out before you. In the center, there is an altar for the goddess of love, and you know that you should not touch or take anything on that altar, though you may leave offerings there.

9. As you wander the temple, you might feel the presence of others there too, also seeking the mysteries of love, but their shape and form might not be clear. You might also feel the ever-present and pervading spirit of the goddess of love around you and now inside you.

10. You find at least one mirror in the temple, if not more, and think back to your mirror affirmations. Gaze into the mirror and think about your previous affirmations and how they made you feel. As you think about them, notice your self-image changing again. How does your self-image change in this mirror, revealing your true self? More importantly, how do you feel when you gaze into the mirror? Is it how you want to feel? If not, what can you do to change the image and yourself?

11. See the image of the mirror shift and change and show you someone else in your life. The mirror reveals someone else you have had a loving relationship with—a family member, friend, covenmate, lover, or partner. What does this person look like in the mirror, and is it different from how they look in the world? What does this image communicate to you through words, pictures, or feelings?

12. After experiencing the goddess's mirror, you feel compelled to wander the temple, and you find a gateway that leads outside to a beautiful flower garden with plants, shrubs, and trees. Flowers of all shapes and sizes, all beautiful, grow here. You find roses of every type, poppies, apple blossoms, belladonna, datura, yarrow, and many more. Many of the flowers are five-petalled flowers. You find amongst the plants various raw stones and minerals—copper ingots, turquoise, emeralds, rose quartz, amber, and malachite. As you wander through the garden, a flower, stone, or other natural power catches your attention. You feel compelled to touch it or pick it up and commune with it. You might feel its energy, its blessing of spirit medicine, fill your heart and change you for the better, though you are not yet sure how. You simply know that when you see that mineral or plant again, it will be important and might even be an ally in your

future magick with love, even if you don't know what its magick is about now.

13. Return to the Temple of Love. Now, you will find one of the many faces of the goddess of love there awaiting you. Who awaits you? You might not see anyone specific, but again feel the presence of the goddess of love all around you. For some, the awaiting presence might not even be the goddess but a god of love. The figure awaits with open arms for you, literally or metaphorically, and surrounds you with love. You are filled with the blessings of love and harmony. This deity might even have advice or wisdom for you and your own quest for love. Have an open heart to feel this message. You might ask questions and receive answers from the Divine then and there, or later, through life circumstances and through the words of people who love you. The gods can speak to us through the people in our lives. Be open to the power and wisdom of love.

14. When the deity is done communing with you, you find yourself moving back through the tunnel. You come out of the tunnel, through the gateway of the mirror that is before you, and the gateway closes.

15. Perform steps 8–10 from the mirror affirmation exercise.

Journal your experience with the goddess of love, and keep her message in mind as you are on your quest for love.

SIX

The Love of Nature

Certain substances have a history in attracting the forces of love and romance to us, and by looking at the wisdom of those who have gone before us, we can harness these natural forces to bend and shape our lives, creating the relationships we desire.

European folk magick uses simple correspondences with plants, minerals, and colors. Generally, green is used for love magick involving general happiness, a prosperous relationship, healthy children, and good love. Green is associated with the Goddess as the Lady of many folk traditions, even in the Christian era. Red is used for lust and passion, to incite a lover to action. White is used in fidelity charms to keep a lover true. Folk spells can involve clothing, string, or colored pins and candles, along with tools found in nature.

In elemental magick, the primary correspondences for love magick are the herbs and stones associated with water. Water is the element of love both spiritual and romantic. Our quest for love is depicted by the cups suit in the tarot. All substances associated with water—oceans, rivers, and lakes, as well as plants that hold a lot of water or grow better near water, and minerals with colors that are reminiscent of water—can be used for love magick.

Yet when we craft a relationship, we want something beyond romance and sentimentality. We want something that will last, with some stability. So along with our dominant water theme, our spellcraft could include the element of earth. Are you trying to find a life partner, someone to build a home with and grow old with? Then the earth element is definitely needed. Earth is the element of stability and the home. Use roots or dark stones in your magick. Do you want something with passion and intensity? Then throw in a bit of the fire element. Fire is passion and drive and even sexuality. Use red stones and colors. Pick red, spicy, or prickly herbs. If you are just looking for a passionate affair and nothing long-lasting, then perhaps fire should be the dominant element. Do you want clear communication and someone who will not only be physically stimulating but intellectually stimulating? Then the spell should have some air element in it as well. Use flowers with a strong, stimulating smell; stones that are colored like the sky; or the traditional color of air in ceremonial magick, yellow. Make the correspondences for your spell match your intention. Choose your dominant element for the type of relationship, and then add appropriate modifying ingredients.

In planetary magick, the same rules apply. Planets are simply another way to categorize magickal energy and archetypal forces. Focus on the type of relationship you want, with the appropriate planet's correspondences as the dominant theme in your spellcraft, and add appropriate modifiers from other planets to bring other qualities to the relationship.

The dominant planetary power for love magick is Venus, the planet of love, attraction, and social relationships. Its colors are green, pink, and copper, and its metal is copper. When copper corrodes, it creates a green color. Many minerals with green or light blue (such as malachite and turquoise) are copper compounds, giving them an association with

Venus, though any green or pink stone, with or without copper in its chemical structure, is associated with Venus. Fragrant flowers associated with love, particularly the rose, are also associated with Venus.

Other planetary powers used in love magick include Mars, Mercury, Jupiter, the Sun, and the Moon. Mars is used for passion and lust, for it is a fiery planet. Mercury, like the element of air, is used to improve communication in love magick. Jupiter adds a spiritual connection to the spell, so your paths, even if they are not the same spiritually, will be connected and complementary. The Sun and the Moon are the two most powerful "planets," though they are technically called luminaries in astrology. The Sun confers blessings of health, wealth, and happiness in all things, while the Moon is a powerful attractive force for you to draw the right person to you.

Planetary magick and many branches of folk wisdom also suggest that we time our love magick in harmony with the Moon and the planets. Friday is the traditional day of love magick associated with Venus. All love magick is said to be more successful on this day. We attract relationships and develop them further with magick on the waxing Moon, as the light of the Moon is growing. We banish ills from our relationships, or even banish the relationships themselves, when the Moon is waning.

Moon signs bring their own qualities to the magick. While all Moon signs have an effect, specific signs are particularly good for love magick. The Moon in Taurus brings a sensual and stable relationship. The Moon in Cancer brings a family-oriented partner. The Moon in Scorpio can draw a particularly sexual relationship, while the Moon in Pisces is good for a romantic and idealistic love, or even spiritual love. Older texts such as the Greek Magical Papyri suggest the Moon in Aquarius for love magick, though I'm not really sure why. Chapter 7 contains more astrological information that may be used to understand your compatibility with a lover. This information can also be applied to astrological magick and timing when casting your spells.

Nature's Helpers

Love magick from almost all traditions looks to the powers of nature for aid in procuring love. Since ancient times, humans have learned how scent, color, and texture can stimulate, arouse, and entice other humans. From a larger metaphysical view, we see nature as a source of unconditional love, and when we spend time in nature, we feel connected to our source of creation through the emotion of divine love. Like the creatures of nature—plant, animal, and mineral—we feel less separation from the Divine because we are operating out of our heartspace rather than our intellectual minds.

In magick, we have used the energies of the natural world to help us tune in to specific qualities to make our magick. As nature is part of the whole, anything we can imagine magickally is available to us. Love is one of those specific energies we want to tune in to when making magick. We want to manifest that divine and romantic love in our daily life and use charms from nature to help us do so. They have become the basis of our magickal formulas in traditional magick systems.

While some look to these substances as ingredients, as tools, from a spirit worker's point of view, they are really allies. Everything has a spirit. Everything has an energetic consciousness, even though it might operate in a way much different from humanity. Every animal, every plant, and every stone has a living power, and the best magick workers consciously partner with that living power to be in harmony with nature rather than unconsciously command or compel those powers. They become our helpers in magick. Cooperation, particularly in love magick, is always better than force.

Love Stones

Stones, minerals, and crystals are powerful allies in the quest and sustainment of love because their very nature is solid and dependable. Each anchors a particular vibration of love for us and helps us attune to it, even in the midst of emotional upheaval and reactions. When used in magick, they can return us to our intention of love, even when we are feeling lonely, scared, or angry.

The following stones have been partnered with love magick in the past and can be used in your own spells:

Amber—Amber is not a stone but a fossilized resin, usually orange, yellow, or brown in color, from the sap of a tree. Though variations of it are found all over the world, the magick of amber plays most strongly in the Norse traditions, being sacred to the goddess Freya. In modern Witchcraft, amber is generally considered male and solar in nature, a counterpart to dark jet, another fossil. It is a versatile "stone," with the ability to absorb or project energy as needed. It can be used to enhance any magick; with its associations with Freya, it is an excellent charm for love magick and for healing from the loss of love by absorbing grief and pain.

Aventurine, Green—Green aventurine, sometimes called green quartz, is another Venusian stone. Though an entirely different stone, it is used much the same way that emerald is (though it is much cheaper), opening the heart and even healing vision. It is used as a good-luck charm and can attract love and romance, and generate an overall sense of well-being.

Azurite—Azurite is a deep-blue stone with properties associated with peace, healing, and unconditional love. While it doesn't have traditional correspondence with romantic love, it forms with many other copper compounds that do, such as turquoise, malachite, and chrysocolla.

Calcite—The shiny family of calcite stones is best used to reveal the truth and to reveal illusions. The color of the calcite focuses on whatever level of your consciousness it operates. For aiding in the quest for love and revealing your illusions about love and relationship, green, emerald, pink, and blue calcite would be helpful.

Cat's Eye—Cat's eye is formed from the same mineral as nephrite jade, but it forms with green fibers in it. When polished, it forms a single vertical streak, making a rounded piece look like the eye of a cat. Like many natural phenomena resembling eyes, it's used for protection, to avert the "evil eye" form of curses. It is also said to confer catlike attributes, helping you attune to your instincts, intuition, and playful nature. Because of the green color, like jade, it can be used for love magick, though other forms of cat's eye can be found in brown or yellow.

Chrysocolla—This soft, blue stone is another copper compound. Its energy is soft, feminine, and loving. It is used to soothe pain—physical pain, particularly joint pain, or the pain of the heart to overcome the ending of relationships.

Chrysoprase—Chrysoprase is a stone of spiritual protection and balance. It elevates the mood, preventing depression, and increases physical fertility. The apple-green stone is sometimes mistaken for a form of jade, but it is really of the chalcedony family of stones.

Emerald—Emerald is one of the premiere love stones. Ruled by Venus, it can be used in all manner of magick to attract and strengthen love, as well as heal the heart. Also influenced by Taurus, emerald magick is used to find strong, secure lovers who seek to build a home. Famed for its ability to heal the eyes, emerald can help you "see" your relationship or lover clearly and make appropriately informed choices about your life.

Hexagonite, Pink—A stone recently "discovered" by the metaphysical community for healing, pink hexagonite has the same minerals that form cat's eye and nephrite jade but with pink or lilac color. Current magickal research says that it opens one up to divine unconditional love rather than personal love, aligning the heart, brow, and crown chakras with the energies beyond. It calms the mind to receive true divine love without judgment.

Jade—Two different stones bear the name jade: jadite and nephrite. While they look very similar and have similar magickal uses, jadite has a brighter color and is considered "true" jade. Jade is an all-purpose stone that is used for physical and spiritual healing of all kinds, strengthening the life force of the body, granting longevity, and boosting strength and determination. It is also a stone associated with love and fertility and is given as a gift on the twelfth, thirtieth, and thirty-fifth wedding anniversaries.

Jasper, Green—Jasper is a form of chalcedony that takes many colors and contains many forms and patterns in it, giving it a wide variety of properties and appearances. Most jaspers are considered protective or balancing. Green jasper, due to its color, can be used in love magick.

Kunzite—Being pink, kunzite can look similar to rose quartz, and many would use the two interchangeably. Kunzite has the added benefit of lifting up the emotions. While rose quartz has a sense of "warm and fuzzy" love, kunzite's love vibration can raise you out of depression and inspire you to make choices from a place of love.

Kyanite—Kyanite is the stone to remove thoughtforms and blockages from the energy body. Its straight, fibrous growth is most commonly found in blue and is used to heal the mental body, but it can also be found in green, removing blocks in the emotional body, or black, to bring protection and grounding. Unpolished kyanite can be fragile.

Lapis Lazuli—Sacred to the queen of heaven and earth, Inanna, lapis can be used to bring peace and prosperity to relationship. It grants a sense of royalty to the user, to enhance self-esteem. It's a particularly good stone for women to get in touch with their inner goddess of love, but it can also be used successfully by men.

Lodestone—Lodestone, or natural magnet, is a classic ingredient in love charms everywhere. The attractive forces of magnetism parallel the "animal magnetism" in sexual and romantic attraction. In the Hoodoo tradition, lodestones must be fed with iron powder to keep them active and alive in your magick.

Malachite—Malachite is a very dense and grounding green stone, granting physical and emotional protection as well as prosperity. It grants strength in all matters of the heart. It is one of the few stones that should not be made into a direct gem elixir, for toxins will leach out of the stone into the water, potentially harming the user.

Peridot—Peridot, also known as olivine, is a bright yellowish green stone used to open the heart to love and to keep it open despite fear and pain. Peridot is also known to attract material wealth.

Quartz, Clear—Clear quartz magnifies any intention placed into it. The points, or rounded stones, can be used in love magick of all kinds to increase attractiveness, to magnify self-esteem, and to broadcast a beacon to attract the lover who is correct for you.

Quartz, Rose—Rose quartz is the preeminent love stone. The color comes from titanium tinting the naturally clear or white quartz, and with this addition, the quartz carries the vibration of unconditional love. It is used in all manner of self-esteem and confidence spells and is the heart of charms for true magickal love.

Rhodochrosite—Rhodochrosite is a pink stone banded with white. It is used to attract and nourish love. It is also particularly powerful in healing issues of the past, including past lives. Rhodochrosite heals the heart and cleanses the aura of unhealthy emotions.

Rhodonite—Similar to and often confused with rhodochrosite, rhodonite is a pink stone with black coloring due to black manganese oxides rather than white. Rhodonite can also be used in dream magick to clarify your dreams, work on past-life issues, and dream of your future lover.

Serpentine—Serpentine is used as an amulet to protect you from harm, particularly the bites of poisonous animals and insects, yet it is also used as a charm for love and romance, being a green stone ruled by Venus. Serpentine can help prevent poisoning a relationship with jealousy or mistrust.

Tourmaline—Tourmaline is an excellent stone to remove blocks in consciousness, particularly blocks in the heart chakra and blocks to love. Blue tourmaline brings peace of mind and clears obsessive thoughts. Green, pink, and especially watermelon tourmaline are particularly powerful for heart healing and love magick.

Turquoise—Turquoise is an all-purpose stone. Due to its blue color, it is most associated with Jupiter in planetary magick, but because its blue hue is from being a copper compound, from the metal of Venus, it also has Venusian associations. Turquoise can be used to bring love, peaceful emotions, clarity when making decisions about matters of the heart, and healing when relationships are in turmoil. It is also a stone of protection, communication, and wealth.

Herbs of Love

Along with stones, it is common to use herbs, flowers, and trees in love magick. Herbs are just as powerful as stones, but they are different. Rather than anchoring a specific kind of love energy, they grow and develop in their own journey of love, just as we do; therefore, their spirit can teach us lessons of change that are different from the wisdom of stones. Plants undergo their own sexual relationships and families, and that wisdom can be carried with us when we use them in spells and formulas. Even though human relationships are different, plant magick can help us adapt, change, and respond more appropriately when seeking romance or when we are in a long-term relationship.

Generally, the flower is the part of the plant that attracts. In some traditions of flower magick, the practitioner divides the sexual aspects of flowers so that the harvested pollen of flowers is for the male mysteries, the God of Witchcraft, and is used generally in attracting women; the nectar of flowers is for female mysteries, the Goddess, and for attracting men. Since most of us do not collect our flower, pollen, and nectar individually, such traditions do not have a lot of written lore on them but are worth exploring. The more solid parts of the plant—the roots of herbs and the bark of trees—can be used to gain solidity in any magick. The leaves and stems are used in general magick.

The following plants can be called upon for aid in your love magick:

Adam and Eve Root—Adam and Eve root are two separate
orchid roots, also known as putty root. One is considered
male and the other female. Sometimes the roots are tied
together and/or carried in a bag to attract or ensure love.
They can be bound in a pouch and given to a couple
to ensure happy love and a successful marriage. For
heterosexual couples, the "male" root is carried by the
man, and the "female" root is carried by the woman. It
ensures fidelity and promotes the strengthening and growth

of the couple. If not in a relationship, you can give the corresponding part to your intended lover. In Hoodoo, the roots are anointed with an attraction oil and carried in a pouch of red flannel to attract a lover.

Almond—Almond is ruled by the element of air and the planet Mercury, though it has associations with love magick and Venus. It is best used to grant eloquence and communication skills, along with creativity, in any romance. Almond oil can be used as a good base oil for any essential-oil blend.

Angelica—Usually angelica is used in protection magick, to align yourself with the realm of the angels and to break harmful, unwanted energies. The root of this plant is used in protection, banishing, and healing incense and powders. In love magick, it can be used to add blessings and grace to any relationship.

Apple—Apple is the tree of Venus, with its five-petalled flowers and five-pointed seed star within the fruit. It is filled with magickal and healing lore and has a variety of uses. Faery traditions are associated with the apple, as are Witchcraft and spells. Apple wood collected in the fall and winter is used in magick to commune with the faeries of the underworld. Due to its potentially baneful nature, it should not be used in relationship and love magick. However, wood collected in the spring and summer is used for the magick of love, relationship, fertility, and marriage. Do not use it for communion with the underworld faeries. In general, apple is also an herb of immortality and healing.

Apricot—Apricots can be used in all manner of love spells, as their juice makes any working more sweet. They also have associations with androgyny and diversity, mixing the flavors of peach and plum, and can be used in gay, lesbian, bisexual, and transgender love magick.

Arrowroot—Arrowroot is used to heal the heart's wounds from the "arrows" of love, just as Native American healers used it to heal the wounds from physical arrows. The powder is used in heart-healing powders and incense.

Avocado—Avocado is an excellent food for love magick, being ruled by Venus and considered a feminine food. It can also be used in beauty magick and in oil mixes, as well as in creams and ointments. As a carrier oil, it should be mixed with other carrier oils because it can have a strong scent on its own.

Balm of Gilead—The flowers of the balm of Gilead are used in love spells and incense. It is considered to be a balm to soothe quarrels in the family, marriage, or any relationship. It eases jealousy and hurt feelings, and helps lovers and friends reconcile. In can be used in incense with myrrh to open the channels of reconciliation with someone. It is used to bring peace in magick. In Wicca, putting bowls of salt in the four corners of the home is a traditional protection spell. Add a pinch of balm of Gilead to each of the bowls in order to add the power of peace with protection to the household.

Bay—Bay is a solar and masculine herb, sacred to Apollo. A powerful herb with many uses, particularly the power of prophecy, it can be used to add power to any love, lust, or romance magick. Bay is particularly powerful when used in food magick.

Belladonna—*Belladonna* means "beautiful lady," as it was used to dilate the eyes of women in the European court to give them greater allure and beauty, yet it is also known as deadly nightshade, one of the most powerful and toxic herbs in the Witch's apothecary. Few modern Witches use belladonna for this reason. The spirit of this plant is decidedly feminine and seductive. Spiritually, she opens new doorways of consciousness and shamanic journeys, being one of the ingredients in the classic flying ointment of medieval Witches, but she is also an enchantress. Her leaves and berries can be used extremely carefully to add potency to any love mixture that will not be consumed. Use only with caution, and never consume or use topically.

Bergamot Mint—Associated with both Venus and the Sun, this herb is primarily used in success and money magick. The minty-orange scent also has associations with air, making it more in harmony with a Librian-Venus blend than a Taurean-Venus blend.

Bleeding Heart—Bleeding heart blooms with flowers that remarkably resemble tiny red or pink hearts with a drop falling out. The Doctrine of Signatures, a teaching that suggests the shape of a plant, as well as the name itself, tells us what it is used for and implies it is used to heal the heart, primarily through emotional healing. While the flower can be picked and used herbally like any other, I've found the most powerful application of this plant is through the preparation of a flower essence.

Bloodroot—Bloodroot is a powerful and somewhat toxic herb, used medicinally to treat cancer, warts, and unhealthy growths. Magickally it is ruled both by Mars and Venus. The red dye from the root has reportedly been used in Native American rituals of courtship.

Catnip—Catnip is a Venusian herb used to put you in touch with your inner instincts, like a cat. It is used in love and attraction magick, lust magick, and beauty magick.

Herbally, catnip is used to calm down the nervous system, while magickally it can be used to help calm down the mind, to get your thoughts out of the way so your instincts can be clearer. It is particularly good to use on a first date, when it will help you follow your instincts, be spontaneous, and not overthink your responses too much.

Cinnamon—A versatile spice, cinnamon can be used in love magick to bring warmth and passion. It is particularly powerful in love magick when mixed with rose petals and other Venusian herbs.

Comfrey—Comfrey is generally regarded as a weed, but it is a powerfully regenerating weed that is difficult to get rid of once you have it. Ruled by Saturn, medicinally it regenerates tissues and bones, and magickally it brings permanence, anchoring your intention into reality. Comfrey can be used in love and marriage spells to cement the relationship together and give it regenerative power.

Copal—A South American resin used for protection and purification in a manner similar to frankincense. Copal is also used in some Mexican folk magick for love.

Coriander—Coriander seeds are ruled by the planet Mars and the element of fire. They add lust and passion to any mixture. When consumed in a tea or tincture, they raise the metabolism and increase energy, making them an excellent ingredient for lust and sex magick.

Crocus—Crocus root is used in powders and incense for love, attraction, and inducing visions. The saffron crocus yields the yellow spice saffron, which is considered an aphrodisiac and is sacred to the goddess Hecate, who is said to be clad in saffron robes.

Damiana—Damiana is the premiere sex magick herb of Central America. Reputed to have powerful lust-inducing properties, some say it is ruled by Mars, while others say it is ruled by Venus. A trick of modern sex magicians is to take a double-strength tea once a day for at least two weeks (two tablespoons of damiana in one cup of boiling water) to increase sexual power and augment your aura to attract people to you sexually. While I can attest that it does indeed work, it doesn't always work the way you envision; not everybody who is attracted to you will be attractive to you.

Datura—Datura is one of the Witch's baneful herbs, ruled by Saturn and quite toxic, granting visions of the underworld and land of the dead. Also known as thorn apple, it is co-ruled by Venus and has a spirit of bewitchment, the enchantress or seductress, guiding it. To add magnetism, glamour, and power to a formula, its seeds and leaves can be used very carefully in mixtures that are not consumed.

Dittany of Crete—Though dittany of Crete is associated with Venus, its mythology and lore has very little to do with romance. Traditionally, it is used in healing wounds and removing weapons from open wounds. It is used more in incense for the manifestation of spirits. Many occult suppliers actually sell oregano or marjoram instead of the more rare dittany.

Dragon's Blood—A red resin ruled by Mars, dragon's blood is a magickal catalyst used in all manner of formulas, from power, protection, and exorcism to love and lust. As it gives off a wonderful smell when burned, it makes a great addition to incense, though its cost can make it prohibitive as a base for incense. There are several plants referred to as dragon's blood, including a succulent garden plant, but the dragon's blood referred to in most magickal texts is the resin of the *Daemonorops* draco palm tree.

Fennel—Fennel is used for healing and protection, and also for fertility and virility magick, because of its profuse number of seeds. Sacred to Dionysus, his wand, or thyrsus, is a fennel stalk topped with a pine cone and seen as a phallic symbol. The Italian word for fennel, *finocchio*, can also be associated with homosexuality and therefore is used in gay love magick.

Foxglove—Foxglove, also known as faery bells, is one of the toxic herbs of Witchcraft. The heart medicine known as digitalis is made from foxglove. Because of this heart association, foxglove can be used in powerful formulas for keeping the heart strong and steady, but only in formulas that are not internally consumed. Foxglove should never be consumed as a direct medicine unless directed to do so by a qualified healthcare practitioner.

Geranium—Geraniums are used in protection and cleansing magick, but pink geranium flowers can be used in love magick. The flowers can be soaked in water and made into a wash or spray to increase the feelings of love in the home.

Heartsease—A type of pansy, heartsease is traditionally used for healing the heart and bringing peace and tranquility to the troubled heart. It is considered an herb of Saturn rather than of Venus, and it does seem to soothe the troubles of Saturn.

Hibiscus—Hibiscus is a large pink flower ruled by both the Sun and Venus, used in psychic development, clairvoyance, and divination. It helps the user experience divine knowledge through the heart center. While it can be used medicinally in teas, the typical garden variety of hibiscus is actually poisonous, and the ayurvedic hibiscus, *Hibiscus sabdariffa*, is used in herbal preparations.

Hyacinth—Named for Apollo's male lover Hyacinth. Its flower, root, and oil are particularly potent in gay male love spells, despite the bloody death of Hyacinth due to the jealous actions of Zephyrus. The flowers were said to rise from his blood in memory of the love shared between him and Apollo.

Hydrangea—Hydrangea, particularly white-flowered hydrangea, is used in Moon magick to attract and banish whatever you desire. It is also ruled by Jupiter and used to bring blessings. The root or flower can be used in dream magick, and in terms of love magick, hydrangea can be used to help you dream of a new love or dream the solution to a problem in your current relationship.

Ivy—Ivy of all kinds has a rich magickal history, from being sacred to Dionysus to playing a role in Faery Faith traditions. It is also used in luck and love magick. Due to its binding nature, it's also used in magick for fidelity and commitment.

Jasmine—Jasmine is a delicate flower ruled by the Moon. It can be used in love and attraction formulas. Jasmine also has the power to uplift any combination it is in and can be used in tantric sexual formulas to raise the vibration of lustful sex to spiritual union.

Lady's Mantle—Lady's mantle is the premier feminine magickal herb. Ruled by Venus, it is not only used in love and attraction magick, it is used for the attunement of nature and the mysteries of the Goddess. Its Latin name, *Alchemilla vulgaris*, shows its sacred nature to the alchemists, seeking to unlock the spiritual powers of nature. Dew collects in the little "cups" of the leaves, and this water is used to guarantee beauty and youth when used as a face wash. Medicinally, it is used to heal and tone the feminine reproductive system.

Lavender—Generally seen as an herb of Jupiter due to the purple color, or Mercury for its relaxing properties, lavender can be used to dispel stress, sorrow, and darkness, and to conjure a happy home and peaceful relationships. In the modern era, it has a reputation as a gay male love herb, primarily through the formulary work of Herman Slater and his former shop, The Magickal Childe.

Lettuce—While not a love plant, lettuce is reportedly used to induce chastity for those who are overly sexual. Though I've never used it as such, this knowledge can make you think twice about ordering a salad on a date.

Lily—Lilies are a pure, spiritual, and androgynous plant. While not used to conjure love and sex, they can be used to break love spells cast specifically upon someone. The flowers or root are used in a purification bath and/or floor wash to cleanse the unwanted influence. Flower essences made from lilies are used to heal betrayal.

Lily of the Valley—Lily of the valley is a powerful and potentially toxic herb, associated with both Venus for its effect on the heart and Mercury for its strong scent. Lily of the valley is used as a less toxic substitute for foxglove in treating heart disease, and both are associated with the faeries. Though it has a strong scent, most commercial oils of lily of the valley are synthetic, as it can be difficult to extract, but thankfully natural ones are becoming more available. The scent is best extracted by macerating the flowers in a base oil such as olive or almond, though it doesn't last long. Due to the heart and faery associations, along with the enticing smell, it is used in love magick to attract a love. In modern times, it is used in bridal bouquets for marriage and longevity. As a flower essence, it returns hope in times of hopelessness and despair.

Lime—Lime is used in love and faery magick, and herbally it is used to relax and lower stress. For both uses, lime combines well with lavender. It can also be used to cool down the excitement of love or lust.

Lovage—The herb lovage, as its name suggests, can be used in love magick. It can increase your appeal to the opposite sex and can be used in potions and baths, either in combination or alone, to attract a new lover. In Hoodoo traditions, one can bathe in the tea, early in the morning, for nine days. After bathing, take the basin to the crossroads, turn your back on the rising sun, and throw the water over your left shoulder, toward the sun, while saying the name of the one you seek to attract. After repeating this for nine days, your lover is said to come to you. It can also be used to attract a nonspecific lover, or simply the one that is best for you, by calling out the qualities you want in a new lover.

Mandrake—Mandrake is one of the most magickal plants and is associated with strange and sometimes disturbing lore. True mandrake, *Mandragora*, is quite difficult to obtain or grow and grows best in warm climates. There are other plants completely unrelated botanically but given the folk name mandrake, such as white bryony, or false mandrake, and mayapple, or American mandrake. Mandrake is ruled by both Saturn and Venus, with roots that look like a human poppet. It can be used for love, healing, or hexing, with the root as a poppet. It is said to be an aphrodisiac, but it is also a powerful and toxic entheogen, so it is not suggested for internal use.

Mistletoe—A parasitic plant that grows upon trees, mistletoe has always been considered a gift from the gods, with a variety of magickal properties. Sometimes the white berries are described as the "semen" of the gods, and the Druids had very particular rituals about harvesting the mistletoe, lest it touch the ground and lose its heavenly virtue. Most popular around the yuletide holidays, the tradition of kissing under the mistletoe strengthens its love and passion associations. Many modern Witches use it as a magickal catalyst—not in formulas to consume, as it is considered toxic by most, but in small amounts added to topical formulas, charms, and powders to catalyze even more powerful properties of magick, similar to other power plants like mandrake and dragon's blood. Though it's famous as a love herb, that is not its primary purpose. It is better used in protection, blessing, and banishing.

Myrtle—A powerful herb used in preserving love. Sacred to Venus, historically it has also been used in the temples of the war gods Minerva and Mars. It has been associated with jealousy—both in punishing jealousy and in protecting others from the danger of jealousy.

Orange—This citrus fruit is ruled by the Sun and used in health, happiness, and inspiration magick, as the fruit reminds us of the Sun itself. The healing properties of the juice are powerful, described as liquid sunshine, and the juice can be used in food magick for love. The peel and essential oil can be used to add brightness to love potions, powders, philters, and bath salts. Orange is a very cleansing and brightening plant spirit that helps when one is depressed or pessimistic about love, as it can raise the spirits and bring optimism.

Orchid—Orchids are used in sex and love magick because the flowers can resemble the sex organs of both genders.

It is associated with Venus and Mars, but also Mercury for this androgynous quality. It is also helpful in all forms of homosexual love magick. The root is particularly powerful; known as satyrion root, it can be powdered for an aphrodisiac or left whole and carved into a charm. In folk magick, it is used to attract others, and when recipients consume a small part of it through food or drink, they traditionally will become attracted either to the person who gave it to them or the first person they see. In high magick, the powdered root or root charm can be placed in the chalice of the Great Rite as a token to empower the wine, water, or other ale with the powers of love and magick. If you grow orchids, the dried flowers and seeds make a wonderful addition to incense. Lucky hand root can be used as a substitute for satyrion root.

Oregano—Oregano is an herb of love and passion, particularly good in food magick or in incense. It is activating and revitalizing. Oregano is used in magick for happiness and brings a bit of zest and vitality. It is also used in protection magick and in helping break away from bad relationships.

Orris Root—Orris root, the root of the iris, is used as a fixative for scent in herbal products, but magickally it is about calming the mind to do deep magickal work and meditation. Ruled by the Moon, its power is to open the gateway to the deep mind, past the subconscious. It has also been traditionally considered an herb of Venus and is used in love magick for both drawing love and "fixing" it in terms of fidelity and commitment.

Parsley—Parsley historically has been associated with both death and dark magick, as well as good luck and life. For our purposes here, parsley tea can be used to increase lust, passion, fertility, vital life force, and strength.

Passionflower—Passionflower is associated with Venus, the
Moon, and Neptune. Herbally, it is calming and sedating,
yet in love magick, it is used to either incite passion (as an
aphrodisiac) or calm passion. It can be used to calm the self
and household, similar to balm of Gilead.

Patchouli—The rich and earthy scent of patchouli gives
Saturn and the element of earth domain over it. It is used
in protection magick as well as for love and attraction.
Patchouli is said to be particularly effective in lesbian love
spells.

Poppy—Poppy is a sedative and a hypnotizer, used in
bewitchment and for altering consciousness. The large
flowers are also associated with love, romance, and the
heady feeling we get when we fall in love.

Primrose—The evening primrose is associated with the Moon
and feminine reproductive systems, but it has a wider range
of associations. It is associated with hunting, possibly due
to its connection with Artemis as a lunar goddess. It has
associations with the Faery realm. The incredibly well-
researched website of Alchemy Works herbal company
suggests it can also be used as a shapeshifting herb, due to
its association with fickleness in the Victorian language
of flowers. The flowers usually open at dusk; later in the
season, they open at dawn but have no scent until evening.
The fickleness—the ability to seemingly change on a
whim—and its associations with the changing Moon lend it
shapeshifting powers.

Raspberry—Raspberry leaf is used in herbal medicine,
particularly for feminine reproductive health. The leaves
and berries can be used in love and sex magick, as well as
fertility magick for women. The berries themselves are best
in food magick for love and seduction.

Rice—Rice is a grain used to bless marriages with fertility and prosperity.

Rose—Rose is by far my favorite plant for love magick. Roses have been associated with love so strongly that even if you have no prior knowledge of magick, you will know and understand this correspondence. Red roses, in particular, are for romantic and passionate love. Pink roses are for a more delicate love, being both for romance and courting. White roses are for pure and spiritual love not yet consummated in the physical.

Rue—Sniffing fresh rue, with its vaguely vanilla scent, can make you forget problems in love and find optimism instead. Rue is protective and brings blessings. Be careful, as rue causes contact dermatitis in those with sensitive skin.

Sarsaparilla—Sarsaparilla root, traditionally used in root beer and many medicinal tonics, is ruled by Jupiter. At first glance, it doesn't have a lot of associations with love, yet the Jupiterian power brings blessings and spirituality to love magick. In Hoodoo traditions, it can be used specifically to increase sexual passion when combined with damiana, juniper berries, and other love herbs.

Spearmint—Spearmint is the sweetest and coolest of the mint family. Ruled by Venus, it can be used in healing and beauty magick, as it's great for the skin. It calms and cools, and can be used when the fires of lust run too high in the body.

Strawberry—Strawberry is a plant of passion and intensity, with a sweet, intense flavor. Strawberries can be used in food magick as well as fidelity magick to bless a marriage or ensure passion on the honeymoon. Strawberry mead can be a particularly potent handfasting or honeymoon drink.

Sugar—Though technically a plant product, not a plant, when derived from sugar cane, sugar in all forms can be used in love and relationship magick to sweeten up any connection between people and bring blessings.

Sweet Pea—Sweet pea is a plant of friendship, luck, chastity, and protection, particularly associated with the Moon, Mars, and Mercury. Sweet pea flowers have an alluring scent yet are self-pollinating, so they make the scent simply for the joy and beauty of doing so, not for reproduction like other plants, so sweet pea can be used in beauty magick and spells to simply feel good and attractive. Though it is strongly scented, no natural essential oil is available as of yet, but sweet pea bouquets, combinations of other scents to mimic sweet pea, can be used.

Tansy—Tansy is traditionally known as a Venus herb but most strongly associated with death, funeral rites, immortality, and transformation. Its scent is said to lead the dead to the otherworld. It can be used in magick honoring the dark aspects of Aphrodite and the Dark Goddess in general. It can also be used in magick to end relationships or to protect yourself from past lovers who wish you ill.

Thyme—Thyme is sacred to the planets Mercury and Venus, and is used in incense, powders, and food magick. Thyme promotes not only love but also fidelity, happiness, friendship, and self-improvement. The scent of thyme is considered an aphrodisiac, but it is also used in dream pillows and journey magick.

Tomato—Tomato is traditionally used in love magick, which always struck me as strange until I realized that it is part of a very powerful magickal family of plants, including mandrake, tobacco, and belladonna, the beautiful lady of the plant world. As a flower essence, the tomato is used to remove energetic blockages, and in love magick, as flower or fruit, it can remove blocks to a successful relationship.

Tonka Bean—While the vanilla-like scent of tonka is used in money and prosperity magick, other traditions and systems of herbal magick use it for love and romance. The hard bean can be used in the "heart" of an herbal charm pouch instead of a stone.

Vanilla—Vanilla is a power herb used to catalyze magick and bring potency. The sweetness of it associates it with love and attraction—romance, sweetness, and happiness.

Vervain—Vervain is the Witch's multipurpose herb. Traditionally ruled by Venus, it can be used for protection, blessing, healing, money, and love. Most historic mentions of vervain mean common vervain, *Verbena officinalis*, while most American supplies of vervain are blue vervain, *Verbena hastata*.

Walnut—The walnut tree's lore is rich in love and faeries. The wood, nutshell, and nut itself can be used in all forms of love magick.

Yarrow—Yarrow is another faery herb with associations of love and enchantment. Like damiana, different sources give it rulership by Mars and others by Venus. Yarrow medicinally aids the flow of blood and staunches wounds. Magickally, it aids in the appropriate uses of boundaries and can aid healing the heart when we feel wounded by our relationships, romantic or otherwise. In love magick, yarrow is said to give seven years of happy marriage.

SEVEN

Love Spells, Charms, and Potions

While ethics, theories, and self-improvement are all an important part of love magick, most people looking for aid in romance and sex are really looking for the spells. If you've skipped ahead to this chapter, I highly suggest you go back and read everything in the previous chapters to give you the proper context. Then you'll have the best understanding of how to apply the knowledge in this chapter for your highest good.

I think the best love spells are the ones you create yourself, as each of our romantic needs are unique. But looking at what has been used before and what is traditional helps us craft our spells in a manner that is more successful. Learning the traditional correspondences for love and how they are applied are important parts of preparing yourself for successful love magick.

Love magick is multifaceted, and there is no one-size-fits-all set of rules. They really are determined by the type of relationship you are seeking, so while a love spell that is successful for one person can technically work for another, it may not bring the second person what they truly wanted or needed. Learn techniques to manifest the relationship that is right for you and your potential partner.

This chapter reviews the basics of ritual in modern Witchcraft and shows you how to put the correspondences of the last chapter into greater use through effective spells, charms, and potions. Once you understand the basic formation and execution of spells, you will be better equipped to create your own for your own unique circumstances.

Circle Magick

Most modern Witches conduct their spells in the sacred space of a magick circle. The magick circle is a ritual space constructed through ceremony, marking the boundary of the circle and calling upon the four powers of the elements to guard and aid the magick. Magick done in the circle is said to be "between the worlds," and many of us find its results more effective, as if we have a more direct line to the universe and all the powers available to us than other forms of simple magick. The ritual itself elevates your magick to a form of theurgy, or god magick, for you are asking to work with the divine powers as a part of the ritual, a step that is not always taken in other forms of magick. The cleansing and preparation for the magick circle also helps you focus so you will be in the right magickal state of mind to cast your spell.

While the spells, charms, and potions in this book can be done anywhere, you might find them more effective when done in a magick circle. Here are simple instructions on how to create your magick circle through a very basic ritual.

There are many different ways to cast a magick circle, and different Witchcraft and magick traditions use a basic formula and embellish the ritual with their own mythology and symbolism. The instructions outlined here are based upon my own circles, in particular on my own methods, but are not immersed in any specific mythology or mainstream tradition. If you already know how to cast a magick circle, feel free to use your own method or adapt the instructions in this book to suit your own style when working the love magick of this book.

To cast the circle, defining the boundary of the sacred space, most Witches use a tool like a magick wand or the ritual knife known as the athame. Such tools are usually ritually cleansed and blessed prior to use. If you do not have these tools, you can do what many Witches do: cast the circle with your finger. Most Witchcraft traditions will have an altar set up as a magickal workspace, with candles, a chalice, stones, bowls, oils, and incense readily available, along with the wand and blade. If you are just starting out, you don't need a full altar. Just make sure you have all the tools you need for the specific spell you are doing.

First, start in the direction of the north and hold your casting tool or point your finger toward magnetic north. (Witches in the Southern Hemisphere can start facing south and moving counterclockwise.) Imagine a beam of light coming out of the tool/finger, creating a ring of light as you slowly move clockwise, reciting the words below to consecrate your circle. Traditionally the light is blue, though it can be of any color, with white and violet being popular colors to visualize. The circle is traditionally nine feet in diameter, but you can make it fit your room space if indoors. Cast the circle three times around you clockwise, reciting one line for each cast circle.

I cast this circle to protect me from all harm.
I cast this circle to attract only the most balanced, perfect energies for my work.
I cast this circle to create a temple between the worlds.

Second, face the north again, as you began, and invite the elements from each direction, moving clockwise (these are known as quarter calls). Different traditions associate the elements with different directions and specific beings, but these are standard quarter calls that can work for anybody. (If you have relationships with specific elemental beings or deities aligned with the elements, you could call upon them.

For multicultural love magick, you might want to call upon Aphrodite for earth, Inanna for air, Freya for fire, and Hathor for water.)

> *To the north, I call upon the guardians of the element*
> *of earth. Guard and guide me. Hail and welcome.*
> *To the east, I call upon the guardians of the element*
> *of air. Guard and guide me. Hail and welcome.*
> *To the south, I call upon the guardians of the element*
> *of fire. Guard and guide me. Hail and welcome.*
> *To the west, I call upon the guardians of the element*
> *of water. Guard and guide me. Hail and welcome.*

Third, invite the Divine to manifest as Goddess, God, and Great Spirit, or in any forms you recognize, as well as your own spiritual guides and protective guardians, ancestors, angels, and animals. Witches traditionally see the Divine as both male and female and recognize a whole host of spirits from the otherworlds, as well as the spirit of nature all around you. As you learn about specific gods and goddesses associated with love (see chapter 5), you might decide to call upon them specifically at this point in the ritual. If you have any other candles, incense, or tools that need to be lit, sprinkled, or scattered, such as salt, water, or oil, do so now. A black candle is usually lit for the Goddess and placed on the left side of the altar, while a white candle is lit for the God and put on the right side of the altar. A central candle can be used for Spirit—black, white, gray, or a color specific to the ritual at hand such as green or pink, as these are the colors of love magick.

Fourth, a traditional blessing of protection is done before any magick. Usually a protection potion is used, anointed on the wrists and sometimes the brow or other chakra points. If you have *The Witch's Shield* or *The Outer Temple of Witchcraft*, you will have the formula for a protection potion, but many Witches simply use a pinch of sea salt in clear spring water as their protection/blessing potion. For tradition-specific magick circles, other religious elements would be added at this point, such as the Great Rite, offerings to the gods, or the blessing of cakes and ale. Since this is a simple outline, I've omitted those parts, but you can add and extend the ritual based on your own guidance, tradition, and previous experience.

The fifth step is called the work of the circle, and at this point you would perform any spellwork, meditation, or any other work to be done in the circle. This is the point you would cast the love magick spells in the rest of this chapter.

Sixth, if you are doing simple spellwork, such as reading a petition spell that you've written out, raise the cone of power to send out your intention. If you are empowering a physical charm or potion, raising the cone of power is not always necessary and is up to your discretion. Empowering an object (also called charging, blessing, hallowing, or consecrating) simply means holding it in your hands, thereby directing energy via your hands or third eye into it with a specific magickal intention. I visualize the energy that would have gone into the cone of power going into the object to be empowered. If you do raise the cone of power, raise your arms up and sweep the energy out the top of the circle in what is called the Goddess position. When you bring your arms down, cross them over the heart in the God position, mimicking the position of an Egyptian mummy, to reflect on your work. Then ground yourself as necessary.

Seventh, start to release the circle as you built it. Some traditions release the spirits first, then the quarters, while others release the quarters first, then the spirits. As long as you release both, it works. For this version, thank and release the powers and spirits who have gathered with you, including the Goddess, God, and Great Spirit. Any entities you have called by name, thank and release by name.

Eighth, release the quarters, starting in the north and going around counterclockwise to dismantle the circle. (If you called on specific guardians, make them a part of your release of the quarters.)

To the north, I thank and release the guardians
of the element of earth. Hail and farewell.
To the west, I thank and release the guardians of
the element of water. Hail and farewell.
To the south, I thank and release the guardians
of the element of fire. Hail and farewell.
To the east, I thank and release the guardians
of the element of air. Hail and farewell.

Ninth, release the circle. Starting in the north and moving counter-clockwise once, with your casting tool facing north, say:

I release this circle out into the universe as a sign of
my magick. The circle is undone but not broken.

While these abbreviated instructions are complete by themselves, if you desire a more detailed lesson on casting a magick circle and a deeper spiritual understanding of each step, review the lessons in my book *The Outer Temple of Witchcraft*. You can use the basic ritual outlined here for all the spells listed in this chapter.

Petition Spells

Petition spells are simply written statements that are burned in a cauldron or other flameproof vessel in the magick circle. They are petitions to the gods and the universe in clear and concise words for exactly what you desire. Here is where your previously created list of qualities will come in handy for clarity in your spellcasting.

Generally, petitions announce the spellcaster (you) and petition either specific deities or a more universal form of the Goddess and God. You state exactly what you desire in the clearest terms possible. You thank the gods and put in any conditions you have for the spell. I suggest "for the highest good, harming none" as your most important condition. With the words "so mote it be" you affirm it, and then after speaking it one to three times in the circle, you burn the spell. Smudging the paper in a Venusian incense or anointing the paper with a Venusian oil can certainly help. A commercially available ink known as dove's blood is best for love and sex magick. Many believe the root of this ink was actually the blood of a dove, the animal sacred to Aphrodite. Today, many commercial magickal inks are just red ink, though the formula of dove's blood ink should contain dragon's blood resin and rose oil. You can add your own to red ink.

Here is an example of a clear love petition:

> *I, (state your name), ask in the name of the Goddess, God,*
> *and Great Spirit to immediately grant me a girlfriend who*
> *is correct and good for me, between the ages of twenty-five*
> *and forty, who is intelligent, attractive, and spiritual.*
> *I thank the Goddess, God, and Great Spirit and ask this*
> *be for the highest good, harming none. So mote it be.*

Love Potions

Love potions are the most famous form of love magick. A potion is an herbal preparation that stores a magickal charge, and it can be a spell in and of itself, with a specific intention for a specific user, or a tool made with an open intention—love in a general sense, love in a romantic sense, or even plain old lust and sexual attraction. The potion, worn like a perfume, can then be used when one wants to use that energy. It can be used to cast a specific spell, enhancing your energy by infusing it with the vibration of the potion. The potion can be used in the ritual, anointed on petitions, candles, statues, talismans, and other tools to enhance their vibration and align them with your intention. A well-crafted potion can last for years, allowing a Witch to "capture" an auspicious time for love magick (see chapter 9) and then use the energy of that moment at a later date.

Potions can be made in a variety of ways. Those with the best scent are made from essential oils in a base oil to dilute their chemical intensity. Base oils include olive oil (the most likely to go rancid quickly) to the more stable almond, grapeseed, or apricot kernel oil. Jojoba oil is the most expensive and the one with the longest shelf life, theoretically never spoiling as it is technically a liquid wax, not an oil.

Potions can also be made in water. Those that are meant only for anointing are preserved with sea salt or a measure of high-proof alcohol added to the base. Those meant to be consumed are brewed and drunk like teas, and great care must be taken to ensure no toxic herbs or those that would interfere with the drinker's health or prescription medication would be used. Alcoholic potions can be made to be consumed with a longer shelf life than a tea, from the medicinal-tasting tincture to the sweeter cordial liqueur. Dry potions, such as powders and incenses, can be made to be burned in ritual, scattered in the area where they are to take effect, or even traditionally slipped into food and drink. Again, consumed powders should be made with only nontoxic herbs. Check with a good medicinal herbal for toxicity levels and potential medicinal interactions.

POTION} **Venus Oil**

14 drops almond oil base

3 drops myrtle oil

2 drops yarrow oil

2 drops rose geranium oil

2 drops palmarosa oil

2 drops ylang-ylang oil

1 drop bergamot mint oil

1 drop rose absolute (can substitute rosewood or a diluted rose absolute if the cost of undiluted true rose is prohibitive; simply add more than one drop until the scent is suitable to you)

POTION} **Venus Incense**

    3 tablespoons orris root

    2 tablespoons red sandalwood

    2 tablespoons apple wood, powdered

    1 tablespoon rose petals

    ½ tablespoon vervain

    ½ tablespoon lady's mantle

    ½ tablespoon tansy

    ½ tablespoon raspberry leaf

    1 tablespoon honey

    5 drops rose geranium oil

    3 drops yarrow oil

Store in an airtight container and let the scents mingle for at least a month.

POTION} **Love Potion No. 13**

This is a formula I created for my friend Rowan (see chapter 2), who was recovering from a series of difficult relationships. Its purpose is to bring back into your life the feeling of love and, when you are ready, an actual relationship.

The base of the potion is water, and this particular batch was made from spring water, melted snow, and well water from the red well at Glastonbury Tor. That's not available to most of us, so you can start with two cups of fresh spring water and add three tablespoons of sea salt.

Add to the water a copper ingot, wire, or coin while it simmers on a low heat to infuse the metallic power of copper, Venus's metal, to it. Grind each of the herbs, ideally in a mortar and pestle to add your energy and intention to the herb, even if you cannot grind it to a fine powder. The beans in particular would be difficult to grind by hand, but bruising them helps release their power and scent. Add one at a time to the potion, stirring in each one thirteen times:

1 tablespoon rose petals soaked in rose water

1 tablespoon rue

1 tablespoon jasmine flowers

1 tonka bean

1 tablespoon vervain

1 tablespoon star anise

1 tablespoon raspberry leaf

1 tablespoon damiana leaf

1 tablespoon yarrow flower

1 tablespoon basil leaf

1 tablespoon red clover tops

1 pinch dragon's blood resin

1 vanilla bean

Let the mixture cool and strain out the herbs. If available, add nine drops of sea water to the potion to truly activate its Venusian sea foam powers.

This potion is not for consumption but for anointing the body, including the chakras and nape of the neck. One of the ingredients, rue, can cause skin irritation in some people and should never be used by pregnant women. Omit it from the formula if necessary.

POTION} **Romance and Self-Love**

2 cups spring water

3 tablespoons sea salt

1 teaspoon yarrow

1 teaspoon orris root

1 teaspoon rose petals

1 teaspoon patchouli

1 teaspoon lemon verbena

3 drops hyacinth oil or jasmine oil

2 drops rose oil

1 drop patchouli oil

Copper wire, penny, or ingot

Rose quartz

This is one of my favorite love potions both for self-love and for use in romantic love magick. It is another saltwater-based anointing potion. Add the herbs and salt to the water and let it simmer. Add the copper and rose quartz as it simmers. Strain it out when cool and add the oils for scent before you bottle it. The hyacinth oil was another oil specifically for gay love. Jasmine makes an excellent substitute from the original recipe for those not specifically using it for a gay male love, and I've had students use jasmine to good effect. You will have a potent potion for love magick. I wore it every day for quite a while, both when seeking romantic love and when doing healing work on self-love in preparation for a healthy romantic partner.

POTION} **Apple Love Elixir**

Apple blossoms

Brandy

Mason jar

Plastic wrap

The magickal power of apples can be harvested to make a very powerful love elixir. The blossoms must be lovingly gathered, filling a small jar. The jar is then filled with brandy, covered in plastic wrap, and capped so that no metal touches the flowers or alcohol. As a folk recipe, exact measurements are not as important. Simply fill the jar with blossoms and then cover them with brandy. Let it steep for seven days. A few drops can be taken on the tongue or in a small glass of water to transform your relationship with love by the power of the apple tree and its Venusian correspondences. You will feel more attractive and more magnetic, and be able to draw love and romance to you if you desire. It works first on kindling your own inner powers and a relationship of self-love. I suggest taking a few drops every day for a week. You can also add a few drops to the drink of a lover, and drink it together to unite your love and further your commitment.

Love Spells

Love spells use a variety of tools to evoke passion, affection, and, most importantly, the magnetic energy to attract two (or more) people together in relationship. They work through the power of correspondence and sympathetic magick, and can also include prayers to the deities of love, circle magick, and use of the potions, oils, and incense described above.

SPELL} Rose Quartz

A simple love spell involving the most beloved of all love stones can be done by anybody. Take a rose quartz crystal. Cleanse it under cool running water; ideally we should use the water of a stream, but faucet water will do in a pinch for those of us without a stream in our back yards. Hold the stone up to the full moon and imagine the stone filling with moonlight. Ask the moon goddess and the spirit of the rose quartz to bring you love. Specify what kind of love you wish—self-love, relationship love, spiritual love—and then carry the stone in an appropriately colored bag. Use pink for self-love, green or red for romantic love, and blue for spiritual love. Repeat the spell as often as needed. This can also be done with rose quartz jewelry. Simply omit the carrying bag and wear the jewelry.

SPELL} **Candle**

> Green taper candle
>
> Pink taper candle
>
> 2 candle holders
>
> Venus oil or other love potion
>
> 14 pins

This spell works through the power of sympathetic magick, gradually bringing you and your potential love closer and closer together until you meet. One of the candles is representative of you, the other of your potential, unknown love. Determine which candle is which in your mind.

Start this spell on the first Friday of the waxing Moon. Pass the candles through a purifying smoke such as sage or a mix of frankincense and myrrh to cleanse them. Anoint the candles with a Venusian oil or other love oil. If you have a particular signature scent, perfume, or oil, anoint the candle that represents you with it. Charge your candle to be you, and imagine magnetizing it to attract the appropriate person for you. Charge the second candle to be your potential love, and charge it to only be attracted to you. Stick seven pins in each candle, dividing them evenly along the taper. Set the candles about twelve inches apart. Burn the candles until the first pins, at the top of each candle, fall out. Snuff the candles and move each candle one inch closer. The next day, burn them until the second pins fall out. Snuff them and again move them an inch closer. Repeat each day until on the last day they are as close to touching as possible. Let them burn all the way. Your love is on the way, and the two of you will soon meet.

SPELL} **Dreaming of Your Love**

A traditional folk love spell states that a young maiden seeking to know and attract her love must go out on Midsummer's Eve and collect nine different kinds of flowers (the different types of flowers depend on what's in bloom in the area). The flowers are placed under her pillow, and she will dream of her love and attract her lover to her. St. John's wort is a traditional flower for this spell and one of the most powerful flowers for Midsummer's magick.

SPELL} **Rose Wish**

> Fresh red rose
>
> Vase
>
> Spring water
>
> Brown sugar or honey
>
> Dragon's blood resin

The rose wish spell, also known as the rose life-mate spell, is hands-down my favorite love spell, for it is the spell that brought me together with my husband Steve. I've shared it with a number of people, and those who cast it while in the proper frame of mind have had amazing successes with potential life mates. A few others have had good romantic relationships, if not lifelong matches.

You must do this spell when you are truly ready to settle down and truly ready to find your life mate and build a balanced partnership together. You can do this when you are feeling unsure if there is someone out there for you, and even though you might be somewhat discouraged, you are coming to a place of detachment about a life partner. If you find one, that's great, but you are not pinning all your future plans and focusing your life on it. Only in this frame of mind does the spell seem to work best. I performed it after several years of casual dating, each time knowing the date was not a potential life partner. Only when I let go of my expectations of what a partner should be (but not necessarily lower my standards about the kind of person I wanted) did I have success.

On a Friday while the Moon is waxing, take a live, freshly cut rose to your altar. (You can use a florist's rose; it doesn't have to be grown yourself.) Mix fresh water, a pinch of brown sugar or honey, and a pinch of dragon's blood resin to the water, charging each with your wish to find your life mate. The water is to feed the relationship with pure love, the sugar is to bring sweetness, and the dragon's blood is to bring passion and power. Hold the rose to your heart between both hands, and pray to the goddess of love, asking the spirit of the rose to connect you and open your heart. Through your feelings and thoughts, your inner magickal prayer, ask for your life mate. Imagine the feeling you will feel when you are together. Do not focus on a look, image, or any specific qualities other than the mate being attractive to you (and you to your mate), that your mate be of good character, and that the match be what is for both your highest goods. Hold the rose a few moments longer and you might get a message from the Goddess to aid you in your journey. Then put the rose in the water and let go of your intent. After a day in the water, take the rose out, hang it, and let it dry. Keep the petals in a safe place, such as a small green bag on your altar, under your bed, or in your nightstand. I poured the remaining water out on the land.

When I did this spell, I received a very clear and distinct message that I would know my mate because he would give me flowers long before I ever thought to give him flowers. Being a true romantic, I was the one in a relationship to give flowers, write love poems and songs, and plan romantic surprises, but I never received them. So I had resolved to back off from broad gestures of affection until I was certain about the relationship. On our first date, a blind date, I walked him to his car and he stopped me for a moment, pulled out a single long-stem red rose, and said, "I don't know why, I felt strongly compelled to get this for you on my way here. I hope it's not too forward." I was shocked, but that night was the start of a lifelong romance.

Polyamory Spells

Though I've been in both traditional and polyamorous relationships, I've never specifically done a polyamorous love spell. Though our relationship is very magickal, the third in our triad partnership came into our life without any overt magick on my end, though Adam certainly performed a love spell for the partner that was correct for him, and in the end found two partners instead of one. Any of the spells and formulas can be adapted to suit a polyamorous intention. You can also adapt these principles to create a spell specific to a polyamorous intention.

Polyamorous relationships are often described in terms of geometry. Triads are described as triangles, where all three have relationships with each other, or "V's" with one person serving as the focal point. Foursomes are described as squares, and so on. In this spell, do you have an ideal configuration in mind? If so, draw a sigil, using the configuration you've chosen, such as a triangle, V, or square. Place a candle for every person you desire in the relationship. If you already have a partner and are seeking others, separate your candle and your partner's candle from the candle or candles you have designated as the person or people you seek to attract. In the center of the candles, put an incense burner, cauldron, or censer with charcoal, and burn a love incense. Let the candles burn as the incense burns and be open to your new love.

Love Symbols

A variety of symbols may be used to attract love, romance, and sexual desire, and to increase charm and beauty. To use these symbols, they are traditionally made into some form of charm and are carried or worn by the person. They can be carved in wood, molded from clay, etched on metal, or even written on parchment paper. They can be carved into candles, written on petitions, or placed beneath candle holders or potion bottles to enhance other forms of magick.

The best wood for such magick depends on the type of love charm you are making. Apple and willow work wonders for love and romance, as does whitethorn and rose if you can get it. For a strong relationship, oak of any kind is powerful and enduring. Clays can be mixed with oils and ground herbs to align them with the forces of love. Copper is the best metal to work love charms, while parchment papers should be colored green or pink and ideally red or green ink should be used.

Love Runes

The following runes from the Norse Elder Futhark are used by Witches and modern magicians for the purposes of love. Most have a more agrarian concept of fertility than romance, but the powers of fertility can be directed toward a successful and fertile union, even if the fertility is a harvest of joy, happiness, and health as a couple, and not necessarily the conception of children. I've found them particularly inspiring when inscribed in wedding rings.

Uruz—Uruz (ᚢ) is the rune of the wild ox. Its power is embodied by the animal nature. It is vitality, physical health, and strength. In love magick, this rune can be used for increasing sexuality and fertility, encouraging one to go with primal urges and passions. On the highest level, Uruz is connected to the wild and vital shamanic and initiatory rituals that get you in touch with your primal self, and for many of us, sex can be a ritual that gets us in touch with our primal, vital self.

Kenaz—Kenaz (ᚲ) is the rune of the torch, of fire and inspiration. Though it's not explicitly a rune of love or romance, it can be used for energy, inspiration, and fertility. The fertility associations come from the light of the torch, seen as a masculine symbol, entering into the darkness of the night, or the darkness of the cave, penetrating the feminine mysteries. Some Stone Age sites have alignments of sunlight entering a cave or crypt to bring illumination and perhaps to symbolize the sun entering and fertilizing the deep earth for the coming year.

Gebo—Gebo (X) is one of the best runes for love magick. It translates to "gift" and refers to a freely given offering, an unexpected gift or good fortune. In readings, this rune shows up for relationships, love, and marriage, as the gift can be an exchange between two people bonding them, such as the exchange of wedding rings. Magick with Gebo can find or strengthen a relationship, or bring new and unexpected delights to an existing relationship.

Wunjo—Wunjo (ᛈ) is the rune of joy, and when it occurs in a rune reading, it indicates success, bliss, and a happiness that occurs when everything goes the way you want it to go. While not specifically a love rune, I've used it in love spells to draw forth the blessings of joy and happiness for a relationship.

Sowulo—Associated with the Sun, Sowulo (ᛋ) is the power of the increasing, fertile sun, used in all magick to bring strength and success. The solar correspondence gives it power with fertility, particularly the fertility of the land, but that can be translated into human fertility and sexuality as well as success and optimism in relationship.

Berkana—Berkana (ᛒ) is a feminine symbol of fertility and the earth, associated with the birch tree. It is another rune that is not specifically for love but for conception, healing, and fresh starts. Birth has been associated with spring fertility rites and young love. Berkana can be paired effectively with Sowulo or the rune Teiwaz (ᛏ) for a female/male balance to the rune magick.

Ing—Ing (ᛜ) is the rune of the fertility god, associated with Ing and the god Freyr, brother to Freya. Again, this is not a rune of romance or love but of our connection to the land and the fertility of the land. Ing has the male, virile power of the land and animals, a power that can translate to the relationship between people, to add lust and attraction to our magick.

The Seals of Venus

For those seeking a medieval flair to their love magick, the Seals of Venus are powerful tools in your quest for love. These complex geometric symbols are also called Venusian pentacles, though they are not always based on the five-pointed star. They originate from the *Clavicular Salomonis*, or *The Key of Solomon*, popularized by the Hermetic Order of the Golden Dawn through a translation from the order's founder, Samuel Liddel MacGregor Mathers. In it, each of the seven classical planets has several seals described, along with specific instructions on how to create them and what each does. The system is heavily Judeo-Christian, using the Hebrew names of God and traditional archangels. They have been adapted into Witchcraft, and you can even find them cast in pewter and silver as items of occult jewelry.

Venus has five pentacles from this text, and any one of them can be used in Venusian love magick, but the ones most strongly associated with our work are the third and fifth pentacles.

The third pentacle is said to be ruled by the angel Monachiel, and this angel should be invoked in the day and hour of Venus. For those not wanting to bother with calculating planetary hours, dawn on Friday is the easiest hour of Venus on Venus's day and requires no mathematical calculation. If the third pentacle is shown to a person, it will attract their love.

The last pentacle of Venus is shown to a person to "inciteth and exciteth wonderfully unto love." Like the previous pentacle, you must be sure of whom you show it to, for it can conjure strong emotions when used correctly.

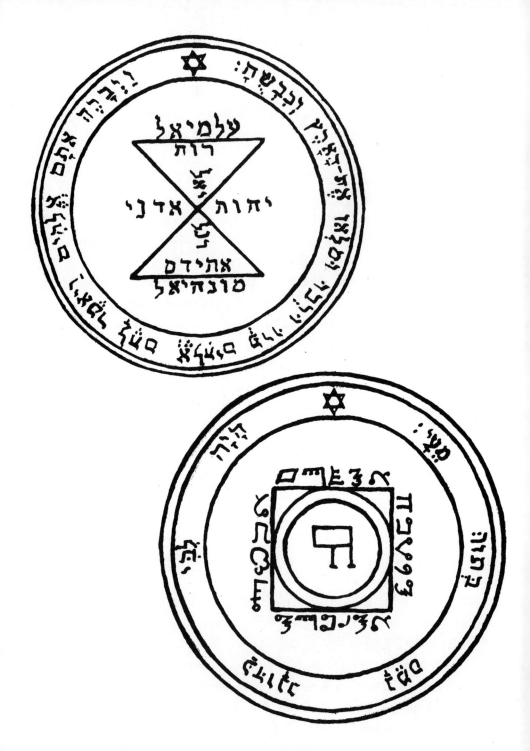

FIGURES} Top, the Third Pentacle of Venus;
bottom, the Fifth Pentacle of Venus

While tradition gives us specific instructions suitable to the medieval worldview, most Witches I know use the seals much like runes or other talismans, believing the symbol itself has inherent geometric power but the manner in which it is created can be adapted to the modern world.

Another form of ceremonial magick for love involves using the *kamea*, or magick square, of Venus. Your intention for a spell is reduced to a simple phrase that would then be converted into geometry by using the magick square. For example, take a short intention such as marriage, if you are seeking a marriage partner.

Using the alphanumeric conversion chart below, MARRIAGE would convert to 4-1-9-9-1-7-5. Some would cross out the double letters, leaving us with MIGE, or 4-9-7-5.

1	2	3	4	5	6	7	8	9
A	B	C	D	E	F	G	H	I
J	K	L	M	N	O	P	Q	R
S	T	U	V	W	X	Y	Z	

Using the simpler version, plot out 4-9-7-5 on the square of Venus, forming a sigil in harmony with your intention. (See next page for completed sigil on the square of Venus.)

22	47	16	41	10	35	4
5	23	48	17	42	11	29
30	6	24	49	18	36	12
13	31	7	25	43	19	37
38	14	32	1	26	44	20
21	39	8	33	2	27	45
46	15	40	9	34	3	28

22	47	16	41	10	35	
	23	48	17	42	11	29
30		24	49	18		12
13	31		25	43	19	37
38	14	32	1		44	20
21	39	8	33	2	27	45
46	15	40		34	3	28

FIGURES} Venus square, top, and marriage sigil
on Venus square, bottom, made by
connecting 4-9-7-5

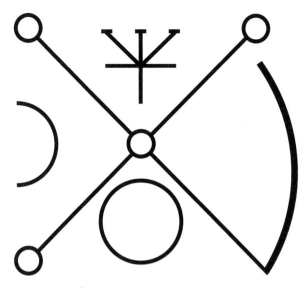

FIGURE} Venus's Planetary Intelligence Seal

A Venus Talisman

This sigil then could be made into a paper, wood, or metal talisman. In qabalistic magick, a more complex talisman can be made, usually using paper. Venus's qabalistic number is seven, so its shape is seven sided, a septagram, and its primary color is green, with a complementary color in red. Cut out two paper septagrams that are connected with a paper link like a paper doll, and put a different Venusian symbol for your intention on each, colored with green and red. Venus has a traditional seal association with the planetary intelligence that can be used for one side (see above); you could also use one of the pentacles of Venus from page 140.

The talisman is then folded over (see next page for an illustration). Sometimes a bit of herb, oil, or a mixture known as a fluid condenser appropriate to the intention would be put in the middle before it is folded over and sealed with glue. For this work, a bit of cotton with four

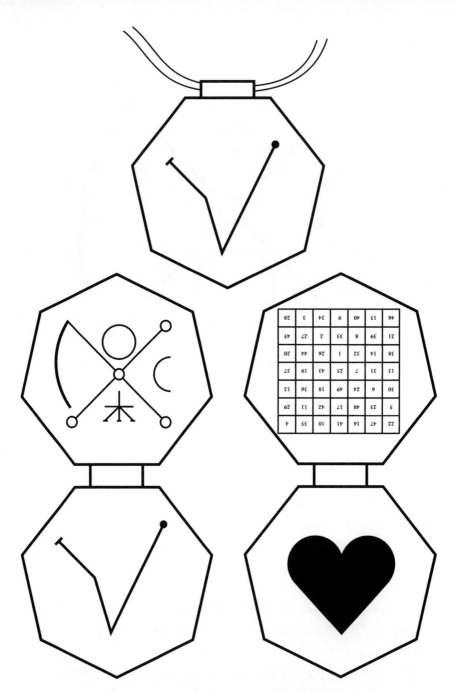

FIGURES} A completed seven-sided Venus talisman, top;
left, the outside of the sigil, and right, the inside
of the sigil; place a bit of cotton with essential oil
in the center before folding it up and wearing it

drops of rose oil, sandalwood oil, or a blended Venus oil would work very well for the center of the amulet. Even some rose water would be quite effective. The connecting paper tab is now a loop where a string can be put through and worn like a necklace. Such talismans were usually kept under clothing, secret from prying eyes.

The Sigil of Archangel Haniel

Haniel is the archangel of the planet Venus and is associated with love, romance, and fertility. Her name means "grace of God" or "beauty of God," and she is said to hold the secrets of beauty and the mysteries of nature and herbcraft. She is also the teacher on the nature of true love and can grant romance and loving relationships, heal relationships and marriages, and bring self-love.

Ideally, her seal is made at dawn on Friday, etched in copper, smudged in the smoke of red sandalwood or rose, and anointed with rose oil or lady's mantle tea. If you can't get the copper and engraving tools, making one out of green or pink paper can still work.

Hold the sigil and tell Haniel what you want and need in a relationship. Speak with an open heart, be true to your feelings, but ask for exactly what you want and need. Carry the sigil upon your person, on the left side, to draw your relationship wish to you. It can be saved until the next time you need to commune with the angel or destroyed upon the completion of your wish. Sigils of Venus are best disposed of in water—running rivers and streams or the ocean itself.

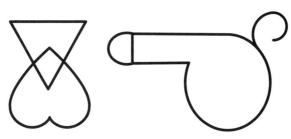

FIGURE} **Seal of Haniel**

Love Charms

Charms are magickal devices created in ritual. They can be contain-
ers of herbs, stones, metals, and animal hair or geometric talismans (as
described with the symbols above) or even pieces of jewelry. Symbols
and sigils can be incorporated into more complex charms. Generally, a
charm is known as a talisman when its magick seeks to attract benign
forces to you, while an amulet sends harmful forces away or repels.
Most love charms are considered talismans by these definitions, unless
you are creating a talisman to ward you from love or sex, or to make
you less attractive.

The item itself is said to contain the energy of the spell. To be of use,
one has to carry the charm, place it in the home, or bury it somewhere
to activate its power. Love charms are an excellent way to empower
another who is seeking love magick. If they can't carry the talisman and
follow any other instructions, then they are not actively engaged in the
creation of their own reality. Carrying a talisman helps your own consciousness interact with the natural virtue of the charm and helps you
co-create your new relationship.

CHARM} **Herbal Mojo**

A love charm that I had a lot of success with in terms of attracting
attention and getting dates was a simple herbal mojo bag I wore as a
necklace. When the Moon was waxing in Taurus—both a sign ruled
by Venus, the planet of love, and my own solar birth sign, adding extra
power for me—I placed the following herbs in a red square of satin
cloth, approximately seven inches in diameter. Seven is the qabalistic
number associated with Venus, and proportions of five and seven are
sympathetic to Venusian magick.

2 teaspoons rose petals

2 teaspoons yarrow

2 teaspoons raspberry leaves

1 teaspoon damiana

1 teaspoon dragon's blood resin

1 teaspoon mandrake root (mayapple)

1 teaspoon lavender

1 teaspoon orris root

1 teaspoon cinnamon

I added a small piece of rose quartz, also charged for love, and the following oils:

21 drops hyacinth oil

9 drops rose oil

5 drops patchouli oil

3 drops jasmine oil

I wrapped up the herbs and stones, gathering the corners of the cloth together, and then the edges, tying them together with a black cord. I left enough cord on each end to be able to create a necklace and placed beads on the cord to make it decorative. I wore it almost continuously for five months, particularly when I was out in public. Many people, including many potential dates, were attracted to it, and it began many conversations that led to dating, if not a long-term relationship. Sadly, with this spell I thought that "love" as the intention was enough, but I wasn't clear in my goals, which I thought were implied as being a long-term relationship. But it was effective in getting a temporary sort of love and some dating experience. You can try this charm for yourself, either to get attention for romance or to be very specific in your intention to find the type of love you are looking to find.

I specifically formulated this charm for gay love, being a gay man seeking to attract a man. The use of the hyacinth oil in particular is specific for gay male love, and in some traditions of herbal magick, so is lavender. This charm recipe can be adapted for all types of love and relationships, with some substitutions. You can replace the hyacinth oil with bergamot, palmarosa, or cinnamon oil. Each variation will yield a different quality, the first two being more feminine and the cinnamon being more spicy and masculine, though bergamot, palmarosa, and cinnamon don't have any connotations for specific types of partners. With the proper magickal intention, all three can attract a romantic partner of either sex for a heterosexual or homosexual relationship. Choose the one that has the most pleasing scent to you. If you do not like the smell of lavender, you can also replace it with vervain and be equally successful. For some, lavender is too peaceful for a love spell.

CHARM} Walnut

The walnut tree is associated with love, fertility, and the Faery realm, and the use of walnuts and their shells in magick is very powerful. A simple love charm uses the shell of the walnut, cracked as evenly into two separate pieces as possible. Remove the nut from the shell (ideally eating the nut) and put in a copper coin (in the United States, a penny minted before 1982) and pinches of several different love herbs, depending on what herbal allies suit the type of love you want to draw toward you. Seal up the walnut shell. Tradition will say to use wax or pine pitch, but I've found the best method to assure a nutshell won't come undone is glue. Carry the nut with you to attract love and relationships.

The walnut spell can be changed to draw other things to you. Walnuts with sexual fluids rather than coins can be used to draw sex and generate lust. Gambling charms can be made with silver dimes and prosperity herbs. Cursing nuts can be made with thorns, nails, or sulfur.

CHARM} Apple

The apple tree can aid us in many ways. A potent love charm consists of using a thorn, copper nail, or other sharp or spiked implement (never iron) for carving your spell on the skin of the apple. On a waxing Moon, hold your apple and think about the love you seek. Take three qualities you wish your lover to possess and write them on the skin of the apple, carving them with your tool. Make the cuts deep. Some Witches find it helpful to translate their three wishes into a magickal language. Runes are ideal, as they are straight lines and easier to carve than some other magickal languages, such as Theban Script. You can let the apple dry on your altar or windowsill; once dried, use it as a traditional charm, carried upon your person or hidden beneath your bed.

A more powerful method consists of disposing of the charm. Take the apple either to its original grove, if you have picked the apple yourself, or to another place of power—a special place in nature, the graveyard of an ancestor, the crossroads, or the beach of a river—and cover the apple in honey. Leave it there, turning around and not looking back on it, knowing the spirit of the apple and the spirits of that place will work with the gods of love to bring you what you seek.

Other fruits can be used instead of the apple, such as pears, but they are not as powerful, in my opinion. Mayapples from the species *Podophyllum peltatum* can be used. Mayapples are considered American mandrake by some. If you should have the fruit of the true mandrake, *Mandragora officinarum*, its fruit can make a potent magickal charm, yet many of us have not been blessed enough to use this plant directly due to it being difficult to grow in colder climates.

Love Spells for Specific People

Though love spells for specific individuals are controversial, as covered in chapter 3, they are quite traditional. You can find many spells in traditional folk magick. No love magick book would be complete without citing at least a few examples for those interested in such ideas and for those interested in protecting themselves from such magick and breaking these spells when they might occur. You must know how they work in order to know how to undo them properly.

All of these spells can be adapted by the clever magician into versions that would conform with more modern magickal ethics concerning love magick.

SPELL} **Sweeten Up to Love**

A traditional spell used to solve all sorts of problems is known as the sweeten up spell. Basically, you have a sealable jar or bottle with some sort of sweet substance in it. Usually the jar is filled with honey, though some will use a sugar water. You place the name of anybody who is not being sweet to you on a piece of paper and place it into the jar and sweet liquid, immersing it. Through the magickal principles of correspondence, you will cause sweetness between you. It's a spell used to quell any arguments you are having with somebody or generally used when you feel you don't get along with a family member or coworker. It makes them more likely to be nice and feel good toward you.

A variation of the sweeten up spell, used for love and romance, is to add essential oils associated with romance and happiness, including jasmine, rose, sweet pea bouquet, vanilla, or even cinnamon to the mix. They will alter the sweetness to romantic sweetness, not just niceness, so make sure you have separate jars for the people you just want to be nice and for the people you want to be romantic toward you. You could also use tinctures or the dried herb, but the oils carry the most potency, as we give strong smells a more aphrodisiac quality than dried herbs. The spell doesn't guarantee romance but makes the person more likely to be flirty and romantically sweet toward you.

SPELL} **Red Sock**

A traditional Finnish love spell (which honestly I've never used or known anybody to use but still find interesting) instructs a woman who desires a specific man to pass water through her red sock after she has worn it and to collect the water that passes through it. She must then somehow get the man she seeks to drink the water, and he will fall passionately in love with her. Spells like this work under the principle of the intended target consuming something intimate—body fluids, sweat, hair—in order to bewitch.

SPELL} **Bewitchment Powder**

    3 tablespoons apple wood

    2 tablespoons orchid root (satyrion root)

    2 tablespoons coriander seeds

    1 tablespoon foxglove flowers

    1 tablespoon passionflower

    1 tablespoon yarrow

    1 tablespoon parsley leaf

    ½ tablespoon poppy seeds

    ¼ tablespoon datura seeds

This modern variation of a traditional powder recipe works by having your intended recipient step through the powder, transferring the energy of the magick and the virtue of the herbs to the target. This particular mix of herbs creates an enticing synergy to bewitch and enchant another, as well as raise sexual energy. The results are not necessarily deep romantic love but a fascination and enchantment that is more reminiscent of a faery glamour than a love spell.

Grind each ingredient into a powder individually and then mix them together one by one, starting with the apple wood as a base and moving down the list to the datura seeds. Spread the powder in a line across a threshold of a door where the target of your affections will cross. The trick is to make sure only your intended target walks through the powder or, at the very least, is the first to walk through it. If you can arrange to cross paths with the target of your affection, ideally shortly after they cross the threshold, so much the better.

SPELL} **Love Bread**

1 cup warm water

1 tablespoon plus 2 tablespoons sugar (white or brown)

2 tablespoons yeast

5 teaspoons rose water

1 teaspoon flavored extract (vanilla or almond)

6–7 cups flour

1 cup milk

Dash salt

4 tablespoons oil or melted margarine / shortening

A potent charm to engage a specific lover is to share a magickal bread. Prepare a simple bread using love ingredients that are potent in romance and seduction. While baking and all forms of cooking can be a complex magickal art, bread breaking can be much more simple than you might think.

Mix one cup warm water with one tablespoon sugar in a bowl. To this sugar-water mix, add two tablespoons yeast. Let the mix sit for five minutes.

Add three cups of flour to the bowl. Ideally, for love magick, walnut flour, also known as walnut meal, is used as the base of the love bread. Walnut trees and their nuts are powerful aids to love magick. Acorn flour can also be used; some would say it makes the bread more of a fertility charm, while others say it adds more of a sexual element to it. On a practical note, acorn flour can spoil easily if not stored properly, and its bread will be more crumbly than bread made of other flours. Perhaps a small amount added to the walnut or regular flour works best. To the flour, add one cup milk, two more tablespoons sugar, a dash of salt, and four tablespoons oil, melted and cooled margarine, or shortening. Then add five teaspoons of food-quality rose hydrosol (rose water). Make sure the rose water is all natural, because many cosmetic brands of rose water are actually synthetic. A teaspoon of vanilla extract or almond extract can be added as well. Stir the entire mixture. When you are done, the spoon should be able to stand up in the mixture.

Add another three to four cups of flour and mix it into the dough until you can form a good ball. Take the dough out of the bowl, place it on a floured surface, and let it sit out for about ten minutes. Knead the dough for ten minutes. Put it in a large greased bowl for about an hour, letting it rise. It should reach about double its size in the bowl. Punch down the dough, and then let it rise again for another thirty minutes. Divide the ball into two equal parts and shape them into loaves, putting them into loaf pans. Bake them at 425 degrees for about 30 minutes. Take out of the oven and let it cool.

Traditionally, with this flowery and sweet recipe, the bread is made by a woman and given to a man. Men wanting to work this magick might remove the rose water, or at least lessen the amount to only one teaspoon and remove the vanilla or almond entirely. Instead, a teaspoon of ground ginger and half-cup of fennel seeds would be added to the mix, making a fennel bread. This spell bread can also be consciously shared by spouses to rekindle love rather than procure a new lover.

SPELL} Greco-Egyptian Love

Many love spells come from the Greek Magical Papyri text, a Hermetic collection of spells fusing traditions and deities from the Egyptians, Greeks, Hebrews, and Christians. Many of these spells involve the recitation of specific god names to evoke power. One of the simplest involves a special name for Aphrodite, NEPHERIÊRI, which means "the one beautiful to the eye" in Egyptian. The spell specifically states a man winning the love of a beautiful woman, but I'm sure it could be adapted to fit other circumstances. The basic steps of the spell are as follows:

1. Abstain from any sexual activity for three days. (In fact, I would suggest abstaining until the spell is complete, three days before and then seven days after the spell.)

2. Make an offering of frankincense, burning it on charcoal while chanting the name NEPHERIÊRI over it.

3. When you see the target of your affection, say NEPHERIÊRI seven times in your heart while gazing upon her. Do this for seven days in a row.

4. On the seventh day, she will be receptive to your approach. Go and speak with her.

In many ways, I see this spell as one that grants confidence as much as love or sex.

SPELL} Ensuring Love

Another folk love spell to ensure that you and your lover stay together, usually done when the relationship is in trouble, is done at the crossroads. One should take two dolls, naming one for yourself and the other for your lover. In forms of Christian magick, they would be "baptized" with water as you and your love. The dolls are bound together with a cord, brought out to the crossroads at midnight, and buried at the crossroads, binding you both together.

This spell is not the best idea if you are doing it on someone else without their knowledge and consent, particularly if you need to let go of your love to heal, move on, and create a new life. This spell binds you together and makes it almost impossible to move on unless one of you has an indomitable will or the help of a magickal practitioner.

This spell can be a great and ethical spell done willingly with your partner's full cooperation if you openly discuss it and choose to do it together, both of your own free will.

EIGHT

The Power of Lust

While most of us think of romantic love when we envision love magick in our idealistic minds, magick has been used just as much, if not more so, for lust and sex. Physical contact, affection, and simple sexual release are just as necessary to our overall health and well-being as romantic love and partnership.

We all have strong feelings about romantic love and sex, and for many people, the two have become completely linked. Such people can't really conceive of having sex without deep, committed romantic love. Many of the dominant religions encourage sex only between married couples, but this rule was as much for social and political reasons as it was for religious reasons. Such rules helped the Jewish tribes to maintain their identity as a unique people, and it helped distinguish both Jewish and Christian cultures from the Pagan traditions that were much more free in regard to their sexuality.

In some Pagan religious traditions, such as those with the sacred priestess-prostitutes, sex was a part of ritual experience. Today, the

Wiccan ritual of the Great Rite—in token through the union of the chalice and blade, or in physical reality through sexual union between priestess and priest—is a reclamation of Pagan sexual rites such as the sacred or divine marriage, or *hieros gamos*, for modern practitioners. For many traditional covens, the Great Rite, in token or reality, is one of the great mysteries for the initiate to experience, bringing a union between the Goddess and the God through ritual. Through the Great Rite, sex is one of the eight paths of power in traditional Wicca, used to raise energy and open the gates between worlds. Modern magicians borrow from Eastern tantra rituals to explore sacred sexuality as a method of personal enlightenment, seeing and worshipping the Divine within their partner. Sexual energy can also be used, with partner(s) or alone, to empower spells and talismans.

Today, modern Pagans have a range of sexual ideas to explore intellectually, emotionally, and physically if they so choose. This is not a call to do anything you don't want to do. The beautiful part about living a magickal life is that you are called to do as your true will, your soul, dictates. You can follow what our current society considers "traditional values" and reserve sexuality for a committed relationship or marriage. You can be a serial monogamist. You can pursue different sexual orientations or gender identities if that is true to who you are. You can look into polyamory or open relationships. You can explore all range of fetishes, such as BDSM practices. You can view sex distinctly from love, as a different form of expression and sharing yourself with another.

In Paganism, we know that most of our societal moral codes have not come from a Pagan culture, and in our exploration and reconstruction of Pagan spiritualities, we can look at sexuality in new and different ways. Most Pagan cultures understood the differences between sex and love, various types of love, and how to express them all. Some did so well. Perhaps others did less so, depending on the culture or time period, but we know many philosophies and worldviews are available to us as modern Pagans.

We know our religion is one of freedom, not guilt, as the Goddess declares in her Charge that "all acts of love and pleasure are my rituals." As long as we choose actions that are honorable, that do not hurt others and do not hurt ourselves, and we are as clear and honest in our communication as possible, we are free to explore and create new ways of living.

The problem with our modern struggle around sexuality is that there is so much religious and societal guilt about our desires and feelings. If we learned to examine them openly and honestly rather than suppress them, we'd have a much more sexually healthy society.

Cultures with a living magickal tradition have known that sex is an integral part of life for which people are always seeking aid. They have created spells and formulas specifically for sex, not necessarily love, to address those needs. If you are doing a love spell and what you really want is sex, you are not being honest with yourself or with the forces of magick. If you do magick for things you don't really want, you are often shown the error of your ways. If you are honest and work toward the things you want, not only do your desires get to be fulfilled, but you get to explore some hidden emotions and urges. While at first lust magick seems to satisfy only our basest urges, Witches see such base urges as sacred. Sex—even raw carnal sex for sex's sake—is just as sacred as a deep longing to be one with the Divine. Both are divine impulses we have as humans, as both express the life force but in different ways. And the exploration of life force is a huge part of our magickal spirituality.

The concept of lust, of desire, is usually considered something bad by most people. Lust is one of the seven deadly sins of Christianity, yet we come from a tradition that doesn't recognize sin as a theological concept. In the Christian system of seven cardinal sins, pride is also considered a sin, yet there can be healthy pride where one takes pride in oneself or one's community. Many disenfranchised communities hold "pride" rallies, such as Gay or GLBT Pride and the more recent Pagan Pride events. Lust, like pride, has positive aspects.

Many Pagan and magickal creation stories look at the lust and the desire between the Goddess and the God as primal forces to initiate and sustain creation. We emulate them, lusting for deeper union with each other and for union with our source. In the Thoth tarot deck of the modern magician Aleister Crowley, the card traditionally known as Strength is renamed Lust. While it denotes many of the same meanings as the original Strength card, it also adds qualities of rapture and joy in using our strength, the enjoyment of the material world, and in lusting after the material world and the pleasures of strength, the lust we have for the Divine. Through it we find the precarious balance between spirit and flesh, and realize that the mysteries are truly found in that space between. Through the teachings of lust, through desire, through the use of the body and its pleasures, we find the sublime joys of spirit and the union with the All; that is the true mystery found in tantric spiritualities. So exploring our lusts and passions can have a deeper significance than most people might think.

Here are a selection of lust spells, aphrodisiacs and virility spells, potions and charms. I suggest putting disclaimers into any of these spells, such as the intention of the sex being safe on all levels. As with all magick, follow it up with real-world action. Please do not make the mistake in thinking that it is magick, so you are protected from HIV and all STDs. Please practice safe sex and take no unnecessary risks, and if you do, be prepared for the consequences.

Aphrodisiacs

Aphrodisiacs have always been a part of the repertoire of the village spellcaster. Natural magicians believe there are substances—be they vegetable, animal, or mineral—whose virtue inspires lustful thought in the mind, desire in the heart, and vigor in the body. Some have proved to have some scientific fact, but enough of them have so much folklore around their power that they have been relegated to the realm of magick and superstition by most people. They are substances that, when consumed or carried, raise the libido and are most effective when used on yourself or used with your partner, mutually and knowingly. They can be a part of foreplay and sensuality, something to be enjoyed in the process leading up to sex.

There are many substances that are considered to be general aphrodisiacs for both men and women. Honey is considered both a medicine and an aphrodisiac for both men and women. In the thirteenth century, the Arab physician Avicenna recommended a mix of honey, pepper, and ginger as a powerful aphrodisiac. Bee pollen also will help a woman get pregnant.

Chocolate was considered a divine food of the gods in Central and South America, though their foamy drink preparations were a far cry from our modern candy. The Greek name for chocolate is *Theobroma cacao*, with *theo* meaning "god" and *broma* meaning "food." This divine treat is considered an aphrodisiac for both men and women. It contains antioxidants like those found in tea and red wine, and it enhances the mood, giving a boost to serotonin and dopamine.

Other classic aphrodisiacs include almonds, apples, bananas, black pepper, cardamom, cayenne, cinnamon, cloves, damiana, dill, figs, ginger, ginseng, hops, jasmine, licorice, lotus, mandrake, mugwort, saffron, walnuts, and wild lettuce, along with a variety of animals and animal parts—powdered rhino horn, frog, bull testicles, snakes, powdered deer antler, sparrows, lizards, and oysters.

APHRODISIAC} Damiana Cordial

Damiana is a powerful aphrodisiac that will increase your libido. One of the traditional ways of taking damiana is to make it into a cordial. Cordials are usually sweet alcoholic herbal preparations generally thought to be invigorating, stimulating, or otherwise good for your health. They can be made at home, though there are many commercial preparations available.

To make damiana cordial, soak two tablespoons of damiana leaves in two cups of vodka for five days in a sealed jar. Separate the leaves from the liquid by straining them out, and bottle the liquid. Put the alcohol-soaked leaves in one and a half cups of spring water for another five days. Some recipes suggest heating the water and making a tea, while others infuse the leaves in cool spring water. After five days, strain the leaves out again and discard them while reserving the water. Gently heat the water extract. Dissolve one cup of honey in the water, and then add the alcohol to the honey water.

I have to say that damiana alone is traditional, but I personally find such a cordial disgusting. The flavor of it doesn't make me feel amorous. But I've had some excellent homemade cordials that mixed damiana with more flavorful herbs and spices, which enhanced both its aphrodisiac qualities and its taste. Experiment with adding any of the following: cinnamon, mace, allspice, coriander, licorice, orange peel, anise seed, star anise, vanilla (bean or extract), and rose (petals or hydrosol/food-quality rose water). Combinations of these herbs will greatly enhance your cordial and increase its power. Add in another two tablespoons total of herbs and double the liquid proportions of the recipe, using four cups of vodka, three cups of water, and two cups of honey.

APHRODISIAC} **Wine of Lust**

    1 bottle red wine

    3 tablespoons honey

    3 cinnamon sticks

    2 teaspoons allspice

    1 teaspoon cardamom

    1 teaspoon clove

    1 teaspoon ginger

A magickal mulled wine can be shared with your lover(s) to increase passion, lust, and sexual intensity. They are simple to make and are best served immediately after making, as they don't store well for long periods of time.

Pour the wine in a ceramic, enamel, or Pyrex saucepan. Though most people would use stainless steal, it inhibits the magick of this recipe, so I would avoid it. If you should happen to have a copper saucepan, so much the better, for copper is the metal of Venus.

Add all the ingredients into the saucepan and stir them together with a wooden spoon. Special wands for love and lust magick can be used to stir rather than a spoon, such as a wand of apple, almond, walnut, rose, or willow wood, or a wand made from a stalk of yarrow. For those who like a more citrus flavor to the wine, you can slice up an orange and / or a lemon and add the slices to the wine mix. Charge (empower through intention, visualization, or spoken words) all the ingredients as you add them.

Simmer the brew over a gentle heat for thirty minutes. Do not bring the mixture to a boil. Strain and let it cool a bit, but serve it still warm. While a glass or three can loosen inhibitions and intensify the senses, much more can have the opposite effect and inhibit the drinker from taking any action.

Virility Magick

Virility magick is typically directed toward men. They are spells, charms, and concoctions to enhance men's physical performance, working with issues of impotence and erectile dysfunction. While there was a time when virility magick and charms were the only recourse in such situations, magick is not a substitute for seeking medical attention in the case of injury or illness. But today, many men immediately go for prescription medication when essentially nothing is wrong. As we grow older, our bodies and hormone levels change, and the fifty-year-old man should not expect his body to act like a twenty-year-old's, and medication to do so takes its toll on the energetic health in other ways. Simpler remedies like working with both magickal energies and herbal power can be used to enhance a man's physical performance. Virility magick is best when the recipient of it is working with the magick and fully aware of the process, as it involves either imbibing a remedy or carrying a charm, but some forms of magick are used secretly by lovers and spouses to enhance the man's performance.

Please consult a qualified healthcare professional before consuming any of these remedies internally. A few are listed as homeopathic, not herbal, remedies. Homeopathic medicines can be found in health food stores and online. They are dilutions of substances, often stored in a lactose pellet form. The traditional dose is three pellets dissolved under the tongue. Most homeopathic practitioners will also tell you to avoid mint and coffee when taking remedies. They can all be safely used as charms, without ingestion.

> *Cayenne*—Like other herbs listed above, the value of cayenne is in its ability to stimulate blood flow. It is also nourishing to the entire circulatory system and the nerves. Cayenne is useful for both men and women.

> *Conium Maculatum*—The homeopathic preparation of poison hemlock (DO NOT TAKE IN HERBAL FORM!) is a remedy for men who experience erectile dysfunction due to anxiety or prostate issues.

> *Damiana*—Though primarily an aphrodisiac for both men and women, damiana is also a sexual stimulant for many people and is used in virility formulas.

> *Ferrum Picricum*—The homeopathic remedy of iron picrate helps men increase their sex drive when there are issues involving the prostate or urinary tract.

> *Ginger*—Ginger root is a wonderful warming herb with many healing properties. Among those properties include stimulating the loins by increasing blood flow to the genitals.

Ginkgo Biloba—Often spelled simply as ginkgo, this generally improves circulation and blood flow, and is said to improve blood flow to the genitals. Thought of as a stimulant to memory and an herb used against the aging process, the results of ginkgo are controversial and not widely accepted by all healthcare practitioners.

Ginseng—Ginseng is generally used as a rejuvenating tonic, reducing stress and strain and aiding in the release of life energy. It can be used as a sexual stimulant. Ginseng is thought to be a remedy for impotence and infertility, and it will help prevent premature ejaculation. It helps normalize blood pressure and is generally seen as a rejuvenating tonic by natural healthcare practitioners. (Siberian ginseng, or eleuthero, is another plant entirely and not a true ginseng, though it too has healing properties.)

Gotu Kola—Gotu kola is used in traditional Chinese medicine as a general tonic, cerebral tonic, circulatory stimulator, and anti-infection remedy. Often seen as an herbal fountain of youth, it gets its reputation as a cure for impotence by stimulating blood flow to the genitals.

Horny Goat Weed—The plants in the genus of *Epimedium* are known as horny goat weed, as a goat farmer in China supposedly discovered its properties by watching his goats' behavior after eating it. While it is supposed to work on a multitude of levels, having the same active ingredients as the Viagra pharmaceutical, it has been used by modern men seeking a more natural stimulant. It reduces stress, which can aid in performance anxiety issues for many men, while not diminishing excitement. Horny goat weed is also said to be an aphrodisiac for women.

Kava—A controversial plant from the Pacific, kava is generally thought to relax the body. It is used in socialization

after work to relax, and it creates clear thinking and a
sociable atmosphere. Others use it for spiritual and artistic
inspiration and dream magick. The true benefit of the kava
in virility formulas, as well as many other relaxants, is to
relax the mind and lower stress over performance anxiety.

Licorice—Like ginger, licorice has a range of healing properties.
It can affect the endocrine system and testosterone levels as
well as stimulate the physical body. While it is not a main
ingredient in virility magick, it is a wonderful addition to a
formula.

Phallic Charms—Anything reminding the user of an erect
penis can be used in sympathetic magick to stimulate sexual
potency. Today many crystals are carved in a variety of
shapes, from hearts and skulls to penises. They come in all
sizes, from life size and larger-than-life size to small charms
that can be put in a charm bag and carried easily. The larger
stones can be used on altars and shrines, particularly to
sexually virile gods such as Freyr. Smaller ones are used as
charms and jewelry. Ones carved from quartz, rose quartz,
and hematite are common. The Greeks and Romans had a
tradition of phallic carvings and jewelry, and reproductions
can be used today. In India, tumbled phallic river stones,
known as Shiva Linghams, are signs of male virility and
divine masculinity. In Hoodoo, the penis bone of a raccoon,
also known as a "coon dong," usually harvested today from
road kill, can be used in lust magick. The buckeye nut of
the actual buckeye tree, or the related chestnut or horse
chestnut, bears a striking resemblance to the testicles and
can also be used in phallic charms as well as gambling
charms where you must have the "balls" to risk your money
in order to win.

Sarsaparilla—Besides being an ingredient in traditional root beer, sarsaparilla has been used by Native people in Central and South America as a remedy for impotence as well as a general tonic.

Saw Palmetto—A tonic for the entire male reproductive system, particularly the prostate gland. Saw palmetto is also helpful in healing and nourishing the nervous system.

Wolfberry—Wolfberries (also known as goji berries) are primarily used in Chinese traditional medicine for their ability to grant overall health and general wellness. Some describe them as pure *chi*, or life force, in berry form. Medically, they have a high antioxidant content and are used to treat a variety of illnesses as well as function as a general tonic. They are a member of the Solanaceae family of plants, including the witchy belladonna and mandrake as well as tobacco and potato. Wolfberries are said to enhance male virility and increase sperm production, but they are not necessarily known specifically for any erectile enhancement.

Yohimbe—The bark of an African tree is used as an aphrodisiac and to promote sexual virility in men. The active alkaloid yohimbe is used in treating male erectile dysfunction, though most studies have been done on the prescription derivative, not on the herb itself. Many consider it unsafe, as it increases heart rate and blood pressure and can cause insomnia, among other side effects. Generally, it is most effective when combined with a small dose of vitamin C. Some herbalist friends of mine make a male potency tea with it and suggest adding two tablespoons of lemon juice to truly activate the yohimbe.

The herbs listed here are given for magickal purposes specifically, not medical, though through the principles of correspondence we can deduce magickal abilities from the herbs' medical abilities. You should not ingest any herbal products without consulting your healthcare practitioner. If you do not have any outstanding healthcare issues and are given permission by your healthcare practitioner, the following formulas can be used in moderation. If you do have any issues with blood pressure, cardiovascular health, or adrenal problems, are on any prescription or other herbal medication, or have any concerns, please consult with a qualified medical practitioner.

TINCTURE} **Male Potency**

   3 tablespoons horny goat weed

   3 tablespoons yohimbe bark

   2 tablespoons ginseng root

   2 tablespoons damiana leaf

   1 tablespoon ginger root

   1 tablespoon coriander seed

   1 tablespoon licorice root

   Vodka

Mix and grind all ingredients thoroughly. Fill one-third of a Mason jar with this mixture and then fill the jar with vodka, at least 80 proof. Ideally do this when the Moon is waxing and either in Aries, Taurus, or (best) Scorpio, or on a Tuesday, the day of Mars. If you have a phallic stone such as a quartz penis or Shiva Lingham, charge it in a separate ritual for male potency and put it in the jar before you seal it, or place it on top of the jar if you don't want to mix your stone with your herbs and alcohol. A garnet would be a great stone to use, too, if you don't have a phallic stone. Shake well every day for at least six weeks. Decant and strain out the herbs. Bottle the tincture in a dark glass dropper bottle.

To use with maximum efficiency, take a dropper full in a glass of water with a tablespoon of lime juice an hour or so before having sex. Take a second dose a half-hour before having sex.

ELIXIR} **Body-Mind Overdrive**

   2 tablespoons blue vervain

   2 tablespoons damiana

   2 tablespoons nettle

   2 tablespoons ginseng

   2 tablespoons saw palmetto berries

   1 tablespoon passionflower

   1 tablespoon schisandra berry

   1 tablespoon star anise

   1 tablespoon ginger

   ½ tablespoon comfrey root

   1 tablespoon sarsaparilla

   1 pinch American mandrake

   1 Shiva Lingham stone

   13 cups spring water

   1 cup honey

   1 cup brandy

   Vanilla (optional, to taste)

   Cinnamon (optional, to taste)

Sometimes the biggest obstacle to male virility is in the mind. Men get nervous and have performance anxiety and issues around expectation. Stress, lack of sleep, and even excess caffeine can all play a role in these issues, but here is an herbal formula I've used for some male clients with great success. It helps align the body with the mind, to help the man have great sex. They do say the brain is the largest of the sex organs.

Grind the herbs together and place them in a simmering pot with thirteen cups of pure water. Bring the mixture to a boil and let it simmer to half the volume you started with. You can add vanilla and/or cinnamon to improve the taste, but they are not the main ingredients. Stir in one cup of natural honey. Let it cool, and add one cup of brandy to preserve it. Bottle in dark glass bottles and store someplace cool and dry. Take a tablespoon daily to improve your overall sexual health and outlook on sex. Take a shot of the elixir before having sex.

If you wish to invoke the power of these herbs without ingesting them, I suggest the following charm bag.

CHARM} **Virility Pouch**

A red bag

1 buckeye or 1 phallic stone or charm

2 tablespoons damiana leaf

1 tablespoon ginger powder

2 tablespoons gotu kola

1 tablespoon basil leaf

A few drops of a lust oil (see below)

1 match or sexual fluids

Mix the above-listed herbs as the Moon is waxing to full. Place them in the red bag along with the buckeye and the phallic stone or charm. Add a few drops of oil—Satyr Oil if a gay man or King of the Woods if a straight man (see page 179). Light a match and drop the burning match into the bag. Close the bag and snuff out the match in the bag, leaving the essence of fire in the bag. Carry it with you wherever you go. Instead of putting the lit match in it, you could anoint the contents of the pouch with your own semen. If this is meant to increase your virility in the context of a marriage, anoint it with the sexual fluids of both yourself and your partner, and place it under the mattress.

Women's Libido

While the signs of sexual dysfunction in women are not as overt as those of with men, they are just as serious. Originally classified as frigidity in women in early psychological diagnostics, this condition has been renamed hypoactive sexual desire disorder (HSDD). Many forms of herbal magick and ritual can be used to increase sexual desire quite effectively in women.

While so many of the classic textbooks on aphrodisiacs tend to focus on the more visible effects of aphrodisiacs on men, many of the same substances work just as effectively on women. And there are specific herbs that are more strongly associated with women. Many of the herbs associated with curing impotence can also be used with women, particularly those that increase blood flow to the genitals.

Calcarea Carbonica (Calc Carb or Calcium Carbonate)—When taken in a homeopathic preparation, this remedy can help increase low sex drive, particularly if the low sex drive is due to exhaustion, anxiety, menopause, or menstrual problems. It's particularly good if there has been an increase in weight or issues around excessive sweating.

Cimicifuga—The homeopathic form of black cohosh is a remedy for low sex drive in women suffering from any gynecological or hormonal problems.

Dong Qui—Dong qui is a species of angelica (*Angelica sinensis*) that is both a tonic for women and considered a female aphrodisiac, increasing sex drive when taken as a tea or tincture. It is sometimes referred to as the "female" ginseng, as it works so well for women.

Schisandra Berry—Schisandra berry is a popular Chinese tonic because it is said to be the perfect five-flavored fruit, including the tastes of sweet, salty, bitter, sour, and pungent. It is a powerful adaptogen and sexual stimulant in general but is particularly associated with women for increasing sexual desire and vaginal lubrication.

Skullcap—Skullcap generally is used as a nervine and relaxant, but it is powerfully useful for both women and men as a tea or tincture to help with any tension around sex. It tones the body and soothes the mind.

Staphysagria—Larkspur prepared homeopathically will increase sex drive in women who suffer from unresolved anger and resentment, or sexual aversion due to poor health or a surgery such as a hysterectomy.

Sulfur—Homeopathic sulfur helps women increase their libido when suffering from PMS, insomnia, or a general lack of energy. It helps when there is any guilt or feeling of "sin" around sexuality.

Ylang-Ylang—The scent of ylang-ylang in essential oil form is excellent for both women and men, and in particular is good for what was considered frigidity. It is particularly good in a bath mixture.

Yoni Charms—Any charm or object in nature that is reminiscent of the female genitals can be used magickally to increase female sexual power. Charms are often shaped like figs or sea shells; in particular, the popular cowry shell, used in African diasporic divination systems, is also a yoni symbol.

TINCTURE} **Female Power**

  3 tablespoons dong qui

  2 tablespoons damiana

  1 tablespoon schisandra berry

  1 tablespoon ginger root

  1 tablespoon skullcap

Mix and grind all ingredients thoroughly. Fill one-third of a Mason jar with this mixture and then fill the jar with vodka, at least 80 proof. Ideally do this when the Moon is waxing and either in Aries, Taurus, or (best) Scorpio, or on a Tuesday, the day of Mars. If you have a yoni charm or a cowry shell, charge it in a separate ritual for female potency and put it in the jar before you seal it, or place it on top of the jar if you don't want to mix your charm with your herbs and alcohol. A garnet would be a great stone to use, too, if you don't have a yoni charm. Shake well every day for at least six weeks. Decant and strain out the herbs. Bottle the tincture in a dark glass dropper bottle.

To use with maximum efficiency, take a dropper full in a glass of water with a tablespoon of lime juice an hour or so before having sex. Take a second dose a half-hour before having sex.

Empowerment Baths

The following formulas mix essential oils and can be used in bathing magick or adapted for perfume or massage when mixed with a base oil. Magickal baths carry with them the power of healing water.

FORMULA} **Bath Oil to Cure Sexual Anxiety**

    5 drops ylang-ylang essential oil

    3 drops lavender essential oil

    1 drop neroli essential oil

    1 drop sandalwood essential oil

Add these oils to your bath prior to having sex. This mixture helps reduce anxiety and induce a state of relaxed sensuality.

FORMULA} **Sensual Bath Oil**

    5 drops ylang-ylang essential oil

    4 drops sandalwood essential oil

    2 drops frankincense essential oil

    1 drop rose essential oil

This formula is slightly stronger that the first, having a more sensual component to it. Add it to bath water or mix with ⅛ cup of a base oil and use as a perfume.

FORMULA} **Aphrodisiac Oil**

> 5 drops patchouli essential oil
>
> 5 drops clary sage essential oil
>
> 1 drop jasmine essential oil

Another oil to be added to the bath, this is more lustful and primal than the previous two oils. It stimulates sexual desire.

Lust Spells

Beyond aphrodisiacs to get one in the mood or virility magick to enhance the body's physical response, we have spells whose sole purpose is to actually have sex, not just enhance sexual experience. These spells are to draw not a romantic partner but a sexual partner. They don't just make you more desirable or entice another, they attract another who desires to have sex with you—and hopefully, if you do the spell well, one with whom you want to have sex too.

Like love spells, I've found both ethically and practically that these spells are best when you have no specific person in mind but wish to attract the appropriate sexual partner for you at this time. Like all love spells, they theoretically can be "aimed" toward specific people, but you must bear the consequences of such actions when such spells go awry, and even when they are more successful than you anticipate. Often what you think is a spell for a simple one-night stand can attract someone who soon becomes enchanted and obsessed with you, while you do not feel the same. As with all magick, be careful what you wish for, because you probably will get it—but not always in the way you anticipated.

SPELL} **Candle Sex**

One of the simplest spells for when you just want to have sex is a candle spell. Ideally, do this spell on the waxing Moon, though you can do it any morning to work with the waxing energies of the day if the Moon is waning.

Take a red taper candle. While you can cleanse it in purifying smoke first and, if you desire, carve it with any sexual-oriented runes and anoint it with any of the oils listed below, it is most often done simply, with no purification, carving, or oil. While I like to do it as a folk spell without the magick circle ritual, you can do it in or out of a magick circle, depending on your preference.

Hold the red candle in your hands. Think about your desire to have sex. Don't focus on a specific person, but think of the sensations of having sex, the feeling of touch. Imagine yourself having sex with someone nonspecific. When you feel the candle is "full" with your desire, light it, and let it burn down until it's done. Then go out and put yourself in a situation where sex would be more available to you. Go to a club. Go to an online chat room for singles. Attend a party or social function with lots of people. If you make yourself available, within three days you will have sex.

The spell is most successful when you are not specific and have few stipulations in it. The spell doesn't necessarily get you someone very attractive or someone very talented sexually, unless you state it. The more stipulations you put in, the harder it is to manifest. But if you just want sex with few stipulations, then this spell is very successful.

SPELL} **Drawing Philter**

A formula coming from the Cultus Sabbati tradition, found in the *Viridarivm Umbris* by Daniel A. Schulke, consists of mixing vervain, rose petals, and fennel seeds. Though the instructions end there, you could grind them together in equal portions into a powder and make a tea with the ratio of one tablespoon herb to one cup hot water. A tincture could be made by extracting the plant powers through soaking the herbal powder in alcohol or, most powerfully, taking a pinch of the mix and placing it in your magickal chalice filled with spring water and letting it sit overnight. Ideally, put it out under the waxing full Moon. Drink the cup of tea, take a dropper full of tincture, or drink the chalice water to find the virtue of these drawing herbs transferred to you. Then you will have the ability to attract others to you magickally.

SPELL} **Attraction Amulet**

This particularly powerful amulet is traditionally used to attract another of the opposite sex. Mix the following herbs together in equal measure and grind them into a powder, then carry in a red bag. Due to its toxic nature, this powder should not be used as an incense.

Henbane

Poppy seeds

Bachelor's buttons

Coriander

Elecampane

Periwinkle

SPELL} **Sex Incense**

2 tablespoons dragon's blood resin

1 tablespoon red sandalwood

1 tablespoon satyrion root (orchid root)

1 tablespoon damiana leaf

½ tablespoon amber resin

½ tablespoon hydrangea root

½ tablespoon coriander seeds

¼ tablespoon foxglove flower and/or leaves

2 bay leaves

10 drops oakmoss oil

10 drops vetiver oil

1 tablespoon honey

5 tablespoons red wine

This incense blend can be used to increase a lustful vibration. It can be burned prior to seduction, to alter the mood of the location (particularly the bedroom), or it can be burned during sex and particularly during sexual rituals.

Mix the dried ingredients together and grind them to a powder. If you cannot find satyrion root, you can use lucky hand root or orris root as a substitute, but it's not as powerful. Benzoin powder can also be a good base for any love or lust incense, as it relaxes the mind and will enhance the qualities of the other herbs.

Mix them with the wine until the powder is like a thick paste. Then mix in the honey thoroughly. Let the mixture dry over several days, and break it apart into small chunks that can be burned on charcoal.

SPELL} Lust Poppet

A poppet is a ritual doll used to make magick. Most people are familiar with the concept of the poppet through the legendary voodoo doll, but the use of poppets in the African traditions occurred through the European influence. Poppets can be used to heal or to harm. The idea works through the principle of sympathy. When you fashion a doll in the likeness of someone, whatever is ritually enacted on the doll will occur to the living person. Direct healing energies to the doll, even with a pin, and the result is healing energies being sent to the person. Direct curses to the doll, particularly with a pin, and pain and illness are directed. Love and lust can be directed toward the doll, and those energies will be directed toward the person.

What the doll is constructed of, and when and how it is made, will affect the magick. Ideally, if you are working with a specific person, if the doll can be fashioned out of an article of clothing the person has worn or out of a personal object like a handkerchief, it will be very effective. If not, putting a bit of hair or fingernail clippings into the doll will also be powerful. Such personal effects work through the principle of contagion, stating that once two things have touched, they will always be connected. The items can be used to direct magick toward each other.

If you are open to doing magick for a specific person who is not in your life, you can direct the lust poppet to fuel their desire for you. Sadly, this doesn't always work out the way you want. Just because you increase someone's lust doesn't mean that it will necessarily be directed toward you or that the recipient will act upon it. If they are shy or feel forward propositions for sex are improper, they will simply be hornier, but it won't benefit you. It's a powerful spell to do consciously on yourself and/or your partner, however, to increase the passion and lust in your relationship. You can either make one doll for whoever is less sexual or two dolls, one for each of you.

Double up a piece of cloth so that when you cut it, you will cut out two identical copies. If you can use cloth belonging to your intended target, do so, but if not, the color red is best for lust magick. Stitch the edges of the doll together, but leave an opening to stuff the doll. Traditionally, poppets are stuffed with herbs, seeds, cloth, or cotton, depending on the intention. You can stuff the doll with a combination of herbs for lust and sex, but for a truly powerful lust poppet, fill the doll with acorns, charging each acorn for lust and sexual attraction.

In sacred space or in a simple ritual, name and "baptize" the doll to be whomever your chosen recipient of this energy is. Ideally you have to "awaken" the doll in the name of the person it is directed toward, otherwise it's just a doll with very little magickal power. Anoint the doll with salt and water, or an oil, and name it for the person upon whom you are focused. While holding the doll, think of your intention of increasing the fires of lust within this person. Then put the doll in a closed space, somewhere it will not be touched, like a box beneath your bed. If you've made an acorn poppet, the most effective thing you can then do is bury the doll at the grove where the acorns originated. If you made two dolls, you can tie them together with red thread, facing each other, before you put them away to work. The lust of the recipient should soon begin to grow.

For those who want to adapt this spell, you can fill the doll with rose petals and yarrow to make a love, not a lust, spell. You can cast a poppet spell on yourself for self-love using rose, yarrow, and raspberry leaf, and put a rose quartz stone in the heart and/or head of the doll. To deal with conception issues, you can fill the doll with a variety of whole seeds and grains to increase physical fertility in a woman or sperm count in a man. You can enhance any of these spells by stitching appropriate runes onto the doll.

To undo this spell, the dolls must be retrieved and separated, and ideally taken apart in a magick circle during a waning Moon with the intention of dismantling the spell. The remaining parts of the dolls should be burnt, buried, or submerged separately from each other.

Lust & Sex Oils

A variety of scents have been used in sexual attraction magick. Often they come from Hoodoo, New Orleans Voodou, Santería, and other African diasporic traditions. They have made their way into modern American Witchcraft in a variety of forms and recipes. Some are consistent with the original traditions and others have been altered radically, as practitioners will have their own variations of the blends.

Oils work on a variety of levels: as aphrodisiacs, increasing physical response, magnetizing the aura of the wearer to attract others, and they even have aspects of commanding and compelling, so the wearer can get what he or she wants. These oils can be worn on the skin and are traditionally anointed on the neck, wrists, underarms, and pubic region. They can also be used in other charms and spells—added to charm bags, put into poppets, anointed on crystals and talismans, or rubbed on candles.

For these formulas, a base oil is needed to mix the essential oils. Excellent base oils include almond oil, grapeseed oil, or apricot kernel oil. The best oil, jojoba oil, is technically a liquid wax. It is so valued because its waxy nature prevents it from spoiling as quickly as other oils. While olive oil or corn oil can be used as a base, neither lasts long before spoiling, so it's best to use something more stable.

OIL} **Queen**

> 4 drops vetiver oil
>
> 3 drops juniper oil
>
> 2 drops lavender oil
>
> 1 drop honey
>
> 10 drops base oil
>
> Gold coloring or glitter/crushed pyrite

This oil is used by women to attract men and to promote success in general as well as success in love.

OIL} **Q Perfume**

> 5 drops myrrh oil
>
> 3 drops peppermint oil
>
> 2 drops carnation oil
>
> 10 drops base oil
>
> Red coloring

Q perfume is similar to queen oil but is more specifically about romantic and sexual attraction. It's used by women to attract men. It makes the wearer irresistible, though I must admit I don't find the scent pleasing at all.

OIL} **Satyr**

> 3 drops musk oil[1]
>
> 2 drops vanilla oil
>
> 1 drop civet oil
>
> 1 drop patchouli oil
>
> 1 drop cinnamon oil
>
> 1 drop carnation oil
>
> 1 drop bergamot oil
>
> 10 drops base oil
>
> 1 piece satyrion root/lucky hand root

Named after the Greek myths of the goat men known for their lusty powers, satyr oil is used by gay men to attract other men. While it can attract women, it primarily attracts men and is not the best formula for the heterosexual man. It does work quite well for homosexuals, though, and it also tends to make the user more aroused as well. Satyr oil is powerful as a perfume and works well anointed on red candles for attracting sexual partners.

OIL} **King of the Woods**

> 3 drops civet oil
>
> 3 drops musk oil
>
> 2 drops vanilla oil
>
> 2 drops cyprus oil
>
> 10 drops base oil
>
> Satyrion root/lucky hand root
>
> Green coloring

A formula for men to attract women, king of the woods oil is credited with making a man irresistible. Some see it as a domination formula over women, but it can be used as a man's everyday power formula to succeed in the world.

---

1   See "A Note on Synthetics," page 181, regarding both musk and civet oils.

OIL} Aphrodite

4 drops bergamot oil

3 drops rose oil

1 drop orris oil

1 drop sandalwood oil

1 drop ylang-ylang

10 drops base oil

An oil considered sacred to Aphrodite and used both for arousal and enticement.

OIL} Desire Me/Come to Me

4 drops rose oil

3 drops jasmine oil

2 drops gardenia oil

1 drop lemon oil

10 drops base oil

Red coloring

A powerful New Orleans–style formula for sexual attraction, primarily used by women.

OIL} Follow Me, Boy

4 drops vanilla oil

4 drops rose oil

2 drops jasmine oil

10 drops base oil

Piece of coral

Gold glitter/crushed pyrite

Another New Orleans formula, particularly used by prostitutes. Legend says that Marie Laveau formulated it both to entice the customers of the prostitutes as well as increase their fortunes and protect them from the law.

An excellent resource of a variety of traditional and new formulas is *Ancient Wisdom: The Master Grimoire* by Pat Kirven Sawyer. I've found it an excellent addition to my library, as it draws from a variety of resources. I also highly recommend *Hoodoo Herb and Root Magic* by Catherine Yronwode (and her website, luckymojo.com). Many of us who learned New Orleans, Hoodoo, and African diasporic formulas as an addition to Wicca reportedly learned formulas that contain "blinds," or mistakes in them to make them less potent. While such practices have created some new formulas that work in new ways, it is helpful to look at a wide range of traditional sources in order to know the history of your formulas and how to use them.

A Note on Synthetics

Many of the oils and incenses of lust found in older occult texts call for animal oil products such as musk, civet, and ambergris. Most modern practitioners have problems obtaining these ingredients in nonsynthetics due to rarity and expense or have a moral problem using them. Most commercially sold musk and civet oils are synthetic, as they are technically illegal to purchase in most countries. While there is a certain magick to these older formulas, they can be adapted into new formulas without these animal ingredients. I have had success with the psychology of smell using some synthetics, so if you feel an absolute need to have these scents and can find a synthetic that is satisfactory to your own nose, then the magick can still work. There are some herbals associated with musk, including musk mallow (*Abelmoschus moschatus*), muskflower (*Mimulus moschatus*), musk weed (*Olearia stuartii*), musk wood (*Olearia argophylla*), and the most popular and easiest to find and use, musk seed (also known as ambrette seed). Some other substitutes for musk from the plant world include amber, angelica, cedar, clary sage, oakmoss, patchouli, sandalwood, and valerian. Combinations of oak moss essential oil and rose essential oil have also been a substitute for musk, as well as labdanum mixed with oakmoss and patchouli. Labdanum alone is sometimes used as a magickal substitute for civet, though it doesn't really smell anything like civet to me.

Hindu Strikarmani

Though many people seeking spiritual traditions may look down upon Witchcraft and folk magick as "base," similar needs were fulfilled in the Eastern traditions as well as medieval European Witchcraft. In Hindu Strikarmani, a form of "venereal" magick, we can find questionable spells for love, controlling a spouse, sex, virility, frigidity, fidelity, preventing miscarriage, invoking sterility, and cursing rivals. Such lore first came to my attention through the book *Oriental Magic* by Idries Shah. In it, he gives translations of two very interesting spells/prayers, one for a man and one for a woman. They should be done on the waxing Moon and recited at least seven times, if not more.

SPELL} **Arousing the Passion of a Woman**

Make or obtain an arrow to be your "arrow of love" and hold it when reciting this spell. Like many traditional spells, no other instructions of visualization or energy raising are given. One simply recites the spell or prayer like a story, letting it evoke imagery in the mind naturally, without a specific technique.

> *With the all-powerful arrow of love do I pierce*
> *thy heart, O woman! Love, love that causes unease*
> *that will overcome thee, love for me!*
> *That arrow, flying true and straight, will cause*
> *in thee burning desire. It has the point of my love;*
> *its shaft is my determination to possess thee!*
> *Yea, thy heart is pierced. The arrow has struck home.*
> *I have overcome by these arts thy reluctance; thou art*
> *changed! Come to me submissive, without pride, as I have*
> *no pride but only longing! Thy mother will be powerless*
> *to prevent thy coming; neither shall thy father be able*
> *to prevent thee! Thou art completely in my power.*
> *O Mitra, O Varuna, strip her of willpower! I, I alone,*
> *wield power over the heart and mind of my beloved!*

SPELL} **Arousing the Passion of a Man**

Like the spell before it, this one should be done on the waxing Moon and recited at least seven times.

> *I am possessed by burning love for this man: and this love*
> *comes to me from Apsaras, who is victorious ever.*
> *Let the man yearn for me, desire me; let his desire burn for me!*
> *Let this love come forth from the spirit and enter him.*
> *Let him desire me as nothing has been desired before!*
> *I love him, want him; he must feel the same desire for me!*
> *O Matrus, let him become filled with love; O Spirit of the Air,*
> *fill him with love; O Agni, let him burn with love for me!*

Like the love spells for a specific person in the previous chapter, I would personally question the wisdom of actually performing these spells, but it's important to understand the entire history of love and sex magick and realize such spells are in all cultures and time periods.

Sexual Healing

Sexual magick is not just about attracting and enticing a lover to have sex. As this book is about love, lust, and relationships, not a manual on the techniques of sex magick, we cannot go into all the details of sex magick. But aspects of sex magick that prepare one for relationship and aid in the sustaining of the relationship are very appropriate to our work here.

There have been so many restrictions on sexual activities in the past because sex is powerful—magickally, spiritually, and personally. It is intense. It causes change. It gives you the opportunity to touch the cosmos. How we use our sexual energy greatly affects us. Because we are not educated in understanding sexual energy as an energy itself, and because there is so much fear and shame associated with sex, we often use our sexual energy unconsciously and unhealthily. Sadly, this reinforces our shame and guilt around sex, rather than breaking the cycle.

Here are three rituals to help restore a healthy relationship with sexual energy in your life.

RITUAL} Healing Guilt

Many of us have hang-ups and guilty associations with sexuality as remnants from previous religions and societal upbringing. There is nothing in Paganism's theology to make you shameful of your sexuality or feel guilty for anything. While there are wise and unwise choices, actions than can bring us what we want and actions that are self-destructive, they are not motivated by guilt but by a sense of what is cosmically right for everyone sexually. We learn as we live, and hopefully we make more appropriate choices as we grow wiser. Yet guilt lingers, and we feel shameful about our bodies and our desire for another's body.

On the waning Moon, fill a pot of water (at least four cups' worth), bring it to a boil, and add to it the following herbs:

> 5 tablespoons hyssop
>
> 2 tablespoons lemon peel or lemon juice
>
> 1 tablespoon your favorite flower or rose petals

Hyssop is the primary herb in healing guilt, used in Pagan purification ritual and even Christian folk magick. Lemon is very cleansing, and flowers in general, particularly roses, are powerful aids in healing.

Let the brew simmer on low heat for at least ten minutes. Strain the herbs out when it has cooled, but do not let it get too cold. Take it into the bathroom. Get naked. Bathe yourself with the brew either by cupping the water in your hands or using a wash cloth. As you wash each body part with the mixture, say "blessed be" and name the part. Thank that part of the body, being sure to include all the places you receive and give pleasure. Bless your entire body. When done, look at your naked body in the mirror. Thank it. Bless it in its entirety. Then take a shower and wash off any remaining herbal residue. Feel yourself blessed and cleansed.

Reclaiming Sexual Power

Whenever we have sex with another, there is a natural exchange of energy. Even within the context of safer sex, when there is not an exchange of body fluids, there is still an exchange of energy for both partners. When we are in a place of freedom and clarity, feeling the flow of divine love, such exchange can be wonderful.

When we are in a relationship, such an exchange can create long-term connections that develop and teach us over the long-term relationship. When we have casual sex, we can make healthy connections to our partners as long as we are in a place of openness and love—not necessarily romantic love, but that divine love where we inherently know our connection. When we enter into sex with fear, guilt, or shame, or are otherwise restricted in our flow of energy, we can create some unhealthy energetic connections, even in otherwise healthy friendships and relationships.

This isn't a popular view, particularly amongst many Pagans who see it as fear mongering from an ex-Catholic, and I understand. I didn't like hearing such teachings at first and immediately rejected them. But as I've looked to my own life and the lives of my friends, covenmates, students, and clients, I see a truth to this concept.

In the shamanic traditions linked to the controversial figure Carlos Castaneda, particularly in the work *The Sorcerer's Crossing: A Woman's Journey* by Taisha Abelar, sexual connections are described as worms in the belly. Women in this tradition are particularly encouraged to remain celibate for seven years, to "kill off" the worms in the belly. This is supposedly the secret reason spiritual orders teach celibacy.

While I can't say I agree with all the sexual teachings from this tradition, I think there is an idea here, and it's not limited to women. In my healing training, I learned that we make energetic connections to people, cords that are often the basis for limiting relationships with others and with ourselves. These cords form near the energy centers of the body known as chakras and can drain energy from others or let ourselves be drained. When someone is "pulling your chain" metaphorically, meaning their words or actions really upset you, then you probably have a cord with that person. These limited relationships are not rooted in unconditional love, which is limitless. Cords that form near the root chakra and belly chakra, the two most associated with sex, pleasure, and intimacy, have a sexual component, and those experimenting in this energetic healing exercise often find the cords in this area are to past lovers, former relationships, and unhealthy obsessions. Using techniques to release these unwanted cords and to reclaim the personal spiritual energy you have given away in unhealthy ways, as well as to release any energy you yourself have stolen, is a very healing practice. We get hung up on sexual relationships for years longer than any other type of relationship, because sex is so intense and we are not conscious of the energetic connection.

This is not a moral judgment on sex (casual, committed, or otherwise) but an energetic experience. Since most of us enter into sexual relationships not fully conscious of our own energy, of course our actions can have unwanted consequences. This is really a call to be more conscious about our desires and actions, and to make sure we are acting from a place of integrity and spiritual love. If we do, I believe we are free to pursue anything and anyone at any time, without making unhealthy cords and connections.

RITUAL} Reclaiming Your Sexual Power

1. Start this exercise by making a list. On the list, working backwards from the present, list all the people you have had sex with that you can remember. Include those that have been "good" and "bad" relationships and casual sex. Also include anybody you might not have had physical sex with but might have had an unhealthy obsession with, a crush that, looking back on it, seemed too intense or went too

far without it being an actual relationship. Hold on to that list when you do this guided meditation. Choose perhaps the most recent five to work with first, and repeat the meditation until you go through the entire list.

2. Perform steps 1–6 from the journey to the Temple of Love exercise on page 90.

3. In the Temple of Love, call upon the goddess of love. She is the goddess of sexuality and sensuality as well. She holds the keys to sexual power. Ask for her help and her healing. While we most strongly associate with the Venusian figures in this temple, the astrological sign of Libra is also ruled by the planet Venus in astrology, and so the figures of Athena, Themis, and Lady Justice, carrying the scales and the sword, might manifest in this vision.

4. Look for your temple mirror. Call forth the first name on your list. Ask the energy, the higher self, of this person to come forward. Feel, see, hear, or know his or her presence in the mirror. Tell yourself you are releasing all energy that you retain from this relationship that is not yours to keep. You still keep all the blessings—the honest exchanges, memories, and lessons you learned—but if on any level you are holding on to the power of the other person, you are releasing that power now (even if you didn't realize you were holding on to it). Feel the unnecessary energy leave you. You will not be holding on to inappropriate energy from any relationship.

5. Then state your intention to reclaim your personal power from this person, if indeed the lover holds any. Feel the power return to you through the mirror. Not every past lover will be holding on to your personal energy.

6. Then ask the goddess of love to help you dissolve the unhealthy connections between you and this lover. The goddess's power might manifest as gentle waves of water that dissolve the cords between you and the mirrored figure or as the blade of the goddess of justice, severing the cords and dissolving them away in the light. Feel the connection release, freeing you from any inappropriate relationship with the past lover. Not every past relationship will have inappropriate cords to release.

7. Repeat steps 4–6 with the next name on your list. Repeat this cycle until you've healed the relationship with as many past lovers as you feel appropriate at this point.

8. When done, thank the goddess of love for her help and healing aid. She may have a special message for you or ask a boon, or quest, of you in return for her help, involving her mission of love in the world. Listen carefully and do as your heart and soul dictate.

9. When the deity is done communing with you, you find yourself moving back through the tunnel. You come out of the tunnel, through the gateway of the mirror that is before you, and the gateway closes.

10. When done, count yourself up from one to thirteen and then one to twelve, with no visualizations. When you reach the last one, feel your fingers and toes, arms and legs. When you are ready, open your eyes.

11. Bring both hands above the head, with palms facing the crown. Sweep down the front of the body, over the face, neck, heart, belly, and groin, pushing out and then down toward the ground. Say:

> *I release all that does not serve my highest good.*

Repeat the sweeping motion two more times, following
each with one of these two additional statements:

I am in balance with myself.

I am in balance with the universe.

12. Ground yourself as needed. Feel your feet extend into the
    ground, anchoring your physical body in the physical world.

RITUAL} **The Sexual Feast**

The sexual feast perhaps should be renamed the sensual feast, as it's a
ritual that has little to do with specific magickal acts as we know them.
Rather, it's an exploration of the senses, to heighten our awareness and
enhance sexual relationships. This in itself is quite a powerful form of
magick.

A couple must prepare, individually or together, a variety of sensory
experiences for themselves and their partner. Foods and drinks that are
sensual and enticing are laid out, such as whipped cream, chocolate,
berries, caviar, champagne, cordials, and anything else that seems like
a good idea at the time. The sensual feast is not just food, it is feasting
with all the senses. Play music that will put you both in the mood. Have
scented oils or massage creams. Have feathers, silk, leather, and other
textured materials.

Share these items of sensual experience with your partner. Feel
each other. Anoint each other with oils. Even trade different temperature experiences, using heat (perhaps through herbal preparations that
warm) and ice to vary the sensation on the skin. Do so in an erotic and
playful manner. Build up with intensity, starting with the most playful
and benign sensory experiences, and then gradually introduce the most
intense tastes, smells, and sensations. Use this entire sensual process
as an experience in itself or as foreplay to build up to sex or any ritual
of sex magick. Give yourself time to receive as well as give, switching

which partner is active and passive so you can fully immerse yourself in the experience.

The senses are the keys to magick. Each sense is linked to one of the five elements—touch/earth, taste/water, smell/air, sight/fire, and hearing/spirit. Use this experience to awaken the magickal senses, through the stimulation of the physical senses. Only through embracing the material world, including our sexuality, do we come into completeness.

Fertility and Pregnancy

Though the conception of children is rarely the intention of traditional lust magick, it is often the result, and fertility magick is a part of traditional magick. The stress a couple experiences trying to get pregnant or keeping a pregnancy under difficult health circumstances takes its toll on the health of a family and the love between a couple. Much of my own practice in counseling couples has been around issues of fertility and family planning, usually when the couple has run out of mainstream medical options.

From a magickal perspective, fertility has a lot to do with your own energy level and ability to be present in the body. Those potential fathers and mothers alike who are exhausted due to work and other commitments simply don't have the life force to commit to bringing a child into the world. Often the solution is resolving this imbalance in life and getting one or both potential parent to find a more harmonious lifestyle that is filled with more enjoyment of the present moment.

The soul of a potential new child who might want to incarnate through a couple wants the most perfect moment of conception and birth, for those moments influence the course of the child's life. If such a being wishes to come through a couple, there is little we can do to stop it, regardless of the best birth control. Some souls are simply determined to be born through specific people. Likewise, if no souls want to come through a particular couple, nothing can be done. Often it seems that a soul wants to come through, but that soul is waiting for the couple's health—physical and emotional—to improve, to allow the conception of the new baby with full life force and personal power.

The following herbs have associations with fertility and birth, and can be used in magick to aid conception. Consult with a qualified herbalist before using them medicinally to treat any fertility or virility conditions.

Almond—Almond wood is used in wands for increasing fertility and healing. Sweet almond oil can be used in the base of any fertility potion.

Ash—The ash tree is associated with both male virility and female fertility. Associated with the Norse world tree, ash is a powerful tree, capable of reaching between the worlds and drawing forth spirits to be born into the world again.

Basil—Basil is an herb of male virility and power.

Chestnut—Like many nuts, the chestnut is associated with fertility. The spirit of the chestnut protects the user from malign influences and brings peace and tranquility.

Club Moss—Along with spells for protection and power, club moss can be used to enhance male virility and, due to the reproductive spores, increase sperm count.

Dock Seed—The seed from the yellow dock plant is used for increase, from prosperity to female fertility.

Mistletoe—Due to the Doctrine of Signatures, the white berries of mistletoe indicate they can be used magickally to enhance male virility.

Nettle Tea—All parts of nettle, particularly the leaf and seed, are nourishment for the womb. In magick, it can be used to prepare a woman to become pregnant.

Oak—Although the oak tree is traditionally associated with Jupiterian storm and lightning gods, the acorn of the oak tree is used in fertility and love magick.

Orange Blossom—The orange, particularly the orange blossom, is associated with both fertility magick and conception.

Periwinkle—Periwinkle is also known as sorcerer's violet and can be used to open the psychic channels for inner vision, but it also is used in love magick. Specifically, it can call spirits to be incarnated in the flesh, drawing them into the material world to be reborn.

Pomegranate—The classic fruit of the underworld that keeps Persephone in the realm of Hades for half of the year can also be used to reincarnate the souls of the underworld in new flesh. The essence of this plant is the power of the Goddess and empowers all aspects of women, including the reproductive system.

Raspberry and Blackberry—The leaves of raspberry and blackberry are both strongly associated with the Goddess and reproductive power. In herbal teas, they are tonics for the feminine reproductive system.

Red Clover—Red clover is another tonic for the feminine reproductive system. As part of its Doctrine of Signatures, the leaf itself looks to have the image of a uterus printed upon it, revealing its power in feminine health and reproduction.

Watermelon—Through the principle of correspondence, we see that the watermelon is a natural association with pregnancy, as the pregnant belly looks much like the shape and size of a watermelon. Watermelon seeds and juice can be used in magick for conception and sustaining pregnancy. Watermelon flower essence, in particular, is used for conception.

POWDER} **Fertility**

>   1 tablespoon periwinkle leaves
>
>   1 tablespoon cinquefoil
>
>   1 tablespoon vervain

Grind the ingredients into a fine powder. Add two pinches to red wine, let it steep for at least twelve hours, and then drink before, during, and after lovemaking to induce pregnancy.

CHARM} **Fertility**

>   9 watermelon seeds
>
>   1 tablespoon parsley
>
>   1 tablespoon mugwort
>
>   1 tablespoon raspberry leaf
>
>   1 tablespoon red clover
>
>   1 piece of silver (ring or coin)

Put this mixture in a silver, white, pink, or green bag, and carry it or keep it under the mattress to increase fertility powers. For both genders.

CHARM} **Fertility Charm No. 2**

>   3 acorns
>
>   10 pomegranate seeds
>
>   1 tablespoon nettle
>
>   1 tablespoon dock seeds
>
>   1 pinch of rabbit hair from a live shedding rabbit

Like the first charm, carry this mixture in a pouch or keep it under the mattress to increase your physical fertility. Note that it is overkill to do both fertility charms, as that will dilute the magick too much. Either put a charm under the bed or carry charms (either one each or one just for the woman), but don't do both.

CHARM} **Male Fertility**

1 acorn

1 tablespoon basil

1 tablespoon club moss

1 tablespoon licorice

1 tablespoon damiana

1 tablespoon mistletoe (mistletoe berries alone are
preferable, but any part can be used if berries are
unavailable)

1 pinch dragon's blood resin

Carry this in a red charm bag or place it under the mattress to
increase the male's power of fertility.

Crystals and Pregnancy

The following crystals can be useful in healing fertility issues, particularly when they are rooted in the emotions and mind around issues
of love, motherhood, and family. These crystals include moonstone,
selenite, unakite, quartz, rose quartz, amber, carnelian, kunzite, and
hematite.

Animal Fertility Charms

Rather than go the herbal route, some people appeal to animal spirits
that are said to increase a woman's chance of getting pregnant. I was
given a carved rose quartz rabbit by a student who realized it was a fertility charm, as rabbits are known for their ability to reproduce. She gave
it to me for safekeeping, as she did not want to get pregnant. I used it in
a ritual with another woman to aid her conception, and she was soon
pregnant. Carved stones, traditional tribal fetishes, and even drawings
of certain animals can aid the conception process. Rabbits, frogs, cows/
bulls, horses, serpents, salmon, and bees are totems of fertility. In some
traditions, dragons and other serpents represent fertility.

RECIPE} **Pregnancy Essence**

Though I've had great success with couples using straight watermelon flower essence alone, in difficult cases I've used other essences in conjunction with the watermelon. Giving essences to both the man and the woman of the conceiving couple to be able to handle the emotional and mental issue around conception is very important, and each person's issues will require a different blend of essences.

For particularly difficult conception issues, this blend has worked very well for couples. I've used it twice, and both times it resulted in conception.

> 9 drops watermelon flower essence stock
>
> 7 drops pomegranate flower essence stock
>
> 4 drops red clover flower essence stock
>
> 5 drops raspberry flower essence stock
>
> 3 drops rose quartz gem elixir stock

Place all of the drops into a ¼-ounce dropper bottle filled with one-fourth apple cider vinegar and three-fourths spring water. Shake it up every time the woman seeking to conceive takes a dose—I would suggest either three drops three times a day or nine drops once a day.

A stock essence is the level of dilution one can purchase at a holistic health food store or online, and these essences and elixirs are available from a variety of suppliers online. If you have access to the flowering plants, you can also learn how to make your own. Detailed instructions on making essences and elixirs can be found in my book *The Temple of Shamanic Witchcraft,* and simpler instructions may be found in this book.

RECIPE} **Lady's Mantle Spagyric Tincture**

For the toughest healing issues around pregnancy, conception, and motherhood, I've found an alchemical tincture of lady's mantle to be incredibly healing. However, it should only be used in the strongest of circumstances, when the recipient is prepared to do deep magickal healing work and has a competent support system of physical, emotional, and psychological care. It has worked wonders in aiding the healing issues of past sexual abuse, miscarriage, and parental abuse, any of which can be an energetic block to physical fertility.

Lady's mantle is one of the premier Venusian herbs for women and Goddess-related magick. It is reputed to unlock the secrets of nature and creation as well as physically heal the feminine reproductive system. An alchemical tincture known as a spagyric tincture is a bit more complicated to make than a traditional herbal tincture. The process is said to unlock the deepest power of the herb. Tinctures are made by soaking the herb in alcohol to extract the healing medicines from the herb and preserve them. The herbal matter is usually discarded. In alchemical processes, the herbal matter must be purified, revitalizing the entire mixture.

Here are simplified instructions for the tincture. Ideally, it should be done on a Friday, Venus's day, at sunrise, Venus's hour. The process of making the tincture is just as important, if not more important, than actually consuming it. Making it yourself allows you to enter into a relationship with the plant world and heal on a very deep level.

1. Fill a Mason jar one-fourth full of dried, ground lady's mantle. If you could have grown, picked, and harvested the lady's mantle yourself, so much the better, but good-quality herbs from an herbal shop will still work. Grind it up, ideally by hand. Even if the herb is already powdered, still go through the process of grinding it in the mortar and pestle, adding your energy and connection to it. When grinding it, think about the power of the Goddess and your own healing.

2. Fill the Mason jar full of high-proof alcohol. Everclear, at 190 proof, is excellent for this work.

3. Put plastic wrap over the mouth of the jar before you seal it, especially if the cap is metal.

4. Shake well. Keep in a warm, dark place and shake it every day. After you shake it, hold it; feel its energy, and think about the process of working with the spirit of nature, the Goddess, your own healing, and the power of lady's mantle.

5. After four to nine weeks have passed (nine is ideal for this operation, as the number of months in a pregnancy), again ideally on the day and hour of Venus, strain the herb by using an unbleached coffee filter. Seal the jar again with the plastic wrap and lid to prevent the tincture from evaporating.

6. Empty the wet herb into a Pyrex glass baking dish, spread it out, and throw a lit match on it. The herb should burn, though you will probably have to repeat lighting it on fire a few times. You might have to open the windows or do this outside, as the herb can smoke a lot. Turn the herb to black ash and, when cool, grind it to a powder in your mortar and pestle. Still be mindful of the healing process: you are helping break down blocks in your own being as you do this.

7. Place the ash back into the glass baking dish, spread out as finely as possible. Heat the ash in your oven at a very high temperature, and let it heat for most of the day. Again, keep the windows open, as it might still smoke. This is known as calcination, the first of the alchemical operations to purify.

8. The ash should turn lighter, from black to gray or white. When cool, powder it again in your mortal and pestle. Add the ash back to the tincture. Store it in a warm, dark place for four to nine more weeks, and shake it every day.

9. In the day and hour of Venus, strain the tincture again,
   taking out any remaining herbal powder and discarding
   it. The resulting tincture should be bottled in a dark glass
   bottle and a convenient dropper bottle for your own dosage.
   Label them *Lady's Mantle Spagyric Tincture* with the date.

For those wanting to go the extra mile, you can add the following step between steps 8 and 9: You can dissolve the powdered ash in distilled water before adding it back to the tincture. Pass the water through an unbleached coffee filter. Discard the filter and evaporate the filtered water in a glass dish, which should have dried salts at the bottom. Scrape the salts off and then add them back to the tincture.

Take one to nine drops daily, on the tongue or in a glass of water. It can be taken at the start of the day, before meditation or ritual, or at the end of the day, whatever is intuitively appropriate for you. Consuming the small amount of tincture daily will transform your relationship with your body, with your womb, and with the goddess of nature and fertility. Be introspective. Journal. Talk. See a counselor. Things will come to heal and transform you. Lady's mantle will readjust your relationship to the feminine powers within your body and within the universe.

A similar tincture can be made by men for virility issues using Martian herbs such as nettle and parsley.

Detrimental Herbs for Pregnancy

While many Witches and advocates of herbal care popularize the benefits of herbs both magickally and medicinally, there are quite a number of herbs that a pregnant woman should avoid as being detrimental to the health of the unborn fetus. This list is provided not as a guide to herbal abortions, as such a procedure can result in your own death, but to educate herb users as to what is and is not safe during pregnancy. Many of these herbs are used at times to aid giving birth, but such use should be left to an herbal healthcare expert, not home use. This is by no means an absolute and complete list, but it is a good starting point.

Angelica, Chinese (Dong Quai)

Black Cohosh

Blue Cohosh

Cotton Root Bark

Mugwort

Nutmeg

Papaya

Pennyroyal

Rue

Slippery Elm

Tansy

Vervain

Wild Carrot (Queen Anne's Lace)

Wormwood

NINE

Magickal Relationships

While many love magick teachings simply focus on finding either a romantic partner or a sex partner, few really talk about sustaining a relationship. Most of us have the ideal that once we find a perfect partner, it will all work out. All our movies and television shows make the finding of a partner the central theme, the quest of most romantic stories. Once the couple finds each other and truly connects, they ride off into the sunset to live happily ever after, like a fairy tale. No one wants to write a story or film a movie that checks in on the couple twenty years later, or even ten years later, as that ruins the mystique and romantic notion we have of how love should work. While we think love should work that way, in my experience, it doesn't.

Finding your love is only the first step of the journey. We focus on it because everybody can relate to the search for love; it's a common denominator to the human experience. But not everybody can relate to the day-to-day reality of the work put into a healthy and mature relationship. That's less common in life, so it's less common in music, books, and film. The finding is the first step, the bare minimum, while the next step is learning how to care for your relationship, to grow it and sustain it through all its cycles and phases.

One of the most important lessons we can learn as magickal people is that we must put our effort and our magick into our relationship as it is developing *and* as it continues to grow, rather than wait for things to go wrong. When things are good, continue to do love spells for you and your partner—just do different types of love spells. Follow them up with real-world action. But do not wait to use your magick or to put effort into your relationship only when things are failing. Most people look to magick only as a last resort, but if you are living a magickal life, it is a part of your everyday reality, including your romantic relationship.

There are a lot of natural analogies that can be used for the relationship and the wisdom of the Witch. My friend Kris says that relationships are like a candle flame in a room. One problem new relationships often have is the intrusion of other people, rather than focusing on getting to know the new person and building a foundation. If you keep opening and closing the door, bringing in new people to see, judge, and give advice in the relationship rather than giving more attention and fuel to the fire itself and your partner, you risk the breeze from the opening and closing door snuffing out your new flame. Such a danger can occur in a long-standing relationship where the flame has dwindled low and can be easily snuffed as well.

My friend Dave, who is not practicing a magickal spirituality, looks at relationships like a gardener with a flower. One partner is the gardener, tending to the relationship, while the other is the flower, looking pretty and appreciating the tending. Though at the time I thought it was a very astute observation of many people, I think this attitude dooms a relationship to failure. Though everybody has individual strengths, assets, and weaknesses they bring to a relationship, if you look at one partner as solely the caretaker and the other as the "caretakee," then you have a recipe for resentment and imbalance. Many people look at relationships exactly this way, even if they are not conscious of it.

I prefer to think that when two people come together, the relationship they create is an individual entity unto itself, composed of the energy they have both contributed. When a Witch joins a coven or a ritual circle, he or she is joining a collective group mind consisting of the energies placed into the group relationship from the individual members. The same can be said about members joining any magickal lodge. Though it is different, when one has only one magickal partner, a group mind is formed between the two. Such group consciousness is considered a thoughtform, a type of artificial or human-made spirit. That spirit must be cared for and fed. As it grows, it confers special benefits to those practitioners attached to it.

A relationship is much the same way, and to borrow from Dave's flower metaphor, I like to think of the relationship as a complex garden with two gardeners. Each one must take care of it. Each one adds to it. Each one has his or her own space, yet the garden must work together as a whole. Everything each gardener does should ultimately complement the work of the other and add to the overall health and beauty of the garden. The two gardeners must plant together and develop it together. If they have very different styles of gardening, they must work it out through communication. Some like to meticulously plan out the garden, while others like to plant things as they come along, in a whimsical fashion. Their life together must be approached like a garden, and those with complementary styles in their approach to life will get along better than those who don't complement each other. Sometimes they are complementary because they are similar and sometimes they are complementary because they are different, each contributing an aspect the other partner lacks.

Compatibility

Sometimes in a relationship we get swept up in the passion—the intensity of physical attraction and the experience of sex and romance—and forget to look at our potential compatibility. Passion, attraction, sex, and romance are all important, but they are the initial spark, not what sustains the relationship. We have a lot of erroneous assumptions about love—or at least incomplete ideas about what it means to be in a relationship. When we act from these assumptions rather than using our Witch's eye to see things as they truly are (as opposed to how we'd like them to be), we set ourselves up for failure. By looking at our assumptions about love and romance *before* we're in a relationship, deprogramming ourselves from some societal expectations as well as looking at the reality of our relationship once we are in it, we are more likely to have a truly successful partnership.

One folk saying tells us that opposites attract, and we see that in nature as well, with positive and negative charges. Yet opposites also collide, react, and form new things totally different from the originals. While in magick we know that all things have polarities, or opposites, opposition magick is often used to cancel out another form of magick. Some traditions teach us that opposites negate. In magick, similars attract. We use the principle of correspondence, "as above, so below," to show us that an herb will have a similar energy and principle to a planet, and we can use the herb to attract the energy of the planet for our rituals. They correspond. In homeopathy, healers tell us that "like cures like" through the law of similars. Two things that are similar can be used to restore balance. So we have the competing principles of *opposites attract* and *like attracts like*. Both can be true, and both attract in different ways.

When we are attracted to someone who appears to be our antithesis, there is a greater charge of energy. We find such people unusual, captivating, or exotic. We respond both physically and mentally with more energy than when presented with someone similar to us and our background. Yet unless there is a lot of effort and communication on both sides, such relationships are difficult to sustain. There is a lot of initial energy, but the lack of common ground makes it difficult to stoke the fire and keep it burning over time. If there is little kindling in common to add, the flame can burn out. In our garden analogy, you've bred an exotic flower that does not thrive in either of your native soils. You either have to come up with a medium, a mix of the two, or let the flower die.

When we are attracted to someone who shares our values, background, or worldview, we have a common platform even though the initial spark may or may not be as intense. Sometimes people appear to be very different from us, giving us that intense charge, but through the relationship process, we realize we share much in common that was not obvious at first glance. Such commonalities can build a solid foundation.

In either case, couples must then develop new common ground by exploring new realms and exposing each other to their own private worlds if the relationship is going to be sustained. One cannot rely on the past alone. Each individual in the couple must continue to grow and develop as an individual, to have new things to share in the relationship while time is being invested in the relationship itself.

Soul Mates and Twin Flames

Along with the concept that opposites attract and can therefore easily and effortlessly sustain a relationship, we have a cultural belief in soul mates. Many people will ask me how to find their soul mate. In the quest for love, they believe if they just find the right person, everything will fall into place. They will be extremely mutually attracted to each other and be able to take care of each other's needs, knowing what the other needs on a soul level without the need to speak about it. I don't care how spiritual or psychic you are, if you don't learn communication skills with your partner, you and/or your partner will be very unhappy. The idea that one person can take care of all your needs without even being told what your needs are is ridiculous, but it's one of the insidious programs we carry around with us in the notion of romance.

We have this idea that we are incomplete—that something is missing. And as romantics, we think the missing thing is a romantic partner. We all long for it, so if we find the right one, the one that is the other half of our soul, we'll be fine. Everything will be perfect.

In the metaphysical world, the concept has expanded into the idea of twin flames. Though the theology of twin flames is not quite the same as soul mates, and few people define twin flames the same way, I'm not a fan of the terms *soul mate* and *twin flame*. Generally, twin flames are thought of as two halves, two flames, from the same source. I think it sets us up for unnecessary expectations and heartaches, even in otherwise healthy relationships, because it gives many of us the illusion that we don't have to work or grow in a relationship—that once we find the right "one," we will be rewarded with happiness. Life doesn't work that way.

We are complete in and of ourselves and have no need to be completed. Partners complement us, but our souls are already whole. They are not halves. We might find someone whom we have known in a past life or had romance with in a past life and rekindle it this time, yet that does not mean we are destined for a perfect relationship. We have "soul family" in many roles, and sometimes what I think of as our soul mates have nothing to do with romance—it could be your mother, sibling, or child that is your soul "mate." From the soul level, it is not about romance or sex, but about spiritual connection. When we talk about romance and life building, I prefer the terms *life mate* or *life partner*. I am also old-fashioned and like *husband* or *wife*. It confers a sense of this lifetime, and the vows you take in this lifetime can be for the entire life but are released in future incarnations. You might need to be married to someone else in a future life, and the mate you have today can reincarnate as your best friend, parent, child, or sibling. Each new facet of the relationship helps the soul grow and develop.

One of the biggest impediments to romantic happiness when one holds on to the soul-mate notion is the egocentric viewpoint, intentional or unintentional, that the partner is here to complete me rather than look to see how the partner views the world and looks at life and romance. One of the ways I've found it most interesting to look at another's point of view is through astrology.

Relationship Astrology

People are always seeking readings to predict their relationship. Those who are wiser use divination tools and sciences such as astrology to help them understand their own patterns and their partner's, and how to communicate better. When discussing what I call "party" astrology, where people will mention their signs and the signs of lovers and spouses, those with a little astrological knowledge will immediately pipe into the conversation things like "those two signs get along very well" or "those signs are doomed to failure." Their knowledge is based on just a smattering of true astrological wisdom and perhaps their own observations of people with the same Sun signs, as well as their own personal biases for and against those signs.

True exploration of astrological compatibility is actually far more advanced than a simple Sun sign comparison. While there are some guidelines to Sun sign comparison, every good astrologer knows that compatibility is based on several different factors, and two people can have zodiac Sun signs that are seemingly incompatible and still have a long and happy life together.

One of my most spiritual astrology teachers told me that no two signs are totally incompatible and no two people are totally incompatible. It all depends on how they manifest the energy of their signs and how much effort they both want to put into the relationship. But that being said, in my experience I've found certain combinations of people, not necessarily signs, to be ultimately incompatible. Perhaps the amount of effort to sustain it simply outweighed the benefit of the relationship and they sought someone with a similar viewpoint.

While this book cannot be a complete course in astrology, you need a simple understanding of the common ideas and terms to talk about compatibility in the astrological charts of two people. When you are born, the position of all the planets and signs in the sky determines the patterns of your life, including your talents, challenges, and likely outlooks. Charts cast for the moment of birth are known as natal, or birth, charts. They are usually looked at to see the forces at work in your life, including romance and sex.

We have four major divisions, or parts, in our understanding of astrology. They include:

> *Planets*—Planets are the larger heavenly bodies in our own
>> solar system. Each has its own orbit, except for the Sun, and
>> while we know intellectually that the planets orbit the Sun,
>> from our perspective they appear to orbit Earth. Astrology
>> is all about how the patterns of the sky appear to us on
>> Earth, so we act as if they do orbit around us. Each planet
>> embodies a component of ourselves, of our psyche. Each
>> has a different function and purpose in our life. The ancients
>> knew seven basic planets: the Sun, the Moon, Mercury,
>> Venus, Mars, Jupiter, and Saturn. With the additions of
>> modern discoveries, astrologers also use Uranus, Neptune,
>> and Pluto, as well as some other smaller heavenly bodies
>> such as Chiron and the larger asteroids of the asteroid belt.
>> Though it's debatable as to what is a planet technically,
>> anything with its own orbit in our solar system can be used
>> like a planet in astrology.

> *Signs*—The signs occupy a specific area of the sky. That area
>> is divided into twelve segments. Each segment of thirty
>> degrees is a sign. There is a pattern to the signs: Taurus
>> always follows Aries, Aries always follows Pisces, Pisces
>> always follows Aquarius, and so on. The planets appear to
>> occupy a sign, and that sign is said to influence the way that

planet operates. The Sun in Libra operates very differently from the Sun in Scorpio. The band of zodiac signs also rotates around Earth.

Houses—Houses are areas in the sky that the signs and planet seem to occupy. Astrologers mathematically divide the sky into twelve sections, six above the horizon and six below. Different methods of calculation yield different types of houses, and each astrologer has his or her own favorite method, but generally the houses are fixed areas in the sky that appear to be larger or smaller, depending on where you are on the planet. The houses look different near one of the poles than they do at the equator. This is why most astrologers ask for a location as well as a time and day to create a natal chart.

Aspects—The aspects of a chart are specific angles made between planets if you consider the center of the chart, the planet Earth, the joint connecting the two planets and creating the angle. Not all angles are considered aspects, only very specific ones, and the angle between the planets determines whether the energy of each planet supports or conflicts with the other. When planets are not making these specific angles, they are considered fairly neutral toward each other. Magickal timing comes from maximizing the times when the planetary energies you need for your intention are in harmony and supporting each other and minimizing the times when the planets you want to call upon are conflicting.

Astrologers interpret the various combinations of a planet in a sign, in a house, and with any aspects to give you a description of the forces at work within your chart and within your life. One analogy my astrology teacher gave me to help understand these various parts and combinations is to look at the planets as if they were actors. Each of us has an array of actors within us. Some of these actors deal with romance, others not as much. The signs they occupy are like the roles the actors play. Each role will color a specific actor's movement, but you can still tell the actors apart. Each actor is unique and has a special area of expertise, no matter the role taken on. The houses are like the scenes where the action takes place. These scenes, however, are in your own life, and the aspects describe the relationships between the actors in their given roles.

A good astrologer can compare the charts of two different people and determine the areas of ease or difficulty between the two. They compare the various "actors" between the charts to see how well they would get along and look for aspects between them. In terms of romantic astrology for compatibility with another, here are some basic points to keep in mind when determining astrological compatibility:

Sun Sign—The Sun represents our basic self. Some astrologers say it is who we are, our ego self, while others say it is who we are learning to be in this lifetime. As the Sun is the largest body in the solar system, it represents the largest amount of energy in our astrological chart. It often is the sign of our most dominant characteristics and traits, particularly if we were born during the day. If we were born during the night, the sign on the horizon, the Ascendant, will appear to be the dominant sign to those observing us. Because the Sun is such a large influence, astrology based solely on the Sun sign can have some merit, but ultimately it's incomplete.

Moon Sign—The sign the Moon is in influences your emotional self and inner nature. Though not specifically romantic, your overall emotions do play an important part in all relationships, and understanding the way you process your emotions, and how your partner does, can be very helpful to the overall relationship.

Venus Sign—Venus is the planet of relationship. It rules over how we express ourselves socially and romantically, as well as how we express our affection for others. Venus is said to be the magnetic quality that attracts people to us, and the sign that Venus occupies determines the style of that attraction.

Fifth-House Ruler—The fifth house is the house of children and lovers. Today it is generally seen as the house where we are most sensitive in terms of our ego development, and the two forces that are mostly likely to build up or tear down our ego development are those that are closest to us emotionally—children and lovers. In terms of lovers, this is the place of romantic and casual lovers, or those that are discreet. This is the house of the romantic and sensual affair. When a deeper commitment occurs, the seventh house becomes dominant.

Seventh-House Ruler—The seventh house is the house of partnership. Though technically it rules all partnerships, including business, most think of it as the house of marriage. It is for publicly declared relationships and public commitments to another. The sign ruling this house determines your view of partnership and your style in approaching and working with a potential partner.

Eighth-House Ruler—The eighth house is the house of sex, death, and transformation, for they all are ultimately things beyond the control of our personality. Some call the eighth house the house of desires, which relates to sex on a physical level. The lens through which we approach our sexuality and sexual experiences is the ruler of the eighth house.

Compatibility is much more than these six points, but they provide a good start for the Witch interested in astrology, and relationship astrology in particular. Generally, it is said that air and fire signs get along well together, and earth and water signs get along well together. This is the basic wisdom of coffee-table astrology, with a few additional notes. Since Venus rules both Taurus and Libra, they are considered compatible, and Mercury rules Gemini and Virgo, so they are also considered compatible. Though each sign's opposite sign will be of the complementary element, and while we are attracted to our opposite signs, particularly our opposite Sun signs, we usually have difficulty understanding and working with our opposite signs. You will also find that the other five points can show the flaws at looking solely at Sun sign astrology. Your Sun signs can be very compatible, but if your Moon and seventh house are less complementary, you can have a very difficult relationship.

Sometimes the biggest obstacle is simply understanding how your partner approaches romance and sex and how they express love and affection. If we know how they view partnership, sex, and relationship, we can better understand their words and actions and how they are different from ours. We can better express what we need and then be able to speak to them in a romantic language they understand.

Here are basic descriptions of the signs, and in particular how they apply to romance and relationship. These ideas can then be applied to definitions of the Sun, Moon, Venus, fifth, seventh, and eighth houses, as needed.

Aries/Cardinal Fire—Those with strong Aries energy like to
    take the lead in love, romance, and sex. They are natural
    adventurers, but rather than the adventure of exploration
    that is typical with the fire sign Sagittarius, they seek the
    thrill of the adventure, the intensity and excitement in
    action. Aries archetypes are warriors, and they can bring
    that energy to the relationship. They can have difficulty in
    expressing love and caring in terms of everyday expressions
    and prefer the grand sweeping gestures. Aries is also the

sign of learning about the self, so their love nature can appear to be very self-oriented and not outwardly expressed, sometimes appearing a bit selfish, unless other signs are mediating their Aries energy in terms of romance. They can be adventuresome in the bedroom and tend to either be very excitement oriented or a bit rough-and-tumble.

Taurus/Fixed Earth—Taurus is both practical and sensual, looking to both receive and give the creature comforts of life. Taureans will give gifts to show affection, particularly gifts with a strong sensual aspect—things with rich smells such as perfumes and colognes; fine textures; expensive and shiny objects like jewelry; good food and fine sweets. Spending money is a way that Taureans show their love and a way they expect love to be shown to them. Little gifts are the language of love for Taurus—the amount spent is not as important as the actual act of getting and giving. Though the gift giving is a lifelong process, Taureans also desire to give security, usually in the home and financially, to their lovers. Taurus is very sexual and likes to both give and receive pleasure over a longer period time, extending foreplay. Sex is seen as playful and recreational, as well as a sign of love and affection. Taurus is fiercely loyal to lovers, present and past, and easily form bonds of commitment through sex and romance.

Gemini/Mutable Air—Geminis express love through words. They tell you they love you and expect to be told the same. Physical signs of love might go unnoticed if they do not come with verbal expressions of love. Geminis will speak and write about love with poems, stories, and short little notes. They love to tell stories of their wonderful times with a lover to others, to show how important their lover is. Sexually, Geminis are very much into the idea of sex and approach it from an intellectual level. They must be intellectually stimulated by sex and can easily get bored without new and different situations and experiences. They bring creativity to the bedroom and usually are open to new ideas.

Cancer/Cardinal Water—The nature of Cancer is to nourish and care for another. Considered the mother sign of the zodiac, lovers with strong Cancer energy will tend to mother their partner, being great homemakers and cooks, seeking to create domestic bliss. Harmony in the home is important to them, and while they prefer to be the nurturer, actions to nurture them or the home will be particularly noticed by them. Food is a sign of love to Cancer. Some do not nurture in a physical way and are purely emotional and seek to shelter and protect their lover, but they are often emotionally sensitive and protective of themselves, sometimes creating the classic "shell" of the crab and reserving their emotions so as not to be hurt. Mature Cancers will support you but not take care of your every need. Sexually, Cancers are emotionally driven and seek emotional intimacy as much as, if not more than, physical intimacy. To be at ease sexually, they must feel secure emotionally.

Leo/Fixed Fire—Leo's archetype is varied, as it's described as the entertainer, the person who likes to show off and be the center of attention. It is also described as royalty—a king or queen who by their very nature is the center of attention. Those with a Leonine energy like to be the center of attention, particularly when it comes to love, romance, and sex. Attention is tied into their self-identity, and they are learning about themselves through how others respond to them, so they need that constant attention and feedback. They are generally romantic and attentive lovers, doing whatever is necessary to keep the attention of the lover, and they are funny, artistic, and entertaining. Showing attention to Leos in big and small ways can build the relationship, and making them feel that your romance together is of extreme importance to you is vital. In astrology, Leo naturally rules the house of children and lovers, the two relationships in which we are most sensitive. Hurtful comments from lovers can devastate Leo's healthy sense of ego, but usually they will not admit it, not wanting their quest for approval to be known.

Virgo/Mutable Earth—Virgo is the sign of service, and those with strong Virgo energy in their chart show their love and affection through service. They do things for their lovers. Virgos operate best when they are needed—or at least feel like they are needed. They might not often express love verbally or through material gifts. Being an earth sign, their material gift is themselves and what they can do. Though Virgos tend to focus on the doing, they recognize love through actions of service, and doing something for someone with strong Virgo energy goes much further than simply saying you love them. Virgos truly believe actions speak louder than words. Virgos can tend to be self-critical as well as critical of a partner, and they express both of these tendencies verbally. Their analytical skills must be put to good positive use in the relationship and generally in their life so it doesn't turn to attacking their partner with unnecessary criticism.

Libra/Cardinal Air—Libra expresses its natural love tendencies through sharing similar pursuits with a lover, often aesthetically pleasing pursuits like art, music, dance, and decorating. Libra is the sign of the scales, and being cardinal air, a great symbol for Libra is the balanced breath, one in and one out. They are seeking balance in relationship, where both their needs and their partner's needs get met. They can go out of balance and either err by doing all the caretaking or doing none of it and expecting to be taken care of. They need to find the harmony between the two extremes. Clear communication is a lesson to be learned by Libras, who need to balance both speaking and listening. Until a decision has been made about anything, Libras can be very indecisive and indifferent to plans. Once a plan has been set and a direction chosen, they can be very stubborn in changing or modifying it.

Scorpio/Fixed Water—A keyword for Scorpio on just about any level is *intensity*. Considering many astrologers think Scorpio is the most sexual of the twelve signs, intensity applies to all romantic and sexual relationships for those with strong Scorpio energy. Scorpios love intensely but can have difficulty expressing their feelings, feeling the need to be private or secretive about their love. They can put up walls and, as a friend has told me, "play their cards too close to their chest," never revealing what they really feel. Those with strong Scorpio energy might also be attracted to the unusual or taboo in the bedroom, exploring different roles and fetishes. Issues of power and control, both sexually and in the relationship, can also come up. Whatever the Scorpio endeavors to do, it is done with passion and psychic intensity.

Sagittarius/Mutable Fire—The love nature of Sagittarius thrives on doing new things and sharing the adventure with a partner. Those with strong Sagittarian energy want to travel, explore, and experience with a lover. While for many it will take the role of a physical adventure—going places, doing things—for others it will be a philosophical bond, wanting a partner with whom they can discuss art, culture, and the world. There is a physical component to Sagittarius, as they can seek out enjoyment through sports and athletics, seeking new experiences and keeping active.

Sometimes those with a Sagittarian love nature will take on the role of tutor to a lover, teaching them about the world, or find a worldly lover and act as student, soaking in all the experience.

Capricorn/Cardinal Earth—One of the key lessons for Capricorn is responsibility. Those with a strong Capricorn energy will take their responsibilities seriously, including the responsibilities of relationship. Their expression of love can be formal and old-fashioned but can also have the aesthetic of Old World politeness and charm. Capricorns typically seek to be the financial provider for the family, being the opposite of Cancer, the domestic nourisher. Most Capricorns will seek out honorable relationships and will always consider their standing in society, be it mainstream society or standing in a subculture. While Capricorns have a reputation for being stoic and formal, the totem of the sign is the goat and the image of Pan, and the exterior can hide a more passionate, fun, and sexually intense streak.

Aquarius/Fixed Air—It's hard to predict exactly how an Aquarian will express their love. Aquarians are innovative, unusual, and unorthodox. They are very modern and forward-thinking in their relationships and tend to have unconventional romances. They are open to trying new things, both in lifestyle and in the bedroom. Being a fixed air sign, they are sometimes perceived as being detached from their emotions and distant. This is not necessarily so, for they simply take an intellectual approach in expressing themselves rather than a passionate one. Aquarians are passionate about social causes, equality, and freedom, and partners who share their same values and goals will do well with them. Partners who are stuck in their ways will have a hard time keeping up with the Aquarian lover.

Pisces/Mutable Water—The nature of Pisces is very dreamy, ethereal, and, in its highest forms, very spiritual. The classic image of Pisces is of two fish tied together. One fish swims towards the heavens. The other fish swims toward the earth, illustrating the conflict in Pisces between the idealized spirit world and the imperfect physical world. Those with strong Pisces energy can be creative, imaginative, and magickal, though they idealize aspects of life. When expressed as a love nature, they have an idealized image of lovers and even of the concept of love, and become easily disenchanted and disillusioned if people and circumstances in the physical world don't conform to their ideas. This can result in martyrdom and self-sacrifice or escapism. The spiritually mature Pisces is very knowing of the ways of spirit and how to serve the divine purpose. In romance, Pisces relates through empathy—by having empathy for you but also seeking empathy from you. Pisces people are very emotionally sensitive, picking up on other people's emotions quite easily. Sometimes such empathic people cannot discern if an emotion originates inside or outside of themselves. They also often don't realize that not everybody is as empathic and use empathy as a substitute for clear communication, assuming that others simply know how they feel. Empathy is not a substitute for communication. Sexually, Pisces can be very sensual and creative, but they are also seeking a spiritual connection or at least a deep empathic connection with a lover, yet they are not focused on a domestic commitment in the way that Cancer is. Though both water signs have similar attributes in terms of empathy, Pisces does not share Cancer's same set of boundaries, and their worldview and goals can easily flow into and then away from the worldview and goals of their lovers.

A very simplistic form of relationship astrology works by looking at the elements of the Sun signs involved. While it can be generally helpful in understanding the signs and their relationships, it's not foolproof. You can have "incompatible" Sun signs but also have many other supportive factors that would make a relationship a success. If you only go by Sun signs and not by the person as a whole, you could miss out on some great relationships. The basic Sun sign relationship astrology is as follows:

- Those Sun signs of the same element generally are compatible. Fire signs understand fire signs, air signs understand air signs, etc. The area in which those signs are focused are the same, so they work well together.

- Signs with the element of the same gender are generally compatible. Fire and air are both considered masculine elements, so they are compatible. Earth and water are both considered feminine elements, so they are compatible.

- Signs that are your direct opposite on the zodiac wheel, even though they are of a compatible element, present challenges and intensity. There will often be a simultaneous attraction and repulsion between these signs, as each represents the shadow of the other:
    Aries—Libra
    Taurus—Scorpio
    Gemini—Sagittarius
    Cancer—Capricorn
    Leo—Aquarius
    Virgo—Pisces

- There will be an attraction to the sign that is adjacent to yours on the zodiac wheel, as it represents the sign that holds the next stage of development, but traditionally it is considered incompatible.

- Signs that were ruled by the same planet in classical forms of astrology will have common elements and have greater compatibility than first believed. These combinations will still have challenges but will also have common points:

    Mercury—Gemini & Virgo

    Venus—Taurus & Libra

    Mars—Aries & Scorpio

    Jupiter—Sagittarius & Pisces

    Saturn—Capricorn & Aquarius

Just as each sign has its own way of operating in the realms of relationship, love, and sex, each sign has a part of the body assigned to it. Traditionally a part of medical astrology and the healing arts of magick, these body parts can also be erogenous zones for those who are strongly aligned with the Sun. The Sun sign primarily, but also the Moon sign and the ruling sign of your eighth house, can give you possible clues to the erogenous zones, or at least places you like to be touched affectionately.

Knowing these astrological placements of your partner can be very helpful, as often we will touch our partner in the ways we like to be touched, not thinking a lover might have very different trigger points than we do.

Aries—Head, face, scalp

Taurus—Neck

Gemini—Hands, arms, shoulders

Cancer—Chest, breasts, belly

Leo—Back, spine, chest

Virgo—Lower belly

Libra—Buttocks, lower back

Scorpio—Genitals, perineum, anus, entire body

Sagittarius—Thighs

Capricorn—Knees, calves, shins

Aquarius—Ankles

Pisces—Feet

EXAMPLE} **Astrological Chart**

The example chart on the next page gives us some great food for thought in interpreting astrological charts. It contains some advanced aspects slightly beyond the basic introduction of this book, but even the base minimum we are looking at for love and relationship will be helpful.

For this example, the Sun sign is Cancer. This person, at their core, is seeking emotional and family security. Being right in the first house, the house of self-learning, they are learning, to some extent, to nurture and take care of the self in this lifetime. This person seeks to explore and express herself but can appear selfish at times. She also emotionally shields herself, like a crab in its shell, when in fear of getting hurt. While she appears tough on the outside, she can be quite vulnerable and sensitive. Generally, Cancer is harmonious with other water and earth signs, such as Taurus, Virgo, Scorpio, and Pisces. While Capricorn is attractive, being the opposite sign of Cancer, it could pose some problems.

The Moon is in Aries, so emotionally, this person is headstrong and fiery. It is in the house of friends and social relationships, the eleventh house, so while friends play an important part in emotional development and connection, she might be competitive with friends or simply need time being alone. She would do well connecting to those with Moon signs of fire and air generally, particularly Sagittarius.

Venus is in Leo in the fourth house. A Leonine Venus indicates one who is affectionate, playful, and romantic, who likes to give a lot of attention but at the same time receive a lot of attention. Physical beauty and charisma will play a big part in life, as this person has a natural

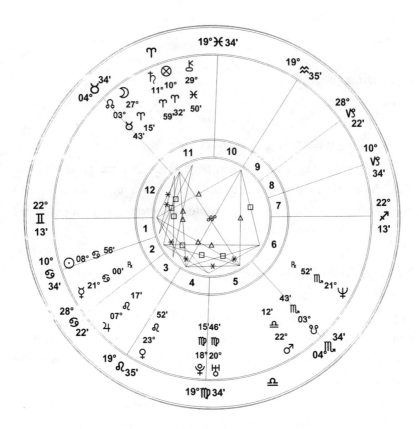

FIGURE}   Sample Astrological Chart
Occupation: actress; birthday: July 1, 1967;
birth place: Ladysmith, Canada; birth time: 4:08 am

ability to attract attention or put on a show in regard to romance and
sexuality. Being in the fourth house indicates a reinforcement of the
Cancerian nature that home and family are important to her as well,
and relationships lead to the security of the family.

The fifth house of children and lovers is ruled by Virgo. The ones to
whom she is most sensitive are also the ones she is in service to. She is
also either particularly critical of children and lovers or feels the sting of

their criticism toward her. The sign of Libra, the sign of balanced relationships, is entirely swallowed up by the fifth house, becoming what astrologers call an intercepted sign. When a house is larger than thirty degrees, it can cause an entire sign to be swallowed in it. The opposing sign, Aries, is intercepted in the eleventh house. Karmic astrologers would say there is past-life karma to deal with around the axis of Aries-Libra, the stress of individuality versus balanced partnership. This will develop into a theme as her life progresses.

The seventh house is ruled by Sagittarius, meaning romance and partnerships will be adventuresome and fun. They will be marked by travel, exploration, and learning new things together.

The eighth house is ruled by Capricorn. Capricorn brings a sense of measured control to the area where we have to let go of control. So even when she is not in control, the appearance is that she is. In regard to sexuality (as this is the house of sex, death, and taxes), the outer, responsible exterior can be hiding a wild, Panlike sexuality just beneath or show areas of control or power over lovers.

Who is the mystery example? It's actress Pamela Anderson. She had one famous relationship with drummer Tommy Lee, whose Sun sign is Libra, and his Moon is not known to the general public but might be Scorpio or Sagittarius. As a Libra, he strikes a chord in her karmic Aries-Libra axis. Her Aries Moon would be attracted to a Sagittarius Moon, or her Cancer Sun attracted to a Scorpio Moon, but ultimately it did not work out. Another famous love of hers is musician Kid Rock. His Sun sign is Capricorn, playing into the shadow attraction with Cancer, his opposite sign, while his Moon is unknown but either Virgo or Libra. Libra too would play into her Aries-Libra karmic axis, while Virgo would align well with the ruling sign of her fifth house.

Astrologers can put two charts together in what is known as a "bi-wheel," where they can compare the interactions of the charts of a couple. A more advanced technique is known as a composite chart, where the two charts are put together into one chart via a mathematical formula. This chart represents the relationship between the two people and can be studied as an individual entity itself, similar to the idea of a relationship thoughtform, as detailed earlier in this chapter. The composite chart can also be used to compare to both individuals' charts, to see your connection with the overall energy of the relationship.

While we've been covering the uses of astrology in compatibility magick, you can more easily use it in terms of your spellcasting. When the Sun, Moon, or Venus is in a sign that represents the type of relationship you want to have, magick for that relationship will be more effective. Generally love magick is considered to be best when the Moon or Venus is in a water sign. If you are looking for a stable love, then earth signs will serve you better. If you are looking for sexual passion, work with fire signs. If you are looking for an intellectual equal, wait for air signs. If you want to be very complicated, you can draw up a chart for the moment of the ritual to determine what is on the cusp of the fifth, seventh, and eighth houses, to add that information to your spell.

Numerology of Love

Just as astrology is used as a method of determining compatibility, numerology—the study of the energetic vibration of numbers—is also used to help us understand ourselves and our mates. Numerology is based upon the numeric value of the letters in our name, as well as the number of our age, the current year, or even our address. One thing that helped me understand the power in the numbers of our name was the first few weeks of dating my partner. My partner's name is Steve, and we discovered that before we met, I was dating another Steve and he was dating another Chris. It was like we were close to finding each other, and the vibration of the names was similar, but ultimately we needed different people attached to those names.

Numerology systems vary from East to West, modern to ancient, so while it's a complete system, there is a lot of variation on how to calculate various numbers, interpret that information, and apply it, particularly to love. The system here is one that I've found to be helpful, yet those interested in a more detailed study of numerology should look at resources that are more specific to the overall study of numerology.

Primary Number

The first number to calculate is the primary number. This number is your inner nature and guiding force. It is calculated by your birth date, as the day of your birth encapsulates the energy that guides your life, much like the position of the planets and signs determines the guiding factors of your astrological birth chart. To calculate the primary number, add the digits together. If you were born on August 13, 1977, add together $8 + 13 + 1977 = 1998$.

The digits are reduced until you get a single digit from 1 to 9:

$1 + 9 + 9 + 8 = 27$

$2 + 7 = 9$

Or add up all the individual numbers:

$8 + 1 + 3 + 1 + 9 + 7 + 7 = 36$

$3 + 6 = 9$

Love Number

Your love number, the force ruling your romantic partnerships, is calculated by converting the letters of your full birth name to numbers and adding them together until they are reduced to a single digit. If your name is Mary Jane Smith, the letters, using the alphanumeric conversion chart on page 141, would convert to:

M	A	R	Y	J	A	N	E	S	M	I	T	H
4	1	9	7	1	1	5	5	1	4	9	2	8

$$4 + 1 + 9 + 7 + 1 + 1 + 5 + 5 + 1 + 4 + 9 + 2 + 8 = 57$$

$$5 + 7 = 12$$

$$1 + 2 = 3$$

Home Number

The last primary number that comes into play is the number involving your home. Generally the home number is calculated by using the digits of the street address only, though if your home only has a name, then that name can be converted using the same alphanumeric conversion chart. If you live on 1624 Broadway, then the home number is calculated

$$1 + 6 + 2 + 4 = 13$$

$$1 + 3 = 4$$

If you live in an apartment, this will give you the building's number, and you can add your apartment number to it, reducing it to a single digit, again, for the energy of your specific home. Generally any numbers in your street name, such as Fifth Avenue or 77th Street, would not be added.

The primary number, love number, and even home number, if residing together, all play a factor in your life, though it's important to know that while the numbers each have a metaphysical meaning, they are open to interpretation. Simply because one book or teacher says two primary numbers do not get along for love, you might find that you personally enjoy a complex and challenging relationship. Common interpretations, even the ones here, are based on simple factors; your personal choices, wants, and needs might go beyond the commonly accepted wisdom and yield success. Many Witches do not choose what is common and have amazing and exciting lives.

The primary number tells you about your general self, much like your Sun sign in astrology. The love number tells you about your romantic self. The information in the primary-number description can supplement the description in regard to your love nature, much like the position of Venus in your astrology chart. "Vibrates to" tells you the number of lovers where there is strong and mutual attraction and compatibility. "Attracts" indicates compatibility. "Opposes" indicates some difficulties in compatibility, while "passive" is neutral, with no particular benefits or detriments. The home number gives you a little information on your home together.

NUMBER} **1**

Primary Number: Singleness of purpose, achievement, action, strength, leadership, self-reliance, centeredness, divine purpose

Love Number: Intellectual attraction, sudden marriage, romance during foreign travel, married life can lead to boredom without continual stimulus

Vibrates to: 9

Attracts: 4, 8

Opposes: 6, 7

Passive: 2, 3, 5

Home Number: House of leadership. Works best with one independent leadership–style personality, not two. Often the home of the self-employed or someone focused on career. It can be lacking in warmth and a homey atmosphere, and should be tempered with relaxed furnishings, music, and flowers.

NUMBER} **2**

Primary Number: Equality, justice, harmony, balance, understanding, passivity, fatalism

Love Number: Seeks comfort and stability in relationship; seeks practical partner to provide security

Vibrates to: 8, 6

Attracts: 1, 7, 9

Opposes: 5

Passive: 3, 4

Home Number: A home of partnership, cooperation, and duality. Comfortable, playful, childlike, with a lived-in feel to it.

NUMBER} **3**

Primary Number: Creative, confident, optimistic, adaptable, enthusiastic, charming, overconfident, indifferent, impatient

Love Number: Idealistic; longs for the ideal partner; intuition is the best guide in the relationship; picks partners with similar interests and ideals

Vibrates to: 7

Attracts: 5, 6, 9

Opposes: 4, 8

Passive: 1, 2

Home Number: A home that is positive and optimistic, creative and artistic. It might be unusual and bold, and attract people who reflect those qualities. Those residing in a 3 might have a lot of ideas but have difficulty finishing what they start.

NUMBER} **4**

Primary Number: Solidity, strong willed, loyal, honest, conventional, routine

Love Number: Seeks stability of marriage; emotional and affectionate to partners

Vibrates to: 6

Attracts: 1, 8

Opposes: 5

Passive: 2, 3, 7, 9

Home Number: This is a home of practicality, integrity, honesty, and usefulness. Such homes tend to attract those who like to "do it yourself" and to design and decorate. One partner might tend to dominate the other in this situation, but if this tendency is not given in to, then it is quite a happy home.

NUMBER} **5**

Primary Number: Health, prosperity, courage, versatility, empathy, friendship, romance, impulsivity, unreliable

Love Number: Seeks companionship; religion and philosophy play a part in the relationship; seeks to marry for life

Vibrates to: 7

Attracts: 3, 9, 2

Opposes: 4

Passive: 1, 6, 7, 8

Home Number: Usually spacious, open, and expensively decorated, these homes are considered happy and versatile. Residents tend to shy away from routine and seek freedom, but are also nurturing to those of artistic or intellectual talent.

NUMBER} **6**

Primary Number: Harmony, completion, happiness, idealism, kindness, excess, martyrdom

Love Number: Shy, difficulty expressing feelings, rash behavior, ardent lover beneath the shell

Vibrates to: 4, 2

Attracts: 3, 9

Opposes: 1 and 8 (mildly), 5 (deeply)

Passive: 7

Home Number: Homes vibrating to the number 6 are harmonious and protected, and tend to manifest the ideal of tolerance, humanitarianism, and social responsibility. They are cozy and comfortable, full of love and tenderness, and tend to be a safe place for those seeking love or healing, or who are simply down on their luck, looking for help.

NUMBER} **7**

Primary Number: Wisdom, completion, evolution, endurance, intuition, intellectual activity, solitude, overly critical

Love Number: Seen as a flirt; intellectually and physically active, and seeks a partner with similar interests; loyal partner when in a relationship

Vibrates to: 3, 5

Attracts: 2, 6

Opposes: 1, 9

Passive: 4, 8

Home Number: This is a home of hard work and independence. It requires a zone within it for quiet and recharging the spiritual batteries. Pets, particularly cats, do well in a 7, and occupants are spiritual, psychic, and natural healers.

NUMBER} **8**

Primary Number: Organizing, loyal, strong, steady, practical, blunt

Love Number: Seeks travel, change, and variety; often seeks an older partner; business with partner usually successful

Vibrates to: 2, 5

Attracts: 1, 4

Opposes: 3, 6

Passive: 7, 9

Home Number: This home is one of power and prosperity. Those who dwell in it are confident and daring, and their home reflects this. They are usually immaculately clean, luxuriously decorated, and comfortable. The occupants usually have the finances to upkeep such a home and are independent and driven.

NUMBER} **9**

Primary Number: Perfectionism, intellect, understanding, logic, philosophy, fine arts, dreamy, lethargic

Love Number: Seeks marriage to complete life, can miss obvious incompatibilities with a potential partner and lead to later difficulties, idealizes love

Vibrates to: 1

Attracts: 2, 3, 6

Opposes: 7

Passive: 4, 5, 8

Home Number: Number 9 homes are artistic, compassionate, and sensitive. Some would describe them as "shabby," but they are still pleasing to the eye. They are filled with unique items from around the world and have a large library. Inhabitants are artistic or in a care-giving profession for a career.

Relationship Cycles

While understanding the compatibility between partners is important, it is not the only factor determining success in a relationship. As mentioned earlier, when two or more people come together, they create something new, a relationship, and that relationship has its own life cycle, spirit, and power. This is the same dynamic that occurs when a group of magickal practitioners come together to form a coven or lodge: they create a collective thoughtform of the group, but it is much more than just mental energy, as implied in the term *thoughtform*. It has its own emotional energy and spiritual awareness. While a magickal group's spirit has a different purpose than a relationship, they are still much the same. Both must be honored, respected, and nurtured to have a successful union.

A powerful way to understand the life cycles of all things, including relationships, is to look at the four elements. Witches, magicians, and many other practitioners call the elemental forces when creating sacred space, as outlined in the "circle magick" section of chapter 7. The circle is a microcosm of creation, and the casting of the circle is like a creation story, a life cycle. Different traditions view this creation story differently, based upon their own mythos and the correspondences between elements and directions, but this life cycle can be seen in all things, including relationships. This concept applied to relationships is best demonstrated in the writings and teachings of the author Starhawk.

While my own tradition is a bit different, a common Neopagan expression of the elements is east—air, south—fire, west—water, and north—earth, with the tradition starting in the east. When you first meet someone, it's a very intellectual process, really. You get to know each other by sharing stories, thoughts, and beliefs. You bond on this mental level of sharing history to better understand each other's viewpoint. At this stage, you can determine if you are mentally compatible. Are your worldviews complementary or clashing?

Fire is the passion of the relationship. Once you determine to step forward, there is passion and sex. You go with your attractions—attraction that is often established, or at least deepened, as you get to know each other intellectually. Passion is powerful, but it cannot be the only aspect of the relationship. If it is, the relationship will soon burn out.

The experience deepens, and the water element, the power of love, begins to have power over the relationship. Infatuation, attraction, and passion all deepen to a sense of love, romantic and/or spiritual. A deeper emotional bond is forged with the partner.

Lastly, a commitment is made. The earth element of stability takes over to guide the relationship as a life is built together, and all the mundane and physical details of money, home, food, and possessions must be sorted out.

While that is one valid expression of the cycle of life, it is not the only one. My own tradition tends to start in the north and the earth element, and fire is placed in the east (air is placed in the south and water in the west). Another interpretation could be given this way: You must come together on the physical plane. This isn't necessarily sex, or even physically meeting face to face, but making a real-world connection to the partner. Many of us dream of a lover or "feel" they are close by, but until we make that connection on the material level, not the psychic level, the relationship has not yet begun. Though there is an earthy "magnetism" that draws us together, it is not successful until it actually brings us together.

After initial contact, it is through the sense of sight, the sense corresponding to the fire element, that attraction begins and passions build up. Some relationships start sexually, some do not, but that energetic exchange begins right away. Passion and sexuality are exchanges of pure energy, of life force, as we learn about each other on a very primal level and have experiences that we struggle to put into words and feelings.

Then, with this bond, we explore the thoughts, beliefs, and views of our partner via the air element. We really share what we think and believe, our view on the world. Although there might be deep magnetic and energetic attraction from the first two elements, it is here we might determine our compatibility or lack thereof.

If we go forward from the air element, the bond deepens emotionally through the water element. We make an emotional commitment to each other. The full turning of the wheel through the elements then brings us back to earth, where we take the step to make a physical commitment and perhaps join our lives together.

While these two are not the only ways of looking at the life of a relationship through the elements, they are two that are most helpful to me. The important thing to realize through any life cycle of a relationship, or anything else for that matter, is that the pattern must repeat to survive. It doesn't end with earth, with stability and sharing a life together, and then you get happily ever after. There is no guaranteed happily ever after, even with magick. Relationships are work. The circle is a spiral that continues to expand and grow deeper over time if you both put energy into the relationship. It becomes both easier and harder. You get to know each other on a deeper level, yet you are challenged to experience the new because you know each other so well. You must go through the cycles of attraction, sharing passion, love, and commitment again and again, constantly renewing your relationship, just as the earth's life cycle is constantly renewed through the turning of the wheel of the year. If you stop, the wheel of your relationship breaks and can potentially end if you are not careful and committed. Many people stay with a broken wheel while keeping their outer-world commitments to each other, and grow unhappy and unhealthy, living a life unfulfilled. Some break commitments by seeking excitement outside of the vows and agreements of the relationship. The only remedy is open communication and working to turn the wheel of your relationship together, to constantly renew and rekindle the life force of your relationship.

EXERCISE} **Contemplating Your Relationship**

In your journal, reflect on your past and present relationships with the elemental cycles in mind. Do you have a particular pattern to the elements in your own magickal practice? Does this pattern, when applied in this manner, help illuminate your experiences and understand the life of your relationship? If you are currently in a relationship, do you see where you are in the cycle? Understand that each part of the cycle has a number of subcycles, so our human experience is not cut and dried. Contemplation of your experience is helpful in making the best future decisions.

Rekindling Magick

Now that you have an idea of how you relate and a greater vocabulary, you can use your magick to help your relationships grow healthy and not need anything drastic magickally or otherwise. As you grow and tend together, you will naturally evolve. It doesn't mean there won't be bumps in the road, but you will face them together because you will be living life together.

The two biggest complaints those in long-term relationships have is the dwindling of romance and the dwindling of sexual intensity. When you first come together, you not only put a lot of effort into romance, but the sex is new and exciting. The more you are with your partner, particularly having sex, the more energy you exchange, and the more like each other you become. The intensity is diminished because a familiarity has grown. The couple must put time and energy into romance and sexuality. They must put energy into the traditional romantic aspect of the relationship and also be willing to try new things to add new energy to their sexual relationship.

SPELL} **Increase Passion**

A spell from Italian folk magick also found in the teachings of author Draja Mickaharic suggests you place a half teaspoon of sesame seeds with one tablespoon of ground coffee (unused) and the hair of your lover into a sealed container, such as a small box or bag. Though this folk magick says nothing about doing things on a Friday or as the Moon waxes, such timing can increase your success rate. The container is then put in the couple's bedroom. If you can do this with your partner so you are putting conscious energy and attention toward it together, so much the better. Traditionally, this spell was done in secret to arouse passion instinctively, without your spouse knowing you did magick.

From personal experience, I have to say this is a very effective spell, but there is something specific about the mixture of coffee and sesame seeds. Once, without referring to my notes, I did the same spell but with equal measures of anise seed and coffee, and it didn't work at all. When I performed it again correctly, there was an instant result.

RITUAL} **Planting an Apple Tree**

An excellent ritual of commitment is to do something together that you will both have to nurture and care for, and as you do, you are magickally reaffirming your commitment to each other. For a couple with property, I've found this apple tree ritual to be helpful: plant a tree together. At first, this doesn't seem like a very magickal operation, but if Witches are truly stewards of nature, revering the old ones of the natural world, then tree fostering is a large part of our work. The apple tree is the best choice for this spell, as it's traditionally associated with love and magick, and most commercially sold apple trees are grafted trees, meaning the root stock is grafted to the top fruit-bearing portions. Magickally, this is symbolic of two lives coming together, grafting together, each with their own attributes and strengths, each with their own weaknesses, and each sharing their life with the other. Over time, as the two grafted portions grow, a ring emerges where the bark meets, reminding us of the image of the wedding ring as a talisman of love and commitment.

Though apple trees can be planted in the spring, they are best planted in autumn, as the leaves are falling. Consult with your local plant nursery about the trees available in your area, as well as soil conditions and planting instructions. If apple trees are not conducive to your area, find a fruit-bearing tree that is. Generally, they should be planted during the waxing Moon, ideally when the Moon is in the signs of Cancer, Pisces, Scorpio, or Taurus for both planting fertility and magickal fertility, though Sagittarius is specifically the sign for planting fruit trees, and the sense of new adventure that is embodied by Sagittarius can be wonderful for recommitment, as you continue a new phase of your life together.

Plant the tree ritually, asking the gods and spirits to bless the tree. Promise the spirit of the tree that you will continue with its care and maintenance. Planting a tree is a commitment, particularly a fruit tree, which is part of the point of this magick.

Each of you should place something important to you as a symbol, token, or talisman of your renewed commitment. It could be a promise written out on paper or a piece of jewelry or a stone. Put it in the hole before you plant the tree. Then plant the tree and fill in the hole. Mix a bit of honey with the water you are going to use to water the tree, and pour it out together as a libation to the gods, to the tree spirit, and to the spirit of your relationship.

Continue the care of the tree together. Do not let one person handle all the responsibilities. Make time to do it together. Make the care of the tree a special part of your relationship. As it grows, watch your own love grow.

RECIPE} **Wine of Love**

1 bottle of sweet/fruity white wine

1 sliced red apple

4 sliced strawberries

2 vanilla beans or 2 tablespoons vanilla extract

1 fresh red or pink rose, or 1 tablespoon dried rose petals

A variation of the Wine of Lust in the previous chapter is a mulled Wine of Love. Again, pour the contents of the wine bottle into a saucepan. Add the ingredients and stir them with a wooden spoon or wand. Let the wine simmer for a short time, fifteen to twenty minutes, and let the wine cool before serving. Strain out the plant matter. Those who drink of this wine will increase their sense of love, romance, and connection to their partner, particularly when the couple drinks it together. It can be used in rituals together, and even as the chalice drink in a handfasting.

SPELL} **Happy Home Wash**

Emerald

Turquoise

Amethyst

1 teaspoon balm of Gilead

1 teaspoon rue

1 teaspoon catnip

9 drops lemon oil

5 drops rose geranium oil (or a handful of fresh geranium flowers)

3 drops frankincense oil

10 of Cups tarot card

Make a weak infusion of balm of Gilead, rue, and catnip by adding the herbs to a large glass bowl of hot water. If you are afraid to use catnip because you don't want to get your cats too "stoned," you can substitute passionflower. Beneath the bowl, place the 10 of Cups tarot card. Place the three stones, each charged for peace and harmony at home, in the water, and allow them to sit overnight. Strain out the herbs and stones, and add the potion to a bucket of water. Add the drops of oil to the water and use this as a floor wash. You can also add a small amount of it to the clothes in the washing machine.

VISUALIZATION} **Astral Kisses**

Distance can play havoc in the growth and development of a relationship. As someone who travels a lot, I understand this well. One technique I've found to be very helpful in reinforcing the bonds of relationship is not a spell or traditional ritual but an act of psychic power. Before going to sleep, count down into a meditative state. Think of your lover or partner. Imagine your partner, wherever she or he is. Simply imagine psychically reaching out to your loved one and giving them a kiss good night, reestablishing the bonds of the relationship on a psychic level. While I've done this mostly in a romantic context, it can be done for any loved one—children, parents, or siblings.

RITUAL} **Aphrodite**

By deepening your relationship with the goddess of love, you can deepen your relationship, heal it, and even transform it. This particular ritual is specifically for Aphrodite, though it can be adapted to suit any other deity of love with whom you feel kinship and connection.

This ritual requires you to make the wine of love (page 238) and the love bread (page 152) as an offering and sacrament. If you cannot make them in time to do this ritual, find another suitable wine and bread to consecrate in this work. Like most Aphrodite work, do this on a Friday.

- Cleanse the space and yourself.

- Anoint yourself with a love potion or oil you feel is appropriate to your intention for this ritual.

- Cast the circle.

- Call the quarters.

- Say the evocation of Aphrodite:

I call to you, O Goddess Aphrodite,

granter of love in all forms,

be here with me. Feel my love for you. Bless me with your presence.

I call to you, Aphrodite Ourania,

goddess of celestial love, goddess of the heavenly ideal of love,

perfect and splendid, love without end.

I call to you, Aphrodite Genetrix,

goddess of marital love, goddess of partnership,

balanced in harmony, love with commitment.

I call to you, Aphrodite Nymphia,

goddess of young love, protectress of the unmarried,

youthful and pure, love with innocence.

I call to you, Aphrodite Porne,

goddess of erotic love, patron of sexuality,

lustful and animalistic, love in the flesh.

In all your faces and forms, dark and light,

I call to you, Aphrodite.

- Consecrate the bread and wine:

In your holy name, I bless this bread. I bless this wine.

Foods of love, given by the gods,

transformed by the hands of humanity,

I offer these to you. I seek to know your ways.

I offer these to you. I seek to grow in my
capacity to give and receive love.
I offer these to you. I seek the mystery of
Perfect Love and wish to embody it in my life.

Take a small piece of bread and dunk it in the wine; eat it. Take a larger portion of the bread and offer it to Aphrodite. Take the chalice of wine and offer it to Aphrodite. If outdoors, place the bread in the west, the direction of water, and pour the wine on it as a libation to the goddess.

May all my relationships—human, animal, plant, and spirit—
be touched by your love and blessing. May I see the love in all
things, creating, binding, and destroying all of nature, all of
the universe, from now until the end of time. Blessed be.

- Meditate. Take this time to contemplate your work. Ask for guidance. Check in with your feelings and senses. Journal. You can even repeat the journey to the Temple of Love exercise.

- Say the devocation:

We thank you, Great Aphrodite, in all
your forms, with all your faces.
Thank you for opening the mysteries of love to us.
May there always be peace between us.
Hail and farewell.

- Release the quarters.

- Release the circle.

Handfastings

One of the most powerful things a couple can do to deepen their relationship is to formally commit to each other through ceremony. Traditionally we think of this as marriage. With current debates raging in the United States about civil unions for same-sex couples and the nature of marriage as a religious or civil institution, many people have strong ideas of what marriage is or isn't. In Paganism, we usually call the commitment ceremony itself a handfasting, as the two hands are joined together with a cord as part of this ritual.

Many Pagan traditions ask that you handfast for a year and a day to make sure you are compatible, somewhat similar to an engagement period. Following that, you are either asked to renew your vows every year for another year-and-a-day period or, after the first, make a formal, and perhaps legal, commitment.

While many consult astrology, tarot, and runes for advice on when the most auspicious time for the event to be performed, we can also find advice in old folk wisdom. An Old English poem for the days of the week and marriage, found in Nigel Pennick's collection of Northern lore, *Practical Magic in the Northern Tradition*, tells us the blessing and curse of each day if you choose to marry on it:

> Monday for wealth,
> Tuesday for health,
> Wednesday the best day of all.
> Thursday for losses,
> Friday for crosses,
> And Saturday no luck at all.

It is interesting to note that in our modern society, most weddings occur on Friday or Saturday to accommodate the work week. Few are held on the first three days of the week. Strangely, Sunday is missing from the poem, perhaps for religious reasons, as the poem is from a

Christian era. I guess intuition won out in my own wedding, as we chose a lovely Wednesday afternoon; the anniversary of our meeting fell on a Wednesday in the year we chose to make a formal commitment, and we wanted to keep the same anniversary date.

For the ritual itself, a handfasting can take many forms. When I have a couple visit me, we discuss many of the life-planning questions that should be discussed by a couple before they plan to get married, though sadly, many don't. They are blinded by the romance of it and don't really know how compatible they are for a long-term commitment.

If you are planning on marrying someone, make sure you've discussed long-term life goals. Are they compatible? Where do you want to live long-term? Do you want children? How involved are your families in your life? What expectations and boundaries do you have toward sexuality? Those are all important things to discuss first.

Once the basics of premarital counseling are out of the way, we discuss how "witchy" or Pagan the event is to be. Some handfasting ceremonies are full magick circles, while others involve different kinds of rituals to create a sacred space. Many are low-key in terms of esoterics, in an effort to be more welcoming to non-Pagan family members. Most Pagan handfastings involve the basic elements you find in many wedding ceremonies. You can have the traditional exchange of vows and exchange of rings. To make it a handfasting, there is an actual ritual of fastening the hands together.

The traditional handfasting uses a cord that is the length of the bride's middle finger to elbow plus the length of the groom's middle finger to elbow and ties the couple's hands together in the ceremony. The couple faces each other, holding hands and imitating the "figure eight" infinity loop as they hold hands. The cord is tied around them (see next page for an illustration).

Usually the cord is released by the end of the ceremony so the couple can walk out hand in hand. A variation of the handfasting for those who want to keep it tied during the entire ceremony is to simply have the

FIGURE} The Handfasting card from
the Well Worn Path deck
(art by Mickie Mueller)

couple hold hands side by side and join the hands together that way, wrapping the cord around them.

Another traditional element is the couple "jumping the broom." The broom is a symbol of hearth and home, and jumping together marks them starting a new life together, joined together and in a new home. Traditionally, Witch's brooms are made from ash handle, birch bristles, and willow to tie it all together, but handfasting brooms can have a variety of different herbs and woods to confer more blessings. The broom is then displayed in their home somewhere to bring blessings, love, health, and fortune.

Here is an example of a simple handfasting ritual to inspire your own ideas. I use this as a template for when I speak to couples seeking a handfasting. We adapt it and draw upon other sources to make each wedding unique for the couple. For some couples, we do a ceremony of intricate ritual and high Witchcraft; for others, we make it Pagan friendly but very down-to-earth for non-Pagan family and friends.

RITUAL} **Handfasting**

- Cleanse and prepare the space and the participants.

- Wedding party procession.

- Cast the circle.

- Call the quarters.

- Say the evocation to the gods:

> *We call to the two who move as one in the love of the Great Spirit. We call to the Goddess and the God, the Great Mother and Great Father of Creation, to bless this union of hearts and lives. Hail and welcome.*

If the couple has a special relationship with any specific goddesses or gods, we also call them or tailor the evocation to suit those deities.

- Welcome and introduce the tradition of handfasting to the guests.

- Poetic reading of blessing by the best man and/or the maid of honor. Here is an opportunity to engage the wedding party or other family members. Sometimes a poem is read, either from traditional material or one composed specifically for the couple. As options, the Charge of the Goddess and the Charge of the God have been read by the maid of honor and the best man respectively, or there may be an offering of song or dance.

- The Great Rite is shared by the couple:

    As the sword is to the grail, the blade is to the chalice, truth is to love. Together, in Perfect Love and Perfect Trust, we drink in the blessings and powers of the Goddess and God. Blessed be.

    One holds the chalice while the other one holds the blade. The blade is plunged into the chalice, blessing the wine or mead.

- Unity candle—In the tradition of the unity candle, which is not specifically Pagan, two candles are lit to represent each family of the couple. Then the unity candle is lit to recognize the joining of the two families with the couple. One of the parents, or a close friend or member of the wedding party from each side, can light the family candle.

I light this candle for the family of (name).
May they shine bright and strong.

Repeat for the other family. Then the couple, together, lights the central flame with both of the family candles.

We light this candle of unity together, joining our lives, our homes,
our families. May our new family shine bright and strong.

- Exchange vows.

- Exchange rings.

- Handfasting.

- Pronouncement.

- Say the devocation of the gods:

  We thank the two who move as one in the love of the Great
  Spirit. We thank the Goddess, the Great Mother; we thank
  the God, the Great Father; we thank all spirits who have
  come in Perfect Love and Perfect Trust to bless this union.
  Stay if you will, go if you must. Hail and farewell.

- Release the quarters.

- Release the circle.

TEN

Be Careful What You Ask For...

...because you probably will get it. But once you get it, will it be everything you thought it would be? Probably not. Many people enter into relationships and love magick thinking it will solve all their problems. If they just find the right person, then everything will be great. It doesn't work that way. Sometimes the overwhelming desire to be coupled outweighs common sense, and we stay in relationships that we intuitively know are not right for us. Sometimes our romantic illusions and erroneous beliefs or attachments to how things "should be" poison our relationships. Magick is not the quick fix to these issues.

Love magick is powerful; there's no denying that. My friend Chris, who has worked in several metaphysical bookstores, likes to tell people that you can always tell when love magick is working. People will call up after doing a spell and be irate that the love spell is not working—the object of their affection is not paying attention to them. How can they fix the spell? They expect to hear that the sign a spell is working includes some tale of grand signs from the gods or the behavior of the person who is the object of desire, but no. Chris tells them that obsession about the spell or person by the spellcaster is the first sign the spell is working—not necessarily working well, as not all love magick is successful, but it is doing something, mostly to the spellcaster. If we can't go into it with an open heart and sense of divine connection, we can still get what we ask for and technically have a successful spell, but it might not be what we really want or need. In the end, it might cause more heartache than be a cure to our loneliness.

There is a power to our obsession that gets us what we asked for but not what we truly need. When a love spell is working in a healthy way, there is a sense of letting go and of being sure that the forces have been set in motion and, when the time is right, will bear fruit. You can't rush a love spell any more than you can rush a plant growing.

In the end, true love magick includes the preparatory work to recognize our own illusions and pitfalls as well as the magick to make healthy and clean separations when a relationship ends. Finally, for love magick to truly be useful, it must help us heal the traumas of previous relationships so we can learn to love again with a full and open heart.

Breaking Illusions

A big piece of successful love magick is not only getting what you asked for but getting what you truly want. We must do the introspective work to sort through our own illusions, the self-sabotaging ideas and behaviors we have that prevent us from having successful relationships, and hope our potential partner has done similar work. While this can be done through serious journaling, talk therapy, or any number of self-help techniques, the ritualistic and meditative practices of Witchcraft can help us greatly to see, understand, and transform our patterns.

Here are some common patterns in the quest for love that we need to be aware of. Do any of them strike a cord within you?

I'm Not Worthy—If a relationship does not turn out the way we envision and expect, or if we've never been able to have a relationship, there is a tendency to think we are not worthy of having a successful relationship. The issue becomes less about our relationship with a potential partner and more about our relationship with ourselves. Self-love and self-esteem are the keys to breaking this illusion. With the way magick works, if you really believe you're not worthy of having a successful relationship, then you won't be able to create one.

Tragic Love—Many people are strongly attached to the idea of tragic love. Love must be a struggle. There must be a dramatic tale before we can truly make a commitment. Those with such beliefs then create drama in their lives and the life of their potential partner so life can live up to their dramatic expectations. Some find a potential partner they have a real connection with and assume the partner is their soul mate and will always be there, despite the drama. They go through break-up and reunion cycles over and over again, and usually one partner gets healthier and ends the cycle rather than be stuck with someone who is not mature enough to make a commitment and work through any issues that arise. Others will find a potential partner but then put career ambitions first, believing they cannot simultaneously work on two aspects of life at once. Anyone in a strong relationship knows that you are working on all areas of your life, including relationships, all at once. If you wait for a time to focus on a relationship only, you'll be waiting a long time.

Prince/Princess Charming—We look to a partner to be the ultimate lover, fulfilling all our fantasies like a prince or princess from a fairy tale. And at first, they can appear to be that perfect, but as the relationship continues, we realize they are not so perfect and have not only their own problems but their own needs. If we focus solely on our needs being fulfilled by a partner, we create a very imbalanced relationship. If our partner wants to satisfy our needs and be the perfect love, they will not always speak up about their own needs, assuming that their partner will "know" somehow. Things are left unsaid until the imbalance is very critical, and most relationships of this nature don't survive unless the imbalance is addressed with open and honest communication.

Unhealthy Apotheosis—Apotheosis generally refers to the deification of another, elevating an individual to the status of a god. In some ritual context, it is the identification of your own godself, but in a relationship, it refers to the glorification and deification of a partner beyond the bounds of humanity. Many people will glorify their partners to such an extent, particularly talented magickal or psychic partners, mistaking magickal gifts for total enlightenment. The partner doing the glorification assumes their elevated partner will know everything they are feeling and doing, therefore verbal communication will be unnecessary. One cannot live up to such a superhuman ideal one hundred percent of the time, no matter how spiritual or psychic one is. Like anyone put upon a pedestal, once they are discovered to have clay feet—to be only mortal—there is disappointment and disillusionment. But only then does the relationship have the possibility of growing into something true and honest.

Codependence—Codependence is a popular psychology term used for those who exhibit caring for others that is excessive and inappropriate in our society. Usually the object of such attention is someone they are in a relationship with, romantic or otherwise, and there is some sense of need or dependence upon the codependent. Actions and patterns of the codependent include excessive caretaking, controlling behavior, distrust, perfectionism, and hypervigilance. Such behavior is more common in families that have undergone traumatic conditions, but the behavior can then affect other areas of life. Those who have lived in a codependent family can seek to re-create those conditions in their own adult relationships. Codependents usually seek out people who are either emotionally needy and want to be taken care of or are emotionally unavailable, creating relationships that are ultimately unfulfilling for the codependent, who attempts to control the relationship. For true happiness, one exhibiting codependence patterns must learn to identify and heal those patterns in order to create a stable, intimate, and healthy relationship.

Unconditional Love vs. Unconditional Relationships—While as spiritual people we aspire to live a life of unconditional spiritual love, we can easily mistake unconditional love for unconditional relationships. In Witchcraft, our Perfect Love is not an unconditional relationship. Too often we fall into the illusion that if we could just love enough, love unconditionally, then our relationship would be fine. You can love someone spiritually and not like them. You can love someone both spiritually and romantically and not accept their behavior and draw a boundary when something unacceptable is said or done. Some relationships can only be healed when both partners are willing to work on all aspects. As a spiritual practitioner, you do not hold the burden for making something work. You must learn to love yourself as well. An ended relationship is not a mark against your spiritual development or qualities; in fact, it can be quite the opposite.

Magickal Stipulations—One of the greatest reasons our love magick "fails" is the conscious and unconscious stipulations we put into our magick. Often these stipulations are safeguards and work well in the end, but when we question why our love magick isn't working right now, this can be the reason. We have to become conscious of our stipulations if we are not already, and then decide to either retain them and wait or break them and hope for more immediate success yet less predictable results. A good friend of mine had a successful love spell to find his husband. In the spell, he asked that the right man for him be at least twenty-eight. He passed his future husband almost every day walking to work for years, but they never spoke until nine days after his future husband's twenty-eighth birthday. I also had an age stipulation but simply worded it as "when we are both ready for each other." I got a direct message that my partner was at a club. I went to that club. I left disappointed that I left alone, without meeting anybody new. I found out years later, he was often at that club at that time, but we were both in a place where we said we wanted a relationship but weren't really ready for it until two years later. While both those examples eventually worked in our favor, some people's stipulations are on how much money a potential lover makes, specific physical requirements of height, eye color, hair color, or specific zodiac Sun signs. I know when I released all my physical stipulations on body, height, build— my "type"—I was open for the perfect partner. My only physical stipulation was "that I find him very attractive and he find me very attractive." It worked out perfectly.

When Relationships End

Everything earthly has a life cycle. Everything is born, everything lives, and everything must eventually end. While we have this romantic notion of true love lasting our lifetime and beyond—and I truly do believe that is possible for many of us—we must face the fact that many relationships do not last our entire lifetime and beyond, at least as romantic relationships. While we put a lot of our magickal energy and time into finding a relationship, and sometimes into sustaining a relationship, rituals of separation and release are neglected. They are just as important, if not more important, for they help us release what no longer serves us or our life and move on, beginning the healing process. They should not be ignored.

Before moving on to the separation rituals for a relationship, one of the frequently asked questions is whether a spell can be done to return a lost love and start over. The simple answer is yes, such a spell can be done—but one must ask if there is wisdom to such an action. When we are in heartbreak and really want our lover back, wisdom and common sense go out the window, and we find ourselves crossing lines, magickally and morally, that we might not otherwise cross. Sometimes we get obsessed with the spells to return our love, and we lose sight of our own spiritual evolution and day-to-day happiness.

Most spiritual practitioners who aid others would suggest doing a return spell only if you feel it is absolutely necessary upon deep reflection. Once you decide to do it, give yourself twenty-four hours to think about it. If you still want to do it, do it, but impose limits for yourself and stick to them. I suggest a limit of doing it three times at most, and if the love has not returned of his or her own free will without you having to manipulate the situation further, then stop. If you have to arrange your paths to cross or otherwise stalk your ex to make contact, then you have gone too far. If the love does not return within six months, give up and do rituals of release and separation. Move on, and focus on other interests and other potential relationships. Realize that your period of "rebound" will be longer because you've put more energy into the end of the relationship and recapturing what you once had, making it even more difficult to move on and recover.

SPELL} Lost Love

Take a piece of amber and cleanse it as you would any ritual object. As the Moon is waxing, hold it and think of your love. Pray to the gods to return your love if it be for the highest good of all involved. Pour into the amber all your emotion regarding the return of your love. Then put it someplace dark, like a box at the bottom of one of your dresser drawers, and forget about it, letting it work its magick. Amber is a great "stone" for this spell, as it has both projective and receptive qualities. If the love is good for you both, it will draw you together, but if it's not, it will project you away from each other. Amber is also very healing and can absorb your hurt emotions as you do this spell, helping you recover from the breakup and prepare to reconcile or move on separately.

Once you are ready to release a relationship, you should do some form of separation ritual. Separation rituals can be divided into two forms. Simple separation rituals are to signal both the universe and your own psyche that you and your lover are no longer a unit, working together, but have separated. If both parties are magickally inclined, it's great to have both involved in such separation rituals, though this is not always possible. Just because someone is understanding doesn't mean they want to spend any more time with you.

The second type of ritual is known as a banishment and can be used both in love and in other relationships. It is used both to end a particularly difficult or toxic relationship and to prevent it from reestablishing. Usually this is done when you want to end the relationship but your partner does not or feels malice or great anger toward you. Banishments are a form of psychic protection. Sometimes with particularly strong relationships, we begin to take on the traits or even illnesses of our partners, and that psychic connection needs to be broken.

SPELL} **Breaking Your Own Relationship**

1 teaspoon rue

1 teaspoon basil

1 teaspoon nettles

Self-igniting charcoal disc

Incense burner

This spell is for those who want to end their relationship, particularly when they live together but for some reason don't want to initiate a direct confrontation. Mix the rue and basil together and burn on a charcoal disc in a flameproof incense burner or other vessel. Another option is to omit the charcoal and simply set a match to the herbs and let them smolder. In either case, fill the house with its smoke. It can be very smoky, so you might need to disengage your smoke alarms. Once you have fumigated the house with this blend, open all the windows. Meditate or pray that the relationship will end immediately. Imagine the energy and vital life force of the relationship going out through the windows. When your lover returns, there will be an incident that will spark the end of the relationship. If you do choose to initiate the end, it will be easier after you've done this spell.

RITUAL} **Separation**

For those who have a magickally oriented ex-partner who understands the value of ritual and is willing to do the separation ritual with you, this is ideal. You both entered into a relationship, and if you did any ritual together, it's best to do a ritual to signal to the gods, powers, and universe that the union is now over.

The ritual can be as simple or as complicated as you desire. If you were handfasted together, it might be a bit more complicated, for you want to undo the parts of the handfasting. In this case, the particulars of the ritual might be based on your handfasting ritual.

Gather these supplies:

3 candles

Cord

Scissors

For a simple ritual, start by casting a circle. Light a single candle at first, and light it in the name of the relationship. Hold a cord or string taut between you and your ex (if you were handfasted, use that cord; otherwise, a string is fine). Then cut the string, signifying that the ties that bind you together are cut freely and of your own will. Each of you take a candle and light it from the central candle, symbolizing how you are taking back your light from the relationship. Together, snuff the central candle. Release the circle. Walk away with your own candle lit, in opposite directions.

If you are doing a "hand unfastening" ritual, you would cut your ritual cord, or at the very least unbraid it. You would also give back each other's rings and recite words to release each other from any vows or promises. If you jumped a broom, that broom should be ritually destroyed.

POPPET} Banishment of an Ex

Sometimes we have a former partner, or even someone with romantic interest that we never consummate with so much as a date, who simply won't take the message that the relationship is not happening and move on. I believe most of these situations can be handled with direct, clear, and forceful communication, but every so often, we have a situation that requires some form of banishment.

Make a poppet of the ex or would-be partner as you would for the lust poppet spell, but rather than fill it with love and lust herbs, fill it with Saturn and Mars herbs. While many Saturn herbs are toxic, the intention is not to kill the ex but to kill their love toward you. Saturn and Mars herbs are also protective. You want to be safe, and, despite the problems caused, you don't want any harm to come to your ex. You can also use calming and tranquilizing herbs. You can fill the poppet with tobacco (Mars), monkshood (Saturn), Solomon's seal (Saturn), nettles (Mars), thistle (Mars), passionflower (Mercury / tranquilizing), valerian root (Mercury / tranquilizing), angelica root (Sun / protective), chamomile (Sun / Mercury / tranquilizing), and myrrh (Saturn). You can also fill it with salt, to kill the love that is growing in his or her heart.

Empower the poppet, baptizing it in the name of the person, and then get rid of it. Say:

> In the name of the gods, I release and banish this person,
> (name them), from my life, in Perfect Love and Perfect
> Trust. May no harm befall you or me from this spell,
> but may we both find joy, blessings, health, wealth, and
> happiness completely away from each other. I ask this to
> be for the highest good, harming none. So mote it be.

Leave it in a crossroads and bless the person away and out of your life, to move on to other places and people. Bury it far away from your home. Bring it to the ocean. Get rid of it somehow, never to return. If you put it in a swamp, make sure it's a true swamp where things rot, rather than a bog that will preserve it. The doll must rot away. You can speed the rotting process by anointing it in a solution of what author M. R. Sellars describes as swamp water, outlined in Dorothy Morrison's book *Utterly Wicked*. Make a solution of aspirin and water, and the acid will help break things down faster. Soaking the doll in swamp water will speed the decomposition process along. Don't throw it in a river, as "sweet" water (unsalted water that is flowing) generally brings things back to us and is not the best place for banishment.

As the doll breaks down, so will the unhealthy attachment to you, and you will be free.

WASH} **Banish an Unrequited Love**

While orchids are known for their love and lust properties and Venusian rulership, they also have a baneful quality granted by the planet Saturn. If you wish to get rid of someone who is very attracted to you or claims to love you, and you do not feel the same, either because you never did or because the relationship is over and you want to move on, arrange to meet with this person.

Before you meet, pick dried and withered orchid flowers, ideally on the waning Moon. Grind them in a mortar and pestle with a little water until you have a paste. Smear the paste on your hands and think of severing the connection of attraction between the two of you. Let it dry, and gently rub your hands to just remove the dried paste but not scrub away the virtue of the spell. Touch the person, flesh to flesh, with whom you wish to disconnect. After you touch, the attraction will be no more, and the person will seek out others, losing any obsession or fixation. Then you can wash your hands.

This spell seems to work best for unrequited, one-way love, rather than ending a past mutual relationship.

SPELL} **Dispelling a Love Spell Placed On You**

If you believe that someone has put a love spell on you, and you intellectually don't want to respond but you feel as if you are being erotically enticed, compelled, or commanded, first sit down and really evaluate the situation. Who do you think put the spell on you? Is it an intentional ritual or simply that they have a strong, untrained psychic will? Do they know how to do this or know others who would teach them? How likely is it, or are you experiencing paranoia? Sometimes we want to blame our feelings on another, or on another's magick, or we want to give in to feelings but not take responsibility for them. If possible, seek out another magickal practitioner who is not personally involved and have a divination done to determine the true root of the issue and if you should break any spell.

If you determine you need to break a love spell cast on you, you need what is called an uncrossing or unhexing spell. They come in the forms of oils, baths, floor washes, and incense. I prefer this bath, for it immerses you in protection, no matter where the spell has "hit" you, and powerfully releases it. Whether you practice magick or not, this spell is effective for anyone. While doing the spell in ritual and with clear intent is powerful, the inherent virtue of the substance does much of the work, so I've been able to give similar formulas to clients who are not magickal practitioners, and they have still performed it successfully.

Mix the following together and either make a tea of it and strain it to add to your bath water or put the herbs in a cheesecloth or muslin bag and make the "tea" right in the bathtub. White lilies are usually available at florists, but if you can't get them, you can substitute a rose.

1 white lily flower

1 tablespoon hyssop leaf

1 tablespoon cinquefoil

1 tablespoon vervain

Fill the bathtub with the tea and warm water and to it add five tablespoons of sea salt and the contents of one can or bottle of beer. The beer helps break all forms of curses and hexes. Bathe in the mixture for at least ten minutes—even immerse your head. Ideally, get out of the tub and towel dry without washing it off for at least a few hours, if not overnight. Then shower and clean yourself, and all ill magicks cast against you should be gone. For persistent spells, you might need to repeat it for three baths total.

When the spell breaks, the caster might consciously or unconsciously recognize it and come calling on you, so be prepared for a final confrontation. Once you are aware and have broken the spell once, it's hard for the caster to successfully recast it, as your resistance will be stronger.

Breaking Up the Heart of Stone

Sometimes love lost can leave us feeling hurt, confused, betrayed, and more alone than ever before. While each relationship can teach us something, if we are not in the place to learn, we not only miss those valuable lessons but cannot truly move on and be trusting and open enough to let ourselves fully love another again. We don't like to feel vulnerable or at risk, and sometimes it's easier to shut our heart down from love than truly heal. Some actually believe the heart becomes hard spiritually, like stone. To curse someone with a heart of stone is a curse to make the heart impenetrable by love.

Part of embodying the Witch's heart is to live from a place of love—love for self, love for others, love for all—our Perfect Love. If we cannot love ourselves or another truly, we cannot foster our connection to Perfect Love. It is our moral duty to heal ourselves from difficult and disastrous relationships so we can continue to walk the path of the Witch.

Healing magick for the emotional self is a very powerful form of love magick. It is self-love magick. Only when we heal—when we crack the casing of the heart of stone and let love in, when we love ourselves—can we truly love another. The following spells help us heal our hearts after a relationship has ended and prepare us to love again.

TINCTURE} **Release from the Pangs of Love**

Even though we can intellectually know that a relationship is over, we don't always emotionally accept the reality. We feel harmed by the pangs of love, even when the love is gone. A spell to help you be released from these pangs of love involves basil, both a purifying and a love herb. The basil can be used two ways. Either put a few drops of basil tincture on the nape of your neck whenever you feel heartache about your lost love, or, for more extreme cases, take a basil bath for seven days in a row, starting on a Friday, ideally on the waning Moon.

To make a basil tincture, take a glass canning jar and fill it one-third full with dried basil or completely full with fresh basil. Then fill the container with 80-proof or higher alcohol. Place plastic wrap on the mouth of the jar to prevent any metal from the lid coming in contact with the tincture. Let it sit for at least two weeks, but optimally for six weeks. This is a preparation that is best to have on hand for future use. For a preparation that is only for this purpose, make it on the waning Moon.

To take a basil bath, heat two cups of water to boiling, and place two tablespoons of dried basil or four tablespoons of fresh chopped basil in the water. Let it steep for fifteen to thirty minutes, strain, and then add this infusion of basil to your bath water. Sit in the bath for at least seven minutes. Do not wash it off, but pat yourself dry. You will feel the pain of love slipping way further and further with each bath and be in a much better place emotionally by day seven.

Flower Essence Remedies

Several flower essences are excellent in helping release the past and heal the heart. Those that I've used successfully with clients include:

Basil—Basil is one of the preeminent love magick herbs, and as an essence it helps us integrate our sexuality with our romantic and spiritual love.

Bleeding Heart—A powerful cleanser of the heart and of heart trauma from previous relationships and past abuse. Use to bring one to a more unconditional state of love and dissolve unhealthy relationships, attachments, obsessions, and addictions.

Borage—Borage is a great essence when we are suffering from depression and discouragement about relationships, or grief from a relationship that we cannot move on from. It helps to give us confidence to move through these feelings.

Evening Primrose—Evening primrose helps us open our heart chakra and trust again. It is particularly powerful if the root of our difficulties comes from a lack of connection to mother figures or early childhood guardians. This essence helps us form deeper relationships, romantic and otherwise.

Foxglove—Traditionally, foxglove is a strong heart healer. It is used to express what is in your heart and heal miscommunications of the heart. Foxglove is for those who feel choked up and use that as an excuse not to express feelings.

Heartsease—An essence for those who are broken-hearted, feeling lonely and rejected. It helps instill feelings of comfort and gently eases the user back into having relationships.

Hibiscus—This essence opens the heart wide to access unconditional love but also shields the heart from harm. It unites spiritual / emotional love with the physical expression of that love.

Holly—The essence of holly helps us overcome "negative" emotions of jealousy, envy, suspicion, anger, and even hatred. It helps us process these emotional blocks and be able to love again.

Rose—Rose opens and protects the heart in potentially vulnerable relationships to help you grow and trust. Use to bring the fire of cleansing to the heart and to release and heal old relationship wounds.

Staghorn Sumac—This essence grants the strength to bend and adapt, yet remain strong and true to your convictions. Brings swiftness and clarity of thought to matters of the heart, particularly regarding continuing or ending relationships.

Most of these essences are available from a variety of commercial flower essence suppliers. Choose one to three that seem to suit your particular healing process. If you choose to make your own, on a sunny day, pick the fresh flowers and float several of them in a clear glass bowl of spring water, and expose it to the sun for a minimum of three hours. Keep the bowl as close to the original plant as possible, and ask the spirit of the plant to transfer the flower's healing essence to the water. You can even make an offering to the plant, such as leaving a strand of hair or libation of wine or beer, or burying a coin or stone near it. Then, using an unbleached coffee filter, strain out the flower, and add the water to a dark glass bottle that has already been filled one-fourth full of a preservative such as brandy, vodka, or apple cider vinegar. Label and date the bottle; this is your mother essence. To make the potency that is sold commercially, take a ¼-ounce colored glass dropper bottle and fill it one-fourth full of a preservative and three-fourths full of spring water. Add 3–7 drops of the mother essence to the new bottle, creating a stock bottle.

To most effectively use flower essences in combination for emotional healing, take a ¼-ounce colored glass dropper bottle and fill it one-fourth full of apple cider vinegar. Apple cider vinegar is a preservative used in flower essences, particularly in short-term dosage bottles, and the apples have an association with Venus and love, as well as other health benefits. Brandy can also be used in the same proportions. Fill the remaining three-fourths of the dropper bottle with spring water. Add three drops of each of the flower essences you have chosen. Take three drops of this new solution, known as a dosage bottle, on or under the tongue or in a glass of water three times a day. Keep a journal and notice the change in your emotions and attitude. The bottle should last about a month. When you are done, you can stop or continue with the same mixture, or try a new combination. Follow your intuition when working with flower essences.

Vibrational essences can also be made of stones and are known as gem elixirs. Rose quartz gem elixir can be added to any combination bottle to enhance the effects of healing the heart. Gem elixirs made of gold are also quite effective in healing and stabilizing the changes that you are going through. Gold is said to magickally enhance any preparation. Gem elixirs are made the same way flower essences are, except the stone is soaked in water rather than the flower. Some stones are toxic or dissolve easily in water, so research your stone before making your own essences.

A very good friend of mine was able to overcome the pain of a past relationship using flower essences for a period of almost a year. For the year previously, other modalities of healing, such as talk therapy, were not helping her much. Combining talk therapy and essences with a qualified practitioner, she grew tremendously in her own self-awareness and spirituality, and finally released the old relationship, making space for a wonderful new marriage several years later.

If you feel your healing process involves more than simply getting over the last relationship but taps into larger emotional issues, I urge you to find a qualified healing facilitator in your area, such as a flower essence practitioner, that you can do deeper healing work with.

SPELL} Valentine's Day Self-Love

Valentine's Day is a tough day for many single people recovering from past relationships. All our mass media and retail gear us toward romantic endeavors, and it's hard to be reminded of it in the midst of our singleness. This is a spell devised for a client undergoing these same feelings near Valentine's Day. She wanted something positive to focus on during the day, rather than get depressed.

> 1 fragrant rose
>
> Glass of wine (or romantic beverage of your choice)
>
> Piece of chocolate (or other food you would associate with love) on a plate
>
> 1 smooth stone (such as a polished rose quartz or favorite river/beach stone)
>
> 1 candle—white, green, or pink

Set up an altar with these objects, with the stone farthest away from you, the wine to your left, the candle in front of you, the rose to your right and the food/chocolate in the center.

Start by holding the stone and thinking about love. Let the stone absorb all blocks you have to feeling love and creating self-love. Ask the stone to fill you with its healing energy. When done, put it down.

Hold the candle. Think about sparking love and igniting passion for yourself and, when the time is right, for a partner. When ready, light the candle.

Hold the wine. Think of filling yourself with love and healing. Think of the waters of life that renew and resurrect you, no matter what you've gone through in the past. Drink a sip of the wine.

Hold the plate with the food/chocolate. Think about nourishing yourself on all levels. Think about the sweetness of life. Eat a bite.

Sit before the altar and feel yourself loved and loving, on all levels. When you are done, the ritual is done. You can finish the food and drink. Snuff the candle. I'd suggest letting it burn as long as possible, snuffing it out, and then relighting it as you would a traditional candle spell. Continue the process until the candle is gone. Wash the stone under running water, and then carry it with you to remind you of this power of love.

ELEVEN

All Magick Is Love Magick

While this is primarily a book on romantic love—modern and traditional lore on how to find and grow a partnership with someone you are attracted to—love magick is so much more. Almost all spiritual traditions value the concept of love, though their vision of love can be different. Most of us from traditional society think of spiritual love as the self-sacrificial kind or the love between parent and child. Usually it is intellectualized and sterilized by scholars and theologians until you can barely recognize it as love, particularly when compared to the carnal love of ancient traditions.

Many of the magickal traditions see the link between romantic and sexual love—the ecstatic union between individuals—and the love of spirit, viewing creation as the act of self-love, creator with creator, sustaining the universe. In Witchcraft, we see the union as the interplay of Goddess and God making love to create, sustain, and transform our universe. Without love, there would be nothing. We are created in the divine image. We want to be filled with this creative force, to flow with it, so we seek love. We seek love in our selves first, if we are wise, for we know if we cannot love ourselves, we cannot truly love another. We seek love with others, making physical connections. As Witches, we see the flesh as divine and the world as divine. We see the unions of nature, of animals coming together in mating seasons, in plants fertilizing, in the unions of the heavens and the earth. Through our physical connection with partners, we find the presence of Spirit that is in all things. We make a spiritual connection and find our godselves. The gods are continuously making love. Love is the fuel of the machinery of the universe.

Love and sex is a path of enlightenment, as sure as any other and perhaps more sure than some of the more aesthetic paths. It's a powerful path, for it requires only our instinct and our willingness to love with an open heart. It is universal. Though there are many texts written on it and many traditions of practice, it really requires no dogma, no institutions, and no structure other than what you put into it as a practitioner. It's natural. We want to love. We need to love, so we do. That is what has made sexuality so fearful to those who run organizations and religions. There is no control over it. It's available to almost any, young and old, and is as natural to us as breathing. That's why society and religious institutions have created so much structure around it, through taboos and shame, to trick us from finding our divine selves through love and the flesh. If we do, then we wouldn't need the power structures of our society as much anymore. Love simply is.

In the Indian *Mahabharata,* it is said, "Love, well made, can lead to liberation." This is the essence of what we think of as tantric practices in the West, though the proper study of tantra is a wide range of topics, and not all of them have something to do with sexuality. In India, Hindus are not afraid of depicting the sexual nature of their gods through art and myth.

In the ceremonial magick tradition of Thelema, ripe with sexual imagery, the holy text known as *The Book of the Law* states, "For I am divided for love's sake, for the chance of union. This is the creation of the world, that the pain of division is as nothing, and the joy of dissolution all." The divine creative spirit is divided and divided again in the act of creation, and it is our chance of union that makes the division worth it. The Thelemic goddess Nuit and god Hadit are constantly seeking union as the infinite space and infinite center within that space. The sexual imagery of Thelema evokes the union between the two, though it was considered shocking at the time, both to Crowley's contemporaries and society at large, to use such sexual imagery in a "religion."

In modern Wicca, influenced by the Thelemic teachings of Aleister Crowley, we have the Great Rite—the union of the lance and grail, the blade and chalice, coming together in token through ritual sacrament or in the flesh through sexual rite. It is the great Goddess and God coming together in union through priest and priestess, and when done in solitary rite, it is the Goddess and God within us reaching union. Both experiences are powerful and necessary in our Craft.

All our magick stems from love. When we perform spellcraft, ultimately it is bringing us closer to the divinity of the universe, and that force connecting us to the universe is love. Our initiatory traditions teach us how to "die" and be "reborn," and in that rebirth we are "free from fate." We learn to live as only those who have died ever truly do. Being free from fate, we learn to partner with the goddess of fate as never before, and we can take a hand in weaving our own fate. It is through love we are reborn. Love is central to our great mysteries. The myth of the descent of the Goddess tells us, "For there are three great mysteries in the life of man: love, death, and resurrection, and magick controls them all."

In some fashion, all our initiatory experiences in the Craft involve the descent to the underworld, the land of the dead and their gods. We emulate Inanna, queen of heaven and earth, and Astarte, goddess of love. Both are patrons to the arts presented in this book. We descend the seven gates of the underworld and find our shadow self, our dark "sister," ruling the throne of the underworld. By not only making peace with the shadow but learning to love it as a part of ourselves, as a part of creation, we can be reborn and rise again. Our love of our shadow is like the love we have for a sibling. It is often difficult but necessary to have a harmonious inner family.

We emulate Osiris, who is reborn through the love of his sister-wife Isis, resurrected and empowered. Isis has since been called upon in matters of love, marriage, and children. It is through their undying love that Osiris is called back from the realm of the dead and resurrected through her powerful magick. If there was not such a link between husband and wife in this myth, Isis would not have been able to work her magick and revive Osiris or conceive Horus to fight the figure of Set. The love of a spouse with a partner is the love of the anima / animus, setting us free.

In European lore, we look to folklore such as the ballad of Tam Lin. Echoing some of the imagery of Isis and Osiris, it is the partnership between true loves that confers the true initiation. Though not a Witch-craft tradition outright, it has decidedly influenced the Faery traditions of the Craft. The future Faery seer Tam Lin is kidnapped by the queen of the fey and brought to the underworld. His true love, Janet, pregnant with his child, is the one to rescue him from the clutches of Faery, as they plan to give Tam Lin as part of their seven-year tithe to hell. On Samhain (Halloween), Janet knocks him off his white horse and grabs him close as the faeries transform him into an adder, a lion, red-hot bars of iron, then burning lead, hoping to scare her and force her to break her grip. She does as she is asked by Tam Lin, not letting him go, and finally the fey transform him back to a human, naked knight. She wraps him up in her green mantle and returns him to the world of mortals. Yet the knowledge and insight, this power he gained in Faery, is intact. The faery queen wished she had cursed him. If she knew he would leave, she would have given him eyes from a tree and a heart of stone, curses to prevent him from seeing the mysteries of the otherworld and prevent him from truly loving another. But she didn't, due to both Tam Lin's and Janet's quick thinking and bravery. Though not a tale of sexual initiation (and it doesn't need to be), it is a tale of the courage of true love and the union of a sacred couple after the initiator's journey into the otherworld. The green mantle of Janet marks her as an emissary of the earth goddess, while the faery queen is her underworld initiatory counterpart.

The mystery of the initiation through relationship, through love and sex, is common in the Pagan world. The story of Osiris is not just the descent into the underworld of the fallen king, mimicking Inanna and Persephone in their descent to the Great Below. It is the story of the sacred king married to the goddess of fertility and the land. The sacred king, the God, rules by virtue of the Goddess. We see it in Isis and Osiris, and we see the theme repeated in more human terms through the mythos of King Arthur of Camelot and his queen, Guinevere. Despite modern retellings and Christian interpretations, the ancient theme is one of a sacred king ruling through his "right" relationship with the land through the queen. When their relationship fails, the land withers, and the wasteland must be regenerated by the grail, the cup, the tool of elemental water and love. If you look further into the myth, you see the same pattern of sexual initiation between Merlin, as seer and magician, with his muse, or tutor, through various stories as teacher or student with Nimue, Vivian, or Morgan le Fay, his wife Guendoloena, and his sister Ganieda. His relationships with these women, for good or ill, bring him deeper along the initiatory path. Without those loves, those attractions, those erotic experiences, the cycle would cease, and the path, as well as his story, would not continue. Love, romance, and sex as a spiritual path has a long tradition in both the East and the West.

The magick of initiation awakens and opens the Witch's heart, the potential for Perfect Love and Perfect Trust within us all. One who has the Witch's heart within has been to the depths of darkness and found the light of life and love. We have been torn asunder by love, both human and divine, like the victims of the ancient maenads, or *bacchante*, the frenzied women worshipers of Dionysus who rip both man and beast apart in emulation of their god.

Those with the Witch's heart awakened keenly feel the world, as they are led by their heart and see through their heart. We feel the pains and joys of the earth and our sisters and brothers in the world. Yet we are, despite our intense connections, separate and apart from our communities—other and different. That is the blessing and the burden of the Witch's heart until we live in an age where everyone is led by their own Witch's heart, filled with Perfect Love.

Until then, our relationships with ourselves and with others—romantic, family, or friends—are great teachers into the mysteries of magick. When we are inspired by our relationships, we are truly "in spirit." We can know the divine presence in flesh by those around us and in ourselves. We recognize that presence through the feeling of what we call love. Attraction, romance, lust, friendship, ecstasy, warmth, and fun all act like arrows pointing us toward this love. This is the feeling we ideally evoke when doing our healing magick, when doing our prosperity spells, when doing prayers and devotions, and ultimately when living life day to day, moment to moment. Every moment of life is potentially filled with this magick. Every moment of life is potentially filled with this love.

Love is the source of our magick. It is our love—the same force that draws the attention of the ancestors, spirits, angels, and gods to our altars and rituals—that attracts lovers and spouses. It is through the love between us and the Divine that we make our magick. All the universe is waiting to receive our love and gives of its own love freely and continuously. We simply have to notice it and awaken our heart. All of our magick is truly love magick, for it is through love we feel our connection to all things, everywhere.

BIBLIOGRAPHY

Abelar, Taisha. *The Sorcerer's Crossing: A Woman's Journey.* New York: Penguin, 1993.

Andrews, Ted. *Animal-Speak: The Spiritual & Magical Powers of Creatures Great and Small.* St. Paul: Llewellyn, 1993.

Beyerl, Paul. *A Compendium of Herbal Magick.* Custer, WA: Phoenix Publishing, Inc., 1998.

———. *The Master Book of Herbalism.* Custer, WA: Phoenix Publishing, Inc., 1984.

Cabot, Laurie, with Tom Cowan. *Love Magic: The Way to Love through Rituals, Spells and the Magical Life.* New York: Dell, 1992.

———. *Power of the Witch: The Earth, the Moon and the Magical Path to Enlightenment.* New York: Dell, 1989.

Cabot, Laurie, with Jean Mills. *Celebrate the Earth: A Year of Holidays in the Pagan Tradition.* New York: Dell, 1994.

Conway, D. J. *The Ancient & Shining Ones.* St. Paul: Llewellyn, 1993.

Cunningham, Scott. *Cunningham's Encyclopedia of Crystal, Gem & Metal Magic.* St. Paul: Llewellyn, 1992.

———. *Cunningham's Encyclopedia of Magical Herbs.* St. Paul: Llewellyn, 1985.

———. *The Complete Book of Incense, Oils and Brews*. St. Paul: Llewellyn, 1989.

———. *Magical Herbalism*. St. Paul: Llewellyn, 1983.

Deerman, Dixie, and Steve Rasmussen. *The Goodly Spellbook*. New York: Sterling, 2004.

Dell, Linda Louisa. *Aphrodisiacs: Aphrodite's Secrets*. Somerset, UK: Capall Bann, 2008.

Dugan, Ellen. *How to Enchant a Man*. Woodbury, MN: Llewellyn, 2007.

DuQuette, Lon Milo. *The Chicken Qabalah of Rabbi Lamed Ben Clifford*. York Beach, ME: Weiser, 2001.

Foster, Steven, and Varro E. Tyler. *Tyler's Honest Herbal: A Sensible Guide to the Use of Herbs and Related Remedies*. Binghamton, NY: The Haworth Press, Inc., 1999.

Foxwood, Orion. *The Faery Teachings*. Coral Springs, FL: Muse Press, 2003.

Goddard, David. *Sacred Magic of the Angels*. York Beach, ME: Samuel Weiser, 1996.

Greer, John Michael. *The New Encyclopedia of the Occult*. St. Paul: Llewellyn, 2003.

Grimassi, Raven. *Hereditary Witchcraft: Secrets of the Old Religion*. St. Paul: Llewellyn, 1999.

———. *The Book of Ways Volumes I & II*. Old Ways Press, 2004.

———. *The Witches' Craft: The Roots of Witchcraft & Magical Transformation*. St. Paul: Llewellyn, 2002.

———. *Encyclopedia of Wicca & Witchcraft*. St. Paul: Llewellyn, 2000.

Guiley, Rosemary Ellen. *The Encyclopedia of Witches & Witchcraft*. New York: Checkmark Books, 1999.

———. *Harper's Encyclopedia of Mystical & Paranormal Experience.* HarperSanFrancisco, 1991.

Heath, Maya. *Ceridwen's Handbook of Incense, Oils and Candles.* San Antonio, TX: Words of Wizdom International Inc., 1996.

Kaldera, Raven. *Pagan Polyamory.* St. Paul: Llewellyn, 2005.

Koppana, Kati. *Snake Fat and Knotted Threads: An Introduction to Traditional Finnish Healing Magic.* Leicestershire, UK: Heart of Albion Press, 2003.

Kraig, Donald Michael. *Modern Sex Magick.* St. Paul: Llewellyn, 2002.

Mathers, S. L. MacGregor. *The Key of Solomon the King.* Mineola, NY: Dover, 2009.

McCormack, Kathleen. *Magic for Lovers.* Hauppauge, NY: Baron's Education Series, 2003.

Medici, Marina. *Good Magic.* New York: Fireside, 1988.

Melody. *Love Is In the Earth.* Wheat Ridge, CO: Earth-Love Publishing House, 1995.

Mickaharic, Draja. *A Spiritual Worker's Spell Book.* Philadelphia, PA: Xlibris Corporation, 2002.

Miller, Lucinda G., and Wallace J. Murray, eds. *Herbal Medicinals: A Clinician's Guide.* Binghamton, NY: The Haworth Press, Inc., 1999.

Miller, Richard Alan, and Iona Miller. *The Magical and Ritual Use of Perfumes.* Rochester, VT: Destiny Books, 1990.

Morgan, Diane. *The Charmed Garden.* Scotland, UK: Findhorn Press, 2004.

Morrison, Dorothy. *Enchantments of the Heart.* Franklin Lakes, NJ: Career Press, 2008.

———. *Utterly Wicked.* St. Louis, MO: Rowan Tree Press, 2007.

Penczak, Christopher. *Gay Witchcraft: Empowering the Tribe*. Boston, MA: Samuel Weiser, 2003.

———. *The Outer Temple of Witchcraft: Circles, Spells and Rituals*. St. Paul: Llewellyn, 2004.

Pennick, Nigel. *Practical Magic in the Northern Tradition*. Northamptonshire, UK: Aquarius Press, 1989.

Pepper, Elizabeth. *Love Charms*. Tiverton, RI: The Witches Almanac Ltd., 2001.

Poche, Henry Z. *Medical Biology of Yohimbine & Its Easy Use in Male Sex Erectile Dysfunction*. Washington, DC: ABBE Publishers Association of Washington, DC, 1997.

Robbers, James E., and Varro E. Tyler. *Tyler's Herbs of Choice: The Therapeutic Use of Phytomedicinals*. Binghamton, NY: The Haworth Press, Inc., 1998.

Sawyer, Pat Kirven. *Ancient Wisdom: The Master Grimoire*. The Woodlands, TX: 7th House, 2005.

Shah, Idries. *Oriental Magic*. New York: Philosophical Library, Inc, 1957.

Silva, José, and Philip Miele. *The Silva Mind Control Method*. New York: Pocket Books/Simon & Schuster Inc., 1977.

Slater, Herman. *Magickal Formulary Spellbook Book I*. New York: Magickal Childe Jr., Inc., 1987.

Starhawk. *Truth or Dare*. San Francisco, CA: Harper One, 1989.

Stewart, R. J. *Earth Light*. Lake Toxaway, NC: Mercury Publishing, 1992.

———. *The Living World of Faery*. Somerset, UK: Gothic Images, 1995.

———. *The Mystic Life of Merlin*. New York: Arkana, 1986.

———. *Power within the Land*. Lake Toxaway, NC: Mercury Publishing, 1992.

Tenney, Deanne. *Yohimbe* (Woodland Health Series). Pleasant Grove, UT: Woodland Publishing, 1997.

Valiente, Doreen. *An ABC of Witchcraft Past and Present.* New York: St. Martin's Press, Inc., 1973.

———. *Natural Magic.* Custer, WA: Phoenix, 1985.

———. *Witchcraft for Tomorrow.* Blaine, WA: Phoenix, 1978.

Whitcomb, Bill. *The Magician's Companion.* St. Paul: Llewellyn, 1993.

Wolkstein, Diane, and Samuel Noah Kramer. *Inanna Queen of Heaven and Earth: Her Stories and Hymns from Sumer.* New York: Harper & Row, 1983.

Yronwode, Catherine. *Hoodoo Herb and Root Magic.* Forestville, CA: Lucky Mojo Curio Company, 2002.

Online Resources

Achland, Abigail. Tam Lin. http://www.tam-lin.org

Alchemy Works. http://www.alchemy-works.com

Encyclopedia Mythica. http://www.pantheon.org

Otherworld Apothecary. http://www.otherworld -apothecary.com/

Yronwode, Catherine. Lucky Mojo. http://www .luckymojo.com

INDEX

The Witch's Shield

Protection Magick & Psychic Self-Defense

Christopher Penczak

Is it possible to gain spiritual enlightenment even in difficult or threatening situations? In this thorough and thoughtful handbook, readers are urged to take responsibility for their own actions, ask what the situation might be teaching them, and hold compassion for those viewed as doing the harm.

Popular Wiccan author and teacher Christopher Penczak takes a three-fold approach to protection magick in this guide for Witches, Pagans, shamans, and psychics. First, find out how to protect yourself using personal energy, will, and intent. Next, discover how to connect with your guardian spirits, angels, and patron deities. Finally, learn how to use traditional spell-craft and ritual for protection.

This book includes a CD that contains the following meditations read aloud by author Christopher Penczak:

- Protection meditations
- Protection Spirit Journey
- Lesser Banishing Ritual of the Pentagram
- The Magick Circle Ritual for Protection Spells

978-0-7387-0542-2, 216 pp, 6 x 9 $19.95

The Witch's Coin

Prosperity and Money Magick

Christopher Penczak

Along with quick-fix money spells, this timely book explores the consciousness of prosperity and how to transform poverty into abundance through magick, meditation, affirmations, and astrological timing. *The Witch's Coin* offers a materia magicka of the most powerful correspondences in wealth spellwork, including gods, stones, metals, herbs, and coins. Unlike most money magick books, it builds upon a foundation of real-world financial principles. Penczak also discusses offering magickal services professionally, including how and when to charge for readings and healings.

978-0-7387-1587-2, 288 pp, 6 x 9 $17.95

To Write to the Author

If you wish to contact the author or would like more information about this book, please write to the author in care of Llewellyn Worldwide, and we will forward your request. Both the author and the publisher appreciate hearing from you and learning of your enjoyment of this book and how it has helped you. Llewellyn Worldwide cannot guarantee that every letter written to the author can be answered, but all will be forwarded. Please write to:

Christopher Penczak
c/o Llewellyn Worldwide
2143 Wooddale Drive
Woodbury, MN 55125-2989
Please enclose a self-addressed stamped envelope for reply, or $1.00 to cover costs. If outside U.S.A., enclose international postal reply coupon.

Many of Llewellyn's authors have websites with additional information and resources. For more information, please visit our website:

HTTP://WWW.LLEWELLYN.COM